The Professional Artist's Manual

Richard Hyman

VNR VAN NOSTRAND REINHOLD COMPANY
New York Cincinnati Toronto London Melbourne

For Roberta, Michael, and Betsy

Printed in the United States of America.
Designed by Loudan Enterprises
All illustrations by the author unless otherwise credited.

Published by Van Nostrand Reinhold Company
A division of Litton Educational Publishing, Inc.
135 West 50th Street, New York, NY 10020, U.S.A.

Van Nostrand Reinhold Limited
1410 Birchmount Road
Scarborough, Ontario M1P 2E7, Canada

Van Nostrand Reinhold Australia Pty. Ltd.
17 Queen Street
Mitcham, Victoria 3132, Australia

Van Nostrand Reinhold Company Limited
Molly Millars Lane
Wokingham, Berkshire, England

16 15 14 13 12 11 10 9 8 7 6 5 4 3 2 1

Library of Congress Cataloging in Publication Data
Hyman, Richard, 1937-
   The professional artist's manual.

   Bibliography: p.
   Includes index.
   1. Art—Vocational guidance—Economic aspects.
I. Title.
N8353.H95   658′.91′7   79-17080
ISBN 0-442-22603-9

for reading that portion of the manuscript.

Allen Hitchcock for kindly contributing illustrations to ''Architectural Blueprint Reading'' and for his advice on that chapter.

Roger Jentink, Commercial Tape Laboratory, 3M Company, for his extensive letter on the use of tapes.

Jim Knox, for kindly contributing the illustration of lettering styles.

George Koch, U.S. Department of Labor, for informing me on Comprehensive Employment and Training Act (CETA) programs.

Frank LaGiusa, Lighting Application Specialist, General Electric Co., for reviewing the lighting portion of ''The Studio.''

Sally Law, American Financial Consultants, Inc., for explaining benefits of financial planning and the functions of financial consultants.

Harry Leutner, Signcrafters, for his copious advice on all subjects freely given over the years; I have learned more from him than any teacher in school. In particular for his help with ''Pricing,'' ''Contracts,'' ''Specifying and Purchasing Materials,'' ''Transferring Designs and Making Patterns,'' ''Paint,'' and ''Installation.''

Roger Marino, Marino Galleries, for explaining the business of framing and for reviewing that portion of my manuscript.

Jim Melchert, Head of Visual Arts, National Endowment for the Arts, for discussing his agency's programs.

Raoul Middleman, for sharing his experiences with the art world.

Thomas Moran, Fuller-O'Brien Paints, for explaining the technology of paint, and for reviewing that portion of the manuscript.

Art Naff, Arnold Factory Supplies, Inc., for all his help with our packing problems, for sharing his knowledge of commercial packing, and for reviewing that portion of the manuscript.

Harvey Nusbaum, Attorney at Law, for his sober counsel, for his generous help with ''Starting Out,'' ''Contracts,'' ''Bookkeeping,'' and ''Lawyers,'' and for reading those portions of the manuscript.

Rohm and Haas for permission to use their skylight construction material.

Israel Rosen for sharing his marvellous art collection with us over the years, and for his insights and anecdotes on collectors and collecting.

Jay Solomon, Administrator, General Services Administration, for sharing his vision of the government's role in assisting the arts.

Bill Somers, signman and artist, for his suggestions on installations and on sign paint.

Joe Schmidt, Senior Marketing Manager, Black and Decker, for his advice on power tools and for reviewing that portion of the manuscript.

Robert Smith, Washington Representative, National Fire Protection Association, for his extensive help with the problems of fire prevention, and for reviewing that portion of the manuscript.

Gordon Strauss, for discussing and reviewing ''Photography,'' and for his help with the photographs.

Anthony Susano, for explaining the ins and outs of installing murals.

Don Thalacker, Director, Art-in-Architecture Program, General Services Administration, for his time spent in describing and showing his program to me, and for reviewing that portion of the manuscript.

Warren and Mandy Teixeira, for their advice and help with ''Presenting Designs to the Client,'' and for reviewing a portion of that chapter.

Richard Wincor, for reviewing ''Contracts.''

Sandra Williams, for discussing General Services Administration schedule and purchase procedures.

Bosley Wright, Milton W. Bosley and Company, Inc., for discussing frame molding manufacture and reviewing that portion of the manuscript.

Vernon Wright, Vice-President, Maryland National Bank, for all his help with ''Banking,'' and for reviewing that chapter.

Preface

Over the past fifteen years, my wife and I have created paintings, murals, wall hangings, sculptures, and serigraphs on commission for contract clients—institutions, supermarkets, restaurants, hotels, schools, and businesses—all over the country. This book is based on our experience supplemented by that of many other experts. My goal has been to provide artists the information essential to producing and selling their work with economy and purposefulness while, at the same time, avoiding major pitfalls.

No book can supplant on-the-spot professional assistance, and I signal when you need the help of an accountant, lawyer, banker, or insurance agent. I furnish a background to your discussions with them and, since professionals usually know the answers but often not the questions, suggest vital topics to cover.

Some subjects, such as transferring designs, are both fundamental and relatively simple, and I explain these in detail. I stress the application of others, like photography, which are too complex to treat fully, and suggest supplementary readings in an annotated bibliography. Several crucial, difficult subjects, copyright or taxes, for example, do not allow facile explanations, and you must apply yourself to understand them.

Occasionally I recommend products that I've found particularly useful. Recognize that they may be modified at any time (not necessarily for the better), or discontinued, or that superior options may appear. Be assured that none of the recommendations has been influenced by payola. I had been concerned with my reaction to the temptations of free samples, but, alas my virtue was never tested.

I've tried to make this the kind of resource I wish my wife and I had when we started out. I hope that it will spare you some of our costly mistakes and ease your journey. Good luck.

I. Starting Out

Working for yourself has both advantages and disadvantages. The *advantages* have mainly to do with control over your own life.

You can, within limits, *set your own hours.* You can operate against the grain of the community to avoid rush hours, go to museums and shops during slack time, take vacations and trips on the off season.

You can, within limits, *create your own working environment.* You can select your human contacts and keep clear of the workplace hassle with its uncongenial people, loud music, and idle chit-chat.

You can, within limits, *trade income for work time.* You can have the option of working longer and earning more money or working less and having more free time (but less money to spend in it).

You can, within limits, *deduct from your income taxes some of the expenses incidental to making art*, expenses like materials, books, work space, and equipment that you would have incurred anyway. In addition, you may save by not needing a business wardrobe, two telephones, day care, or to commute to work.

You can get to know your family better. Your children will understand and share your occupation—you won't be going out to a mysterious "office."

The *disadvantages* have mainly to do with lack of control over your life.

While *income uncertainty* is an endemic occupational hazard of the self-employed, be they salesman, architect, lawyer, or doctor, the freelance artist is more vulnerable than most. But how secure is the income of anyone? Tenured professors lose their jobs; whole industries take nosedives. *Corrective:* Accept the insecurity and try to save enough for some peace of mind, a year's minimum expenses for example. Cultivate the bread-and-butter accounts that provide steady income. Stay out of art. Marry a wealthy spouse.

You must face *feast or famine.* You hate turning down jobs when you're too busy and risk losing a client, but overwork can erode your life: The long-awaited vacation is at hand, the bags packed, Fido with the kennel, and POW! the phone rings. Your best customer has a sudden, rush order (it's been sitting on his desk for six weeks). The job has to open—TOMORROW! What to do? *Corrective:* Ask steady clients for their long-range plans, if they have any, so you can arrange a schedule. Restrict and space your bids and selling forays (but at the risk of being without work when the "sure things" dissolve in a flurry of budget cuts, lower bids, unexpected competition, and artist friends of the boss's spouse). Unless your services are so much in demand that you can pick and choose clients, I have no answer and I don't think anybody else does either.

Without a publicly recognized workplace to go to, you're *liable to personal temptations*; viz, a book that needs reading, or *distractions*, viz, a leaky faucet in need of repair. And, since you're not "really" working, you're a sitting duck for those in need of help, viz, the P.T.A. or your mother-in-law with her trip to the dentist. *Corrective:* Discipline yourself to regular work hours and let it be known to all who'll listen that you're involved in something at least as worthwhile as working for the government.

If you work at home, you will see a lot more of your family. This can be a great joy, but it can also increase the *opportunities for domestic conflict*, especially if a husband and wife share a business. *Corrective:* Build some separation between your work and home life. If you work with a spouse or other love object, consider divisions of responsibilities to diminish arguments over who misplaced which pencil, fouled up whose checkbook, or alienated which client.

You won't have a boss to blame for your failures: *your mistakes are your own. Corrective:* Learn to live with yourself; lower your goals; don't fail.

Perhaps the worst hazard for many self-employed people is the *psychological stress* created by all the above and similar problems. *Corrective:* Each person has to come to terms with his own portion in life. If you can't stand the strain, get out; there's no shame in it. But don't be afraid to work for yourself. You can, as many do, ease into self-employment by working for others in art or related areas. Develop useful contacts while maintaining a regular income source. The first few years are supposed to be the hardest; try to set aside enough money to ease you through them.

Analyze Your Assets and Deficits

A dispassionate review of your assets and deficits may help you.

Personality: Are you made anxious by uncertainties; do you need that regular paycheck; are you willing to hustle, persevere to make contacts and follow through with them; are you willing to put up with aggravation, long hours, low pay, frustration?

Business Skills: Can you discipline yourself to keep systematic records and make sure the bills are paid? Can you submit to normal business practices: punctuality, dependability, legal correctness?

Artistic Skills: Do you think you're really good enough? Do you have the confidence to persevere in the face of the manifest disinterest of others? It's one thing to preserve your self-regard in the sanctity of an art school or studio, and quite another when your portfolio, the cream of years of effort, goes whizzing by a prospective client who interrupts your interview, after you've sat in the waiting room for an hour, to make a few important phone calls (to his hairdresser, garage, or tennis partner).

Are you a specialist or a generalist?: Specialization limits your market. If you only weave and a potential client wants an appliqué hanging, will you do it? Specialization, by the same token, increases your depth. Someone looking expressly for a weaving might approach a weaver before a generalist fabric artist. To extend the thought, when Mr. Big wants a Blockbuster Sculpture for his new building, he doesn't go to a generalist unless that generalist's name is Picasso; he goes to Henry Moore. You can't have it both ways.

How much will you compromise?: You may not know the answer until you've been offered the apple. You can vow truth to your muse in your garret, but ah, in the coziness of the boardroom with the bills due, will you bend a little? And how much? It's often a fine line between reasonable accommodation and prostitution. Is modifying the red of your sculpture a wee bit to keep it from clashing with the brick wall on which it's to hang too much to ask of you?

Training: Your training will impress some people, particularly when you're getting started and have no track record. It can also give you confidence and provide contacts and references. I've found, incidentally, that many art schools do not prepare their students adequately for the business world. This may in part be because their faculty has had little experience with business, an inexperience sometimes masked by an ivory-tower mentality that hides inability, timidity, or the lack of opportunity.

Experience: It's la ronde—you can't get work unless you have experience, and you can't get experience unless you have work. Here are some suggestions:

● Put together a professional presentation of your student work.

● Select potential job sites, make proposals for them, and contact the owner.

● Work for friends and acquaintances at cost or for free.

● Contact local businesses and institutions like schools and offer to work cheap or for free. Think up a scheme and propose it to them. Try to get your materials contributed to you.

● Explore low-cost, low pressure government commissions like those offered by the Comprehensive Employment Training Act (CETA), the Park Service, or local jurisdictions.

● Cultivate a professional friend, such as an interior designer, architect, or builder who'll give you a break.

● Work up a "line," and photograph it in a professional manner on location in a building or home.

● Apprentice to someone and use the work on which you've collaborated for your portfolio (with his permission).

● Work for people in allied fields, like architects, interior designers, manufacturers' reps, and framers to make business contacts and gain experience. Explain your position and, if necessary, offer to take a salary cut as an inducement to being hired.

Working on Commission

Working on commission offers certain advantages and disadvantages.

Advantages

● You don't have a large inventory (artwork) unsold or on consignment tying up your capital and storage space.

● Your jobs are presold. You don't manufacture the goods and then look for a market. You can budget your expenses more rationally.

● If you do your own selling, you can avoid commissions, markups, and fees. Thus, you can charge less than the market price and still make a good profit. You may be able to control your overhead to such an extent that you can compete, if you choose to do so, with catalog art while offering custom advantages.

● You can design your work to integrate with an environment.

● You will have the opportunity to work with professionals in other fields.

Disadvantages

● Regular art is a fait accompli, take it or leave it. With commissioned art there's the chance for plenty of fingers to be stuck in your pie—those of the client, the architect, the fire marshal, the building supervisor, the interior designer, and their uncles, aunts, and cousins.

● It's nice to have the environment fitted to your artwork (The "I designed my living room around my (*fill in YOUR name*").

● If you work solely through commissions, you won't have work to exhibit in sales galleries or shows, which are important avenues to career advancement. If you're too much of a broken-field runner, you won't amass a homogeneous body of work. Without the two traditional channels—shows and a consistent body of work—you may have trouble being accepted as a "serious" artist.

Where to Locate

A region needs a certain population to support an artist as it does to support a doctor or a tractor-repair shop. You can reside wherever you choose, of course, but you must have customers if you want to make a living from your art. The more populous your area, the greater the potential for opportunities, but, alas, the more likely there will be competition from other artists.

Being close to your market is advantageous. You can establish and maintain personal contacts and provide prompt service. When a client knows you're within easy reach and can drop in at short notice for a conference or some trouble-shooting, he'll be readier to do business with you. Once you've established yourself, your clients may stick with you if you move farther away, especially if your product is unique, your prices attractive, and you're cooperative.

If you live in a less populous area, your market will be more diffuse, so you'll have to spread your nets wider and maybe fish harder. But the competition should be less intense, and, hopefully, you'll be appreciated more—a big fish in a small pond. You may have to be more of a generalist, however. Just as your area may support a general practitioner but not a cardiologist, so you may have to do a little of everything—sign work, portraiture, murals—to keep going.

The flight from the cities has brought new businesses to many rural parts of the country,, and some regions have concentrations of particular industries and their satellites—e.g., rubber in Ohio, steel in Pennsylvania—that might provide support for artists.

On the other hand, regional operations may be controlled by central locations. You may, for example, have your tranquility disturbed by a multi-million dollar hotel being built next door to you, but, when you present yourself to the management, find that it's a chain whose decisions are made in design offices thousands of miles away. (Try anyhow. Some chains have local franchisers, or they might be privately owned.)

Urban, Suburban, or Rural?

The principal advantages of an urban location are that it provides a concentration of markets and suppliers, information and cultural institutions, and skilled co-workers and subcontractors. Some disadvantages are: traffic, congestion, competition, the problems of delivery and storage, and the scarcity and expense of good working space.

A suburban location shares the advantages and disadvantages of urban locations, but often lacks the cultural stimulation.

A rural location is farthest from concentrated markets, sources, and resources, but studio space may be cheaper and more available, and there should be less congestion and less zoning troubles. The isolation is oppressive for some and a solace for others.

Zoning

Zoning is a concern if you are operating a business. Contact your zoning agency, which may be found in the county seat, city office building, or town hall, to determine the permitted usage for your general location. Don't tip your hand prematurely; you may find that you'll be able to conform to the permitted usage simply by semantically redefining your operation. For example, in some jurisdictions professional people, such as doctors and architects, are allowed to use a certain percentage of their homes as office space, but the operation of a business is not permitted. If you are accepted as a professional and not as a businessman, then your studio should be approved also, as long as you comply with the provisions of professional occupancy.

Some codes have a zoning variance option that permits exceptions to a property's zoning. You can request a hearing and petition that your studio be allowed in variance to the normal uses authorized for the area.

Your area might be unenlightened in its control over artists' workplaces. With the help of a lawyer and other artists, citizens, or arts organizations, you can compose a model definition and act to amend the code. This is done all the time by various interest groups, why not artists? Remember in your amendation that watercolor miniaturists and junk sculptors both use studios and that their acceptance by the community may differ.

Although many artists continuously engage in nonconforming usages, it would be risky to establish a business illegally. The chances of your actually being caught by a zoning inspector are slim, but you will be at the mercy of your neighbors, who can file a complaint whenever they fancy. I had a neighbor threaten to turn us in anytime we did something he didn't approve of, and I wouldn't recommend that to anyone.

Business Types

There are three fundamental types of business organizations: sole proprietorship, partnership, and incorporation.

Sole proprietorship is the simplest form of organization; it needn't cost anything to set up. Sole proprietors—either an individual, or a husband and wife operating under the individual's name, the husband and wife's name, or an assumed business name—are solely responsible for their actions. The decisions and profits are all theirs, but then so are all the losses.

Partnership is an arrangement of two or more people, who may or may not be married to one another, to share business income, expenses, and decisions. Partnerships can allow the sharing of finite profits and infinite debts. Apportioning the responsibilities and establishing the chain of command can be tricky—like a marriage without bedroom privileges. Before tying the knot, talk to *your* lawyer.

Incorporation is a complex legal entity only for the successful. It requires a lawyer as a midwife. Incorporation establishes a legal persona that relieves the corporation's officers and stockholders of personal liability. Its other advantages can include tax relief for upper-bracket incomes. Decide in concert with your lawyer.

Legal Requirements

The legal requirements for operating a business vary throughout the nation. Check with your state's department of taxation or revenue and your local county, city, or town to find out what is required in your jurisdiction. Also ask other business people in your area. It's always wise to consult a lawyer and/or an accountant as well.

States with a sales tax require businesses to charge sales tax on items sold within the state to final users of those items. Manufacturers, when they sell to wholesalers, charge no tax. Out-of-state sales tax policies differ; your state will inform you of its own policy. Your state will grant you a license that exempts you from paying sales tax on wholesale purchases of materials that are to be resold or to be incorporated into manufactured items that are to be resold. In turn, you must collect sales tax on the items that you sell to final users, keep records of these transactions, and turn the collected revenue over periodically.

Your in-state suppliers will need formal certification of your tax-exempt status. You may buy the forms at a stationer's or make up your own. Often suppliers will provide them to you. Tax-exempt status is a key negotiating point in establishing your bona fides with a local wholesaler; you may not get far without it.

11

2. *Marketing*

I can think of no better preface to this chapter on marketing than the remarks made by Avery Faulkner, the Washington architect, in defense of artwork in public places:

Artwork has a longer cost cycle than most other parts of a building, because artwork doesn't have to be replaced as frequently, if at all. Not only that, but it often actually increases in value with time.

We must not forget that artwork often replaces some other finish—marble, fabric, or wood for example—that may cost as much or even more. Furthermore, when artwork serves as the focal point of a room, other finishes in that room can often be reduced in cost because of their down-graded importance.

Artwork must be thought of as integral to a building and be built into its budget from the very beginning. Any cuts in the artwork should be proportional to those made across the entire building program. Too often art is timidly put in as an afterthought, only to be pulled out at the first sign of trouble.

Donors are much more willing to give to and be associated with buildings that are aesthetically attractive and display good taste.

Buildings, and institutional buildings in particular, need evidence that their operators care for the buildings' users. Art helps in this by humanizing and personalizing buildings. It can lift employee morale and create more positive attitudes. What's more, areas that are attractive ordinarily require less maintenance than ugly areas. People tend to respect and respond positively to the interest shown in improving their environment. The Paris Metro study, which showed a significant decrease in station abuse after a beautification program, is a case in point.

Refurbished stores have consistently shown increased sales volume, often to such an extent that the reburbishing cost is quickly recovered.

Art, according to a Harris poll, is the nation's most popular spectator sport, more so even than football or baseball.

Of course this powerful incantation should only be delivered in its entirety to a sympathetic audience—an artist's consciousness-raising session, for example. Keep the separate points in mind, however, to use in discussions with open-minded prospects at those moments when intelligent argument can be persuasive.

Information Sources

There are a number of research sources available to the artist seeking markets. Some are as convenient as the phone book or newspapers; some are as close as the nearest library; while others must be purchased at considerable cost.

If you're interested in working with architects and interior designers, you'll want to look at the magazines that they read. Formats are similar and cover current trends, notable firms, new projects, new products, and the like. They'll give you ideas about which firms are busy and about current trends. Your prospects may come to you for art prompted by something they've seen in one of these magazines. Each copy will include a reader's service card for readers to use to request free literature from advertisers. See the Bibliography of this book for an annotated listing of useful publications.

Artists' magazines, artists' newsletters, and artists' newspapers are a regular source of what's happening in the art sector, and are listed and described in the Bibliography of this book. (I have omitted familiar magazines like *Art News* and *Art in America*, which don't include much marketing information anyway.)

Artists' publications have been proliferating like mayflies in July, and some are as short lived. That fact, and their constantly changing formats diminish the value of a recommendation. If you want to subscribe to any, look over as many as you can in a library or artists' center, or write for a sample copy.

Realize that most magazines are under constant pressure to stay filled and meet deadlines. Thus the rehashes: "Health Hazards in the Studio," "Beware of Benzol," and "Safety Tips for Artists." Worse are the erroneous or misleading articles. I had, for instance, just completed the chapter on insurance when I received a high priced artists' business letter advising its readers to protect themselves with bad debt insurance, a form of coverage unfamiliar to me. A brief investigation revealed that bad debt insurance did in fact exist, but was available only to those with sales in excess of one million dollars per year, hardly your average artist. Finally, be skeptical of the announcements of lucrative commissions and other such opportunities. These are frequently repeats from previous issues, or may be formalities covering openings long since secured by insiders.

Most art organizations publish a newsletter that is part of the membership dues. These newsletters are a reflection of the interests of the organizations' management and members' interests, and are often a valuable source of information. An annotated listing of these organizations is also in the Bibliography.

Your local and regional newpapers can be a good source of business activity and new building starts. Many of the larger cities have their own magazines which report who's doing what. By the same token, you might try to get written up yourself (see Promotion). Business magazines like *Fortune* and *Business Week* help keep you up to date on economic trends and sometimes provide leads on particular companies or expanding sectors.

The telephone company's Yellow Pages list architects, interior designers, management firms, contractors, galleries, etc. Not all firms or individuals have listings, and some occupations, such as art consultants, are not listed at all. Moreover, except when firms have an informative ad, there is no way to evaluate them as a prospect.

Representatives, wholesalers, manufacturers, and suppliers who deal with the building trades can be good sources of information because they or their sales staff call on clients regularly. They often know who is buying and who is busy.

Architects and interior designers can be good sources of information about work both in their shops and elsewhere. Younger professionals in particular are often on the lookout for employment changes, and, if you visit a number of firms, you can provide them information in exchange.

Business newsletters are good sources of leads. A couple are described in the Bibliography. Also worth investigating are marketing and business directories, which can usually be found in public libraries; they, too, are described in the Bibliography.

Professional meetings, symposia, conferences, and the like are opportunities for you to meet potential clients informally, often people who would be otherwise unavailable. Serving as a guest panelist or talking about your work or field can help you become better known. Contact local chapters of such groups as the American Society of Interior Designers (ASID), American Institute of Architects (AIA) or the Chamber of Commerce.

As you travel about, note new construction and its identifying signboards, which list the architects and owners, and sometimes the interior designers. You can call on them to inquire about work on those or other projects.

Prospecting

Most artists dread contacting prospective buyers. It's understandable—we don't want to expose ourselves to disapproval and/or waste our time. I have a few thoughts to make the experience more bearable.

● Many people do it. If you want to sell your work, at least in the beginning you'll have to hustle. It won't sell itself for you. Why should you, simply because you call yourself an artist, expect things to be handed to you?

● Everyone dances to someone else's tune: The snotty secretary to his boss, his boss to her clients, the museum director to the board of trustees, the gallery owner to collectors.

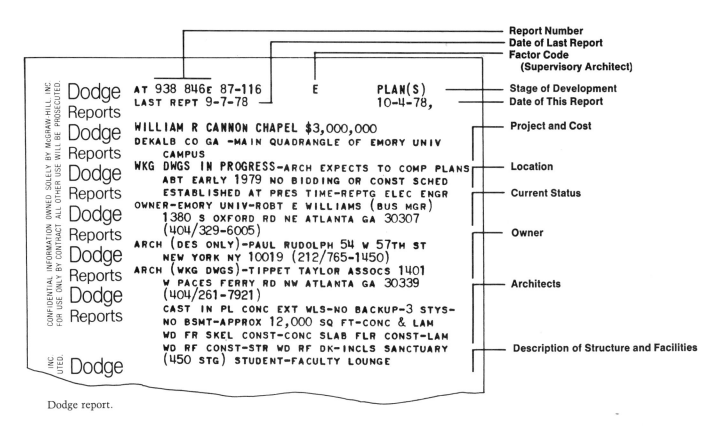

Dodge report.

● The person you're contacting, if he's a designer or architect, has had to work for the project you're after. Is it unreasonable that you should also work to get your share?

● Are you interested in and sympathetic to your prospects' work? Artists sometimes sneer at people in business while hoping for their patronage and praise.

● There's work out there and somebody will get it. It might as well be you.

● You won't please everybody. The more exclusive your art, the narrower your market. You'll hit it off with some and lose out with others. If, after you've given it a good try and found no takers, either you're offering a product for which there is no demand or you're offering a product for which the demand has not yet been created. If we've learned nothing else since Duchamp's *Urinal*, it's that if you say it's art long enough and loud enough, someone out there will believe you.

● Interviews cost firms money. If, for instance, you meet with four designers for fifteen minutes, that's a total of an hour's wage that their company cannot charge off to a client. Consider the number of salespeople (that includes you) who come to call, and you can see why many firms don't put out the welcome mat.

Establishing Contact

Set up an index file of your prospects either alphabetically by name or alphabetically by sector—architect, client, interior design, for example. Record their names, addresses, telephone numbers, and mutual acquaintances. Every time you contact a prospect, note the date with a brief resume of your conversation. If there's a need to call back, write it down in your daily appointment book. You may take your cards with you when you go out on appointments, but you may prefer to keep names alphabetically in a small loose-leaf pocket notebook. Then, when you're out selling and have some spare time to make a few calls, the information will be at hand.

You may either make your initial contact by phone or through the mail. The phone is simpler and more flexible. You can tell immediately if the prospect is uninterested, and you can adjust your pitch to his responses. But a turn-down may leave you with no recourse. A letter gives you the chance to include some background information, so when you do call the prospect will know something about you. Letters, however, take much more trouble to prepare and may not be commensurately effective.

Firms get junk mail and phone calls constantly. To make your communications effective, target a specific person and tailor your message to his interests. If you can refer to a mutual acquaintance, you should at least be given a hearing out of politeness. When you are told that someone might be interested in your work, or if you have an acquaintance who knows someone you'd like to contact, ask the acquaintance if you might use his name as a reference. That's how the grapevine works. Not only is permitting referrals simple goodwill, but people never know when they might be out looking for a job, and you, because you have a different set of contacts, might be able to return the favor.

Occasionally you will need to meet a prospect at some distance from your studio. If you requested the conference, you can scarcely ask for compensation, but if the prospect asked for the meeting, then you're justified in some consideration. Our policy, a common one, is to ask for travel expenses if the meeting is to discuss a potential project, and to ask for travel expenses and an hourly fee if the meeting is for consultation. These expenses and fees would be applied to any resultant job.

When telephoning a firm for the first time, state your name and, if possible, ask for a specific individual by name, say Fernstrom. If he's not the right person for you to deal with, Fernstrom should refer you to someone else, say Rackmeyer. When you reach Rackmeyer, mention that Fernstrom suggested you talk with him. Rackmeyer, assuming you know Fernstrom (as well you might), will be more attentive than if you simply called cold.

Should you not have a contact, if you're interested in a particular project, ask for that project's *project manager*. The project manager is the person assigned to that job who's responsible for overseeing it until completion. After you've talked with him, ask if there's anyone else in the office who might be looking for artwork. Keep in mind that large firms normally work on many projects simultaneously, and the people involved with one job are frequently ignorant of the progress of the others. Once you've got your foot in the door, wiggle it around a bit.

If you haven't a project in mind, ask for the person who specifies artwork. This should be someone who has an overview of all the office's activities, perhaps a principal, or the head designer. Large firms often have librarians in charge of catalogs and samples who also schedule, and thus screen , presentations. If the librarian blocks you, try to escape and start again.

Don't be so nervous that you start jabbering away to the first person who answers the phone—it might be a temporary receptionist filling in for the day. Plan what you're going to say. You'll only have a few moments to get your message across, so don't waste time. If it will help, rehearse your remarks and prepare notes, but don't make your pitch like an automaton. If you're uneasy, you can practice on the most unlikely prospects first.

When you've contacted the right person, note his name and title on your index card. Give a very brief resume including the kind of work you do—medium, technique, scale; how you do business—consignment, commission, direct sales. Ask if they might have any need for your artwork or services. Try to discover if there are current projects or clients that need art. If there are none or no prospects for any in the near future, then your relationship will be academic. You may be asked for some information for their files should something come up in the future, but that can be pie in the sky. Files are often the last place consulted. More likely sources are friends, former suppliers, more recent supplicants, and magazines.

You need not press for an appointment unless you're eager to meet the prospect. It's better to ask if they'd like you to come in, which will elicit a decision on their part. If they're too busy to see you, and you want to see them, or if they're not interested now but may be later, ask if and when you might call back. Put the new date in your appointment book. Call again. Persistence may pay off.

When you make an appointment, you can ask directions for getting there, how many people will be at your meeting, and should you plan to use a slide projector, if they have a screen and a room that can be darkened.

Grouping appointments together will save travel time. As a rule of thumb, allow from ten minutes to an hour for introductory appointments depending on how long you must wait, the number of people involved (and if they come in together or trickle in so you have to keep repeating yourself), and if there are any specific projects to discuss. Budget ample time between appointments to get from one to the other and to recover your composure.

If you are prospecting by mail, address your letter to a specific person using his title if possible. Identify yourself, mention your mutual acquaintance or how you came by his name, explain why you are writing, cite any jobs you have done for similar clients or in similar situations, and ask if you might come in to show your work. Enclose your brochure and any other suitable material. Don't include unsolicited slides or expensive artwork unless you can afford to gamble that they won't be returned. If you have no printed material, then your letter should briefly describe the kind of work you do, how you operate (consignment, commission, direct sale) and something about your background, and include a representative client list.

The following is a sample letter to enclose with a brochure:

Dear _____:

I am an artist specializing in the design and execution of wall hangings and banners in appliqué and stitchery. I recently installed eight, five- by eight-foot appliqué banners in abstract designs for the Western Bank of your city. Ms. Harriet Ames of Interiors, Inc., the designer for the job, thinks that you might also be interested in my work.

I enclose a brochure which includes some personal background, a description of how I work, and a client list. I would like to come in at your convenience and show you my portfolio. I will phone shortly to arrange a convenient time.

Thank you for your consideration.

Yours truly,

Don't call too far ahead for an appointment. Most people will not want to schedule presentations more than one to five days in advance.

The Meeting

If you have a distance to travel, or if you suspect that the prospect may be unreliable, call the evening before or that morning to confirm your appointment. Review the materials for your meeting in advance. Make sure that your presentation is ready, and that you have enough brochures and business cards to cover unexpected people or additional appointments. If you're using slides, check that they are in order and that you have an extension cord and a spare bulb for your projector.

It's arguable, but I think that dress can be important. I prefer neutral business clothes for unknown contacts, subdued but with a bit of flash accessory, like a bright necktie. Traditional firms may feel comfortable with conservative dress, but some will be disappointed if their artists don't look something of the wild man. Go-go firms won't hold it against you if you're unobtrusive. It won't threaten their turf, and you can always take off your jacket, loosen your tie, and roll up your sleeves to show you're one of the boys. Of course, you can deck yourself like an artist if you wish, but you may be mistaken for a dentist.

One successful interior designer used to wear the colors that she planned to sell on that day. When the moment came for her presentation, she would search the air for inspiration and, looking about her, discover that by happy accident she was wearing the very same colors that were absolutely perfect for the new townhouse apartment complex under consideration. I never saw her miss—what businessman could imply that a pretty woman's outfit was unsuitable?

Punctuality will make you more relaxed and help create the impression that you are reliable. If you are using a slide projector or other equipment, see if there's a free room where you can set up in advance. It's tough to keep up your patter while wrestling with a recalcitrant screen.

Your first clues about your prospect will come from the reception area. Is it elegant or frumpy, high style or reactionary, prosperous or down at the heels? Do the employees seem happy and courteous, or are they harrassed and snarling? Are you greeted efficiently and seen promptly, or are you left to fend for yourself? Scan the display areas to familiarize yourself with the firm's style and work. It can provide points of common interest for your subsequent conversation. And receptionists can be excellent sources of information about their employer's current projects and activities.

You cannot be sure who'll attend your meeting. You may line up a project manager and get the file clerk, or you may line up a junior designer and get a partner. Some offices have periodic staff meetings to see suppliers for which attendance is supposed to be mandatory, but seldom is. People may wander in and out, take a peek and stay if curious, or leave if busy or bored. If someone likes your work, he might haul in whomever he can collar. Should this happen, ask your host and the new people if you should begin over again or continue on at the point of their arrival. Note the names and positions of the people present for later identification.

Start your presentation with a brief description of your background, competence, experience, and how you operate. Show enough of your best work to give a clear idea of what you do and how well you do it, but don't overstay your welcome. Fifteen to twenty examples can suffice. If more are requested, then trot out extra. Let the prospect pace the presentation. Don't drag out the clever ways you've solved problems; let your work speak for itself with only modest commentary from you. If there's interest, you can slow down and elaborate. If there's disinterest, speed up. Answer questions frankly and honestly; evasiveness will show. If you don't have answers, offer to supply them later.

Be confident, polite, and persistent. To keep up your interest, you can set yourself the goal of leaving with a job. Ask what current projects you can become involved with and what's in the pipeline that you might check back on. Gentle probing sometimes produces unexpected results.

If there is a job possibility, there are questions you should ask and information that you'll need to decide if, and how, you want to be involved:

- Is there an established art budget, or will you have to set it?
- Is the money locked firmly into the budget or will it be sacrificed to construction overruns?
- Who will pay for the art, and how much control will they exercise?
- How much independence will you have?
- What are the materials, styles, colors, and finishes specified? Get color chips and samples if available.
- Look at the prints of the job and take copies if available.
- What is the schedule? When will the contract be let, the roughs and final art due?
- Is anyone else being considered? How will the choice be made? Will you have to bid?
- Can, and should, you visit the job site?

Post Meeting

Perform whatever you might have promised: provide additional information, estimates, or brochures. If anything substantive was discussed, you may want to submit a record of your conversation that will confirm your accord and protect you in the event of later disagreement. Confirmations of Understandings can be especially useful when dealing with complex projects, devious clients, and multiple participants. For identification, your record may include the conference date, project name, project number, meeting location (or if it was by telephone), subject and the persons present. Following that, summarize succinctly the discussion, noting what was agreed to and by whom. Conclude with a formula such as, "The above is a summary of my interpretation of the meeting. If there are any changes or clarifications, please forward them as soon as possible. Barring these, I assume that the summary is agreed to as written." Sign it and send a copy to all participants.

Timing

When you approach a prospective client is often as important as how you approach him. Consider your timing as it relates to two cycles: (1) The behavior of the general economy, and (2) the behavior of your prospect's sector of the economy. His sector may be noncyclical, like food and health, for which there's a steady demand, or cyclical, like building and steel, for which there's a varying demand.

Your prosperity is, of course, connected to that of the general economy. Your prosperity, if you work with businesses, will also be linked to the businesses with which you work. Construction, perhaps the most important of these businesses, is, unfortunately, quite cyclical. Artwork for new buildings is generally among the last things specified, purchased, and installed. Thus, when a building boom commences, it may be quite a while before the artist feels it. Conversely, at the tail end of the cycle, when architects and construction workers are being laid off, artists may still be occupied. Being last can also mean that when it finally comes time to specify artwork the budget will have been exhausted by cost overruns.

Cyclicity is a good argument, incidentally, for diversifying your client mix. If you have all of your artistic eggs in one basket and the bottom drops out, you'll be in trouble.

If you're canny, you can try sniffing out growth companies when they're still in the formative stages. The time to get involved with a hotel or restaurant chain, for example, is just when it is contemplating expansion, not after it has made its move and everyone's chasing it.

The same is true of the individual prospect. There is a critical period, usually at the beginning of a new project or renovation, when plans are formulated and money is available. Then, if you can get to the right people, you might have some influence over the specification of artwork. Later, if art has been specified, you must make your contact before a contract is let.

When exactly to make an approach is difficult to predict. Too early, of course, is better than too late. If you're too early for a particular project, ask when to check again. I've followed possibilities for years; usually they die somewhere between the second sprinkler system and the cost overrun on the carpet, but occasionally, just enough to keep my interest up, I'm rewarded. Don't depend on being remembered. We've lost plenty of jobs, even for people with whom we've worked for years, because they couldn't imagine that we'd be interested, or had forgotten we could do that sort of work, or just weren't thinking of us. Your chances are better if you provide an occasional memory freshener.

Evaluating a Prospect

Your time and energy are limited. Don't dissipate them chasing after unsuitable prospects. Before you go any further, pause a moment and decide if you wish to work *with* (not *for*, which implies subservience) the prospect and if they, the prospect, can use your services. Few people would characterize themselves as dishonest, and you should assume good will on the part of all with whom you deal, but your notions of honesty and reliability may differ from those of others, and all men do at times falter. Therefore, be prudent and protect your own interests; don't assume others will do it for you.

Some creditors drag out payments to suppliers on principle; others do it, especially to low-leverage souls like artists, so that they, the creditors, may use the money due their suppliers as no-interest loans to themselves. More dangerous are the clients who *never* pay. I mentioned earlier that incorporation absolves personal liability. While it is unlikely that you will ever incorporate, you may do business with a corporation, and corporations (particularly those that are speculative—the splashy developments and resort hotels that like alluring artwork to attract customers) go bust all the time. If you're not careful, you can be another one of those waiting to collect ten cents on the dollar after the bankruptcy sale.

How to keep from getting taken? You have various options depending on the amount of money involved and the apparent soundness of your prospect. The direct approach is often the best. Ask your prospect for references: a list of his suppliers, to see how well and regularly he pays, and his bank, to see what kind of balance he maintains. Have your banker contact the prospect's bank if his bank is reluctant to provide you with information. Your banker may also be able to obtain a Dun and Bradstreet credit rating for you. (See page 86.) Don't be bashful. You should be respected as a hardheaded businessman. If your prospect acts offended, hedges, or is embarrassed, he probably has something to hide. In that case—look out. As my cousin, Cohen the Builder, puts it, "If he pays his bills, he'll be delighted to say so."

There are some clients with whom you'll always be uneasy. These include those clients who are hard to get a handle on, like the management intermediary firms that design, specify, purchase, and bill for other companies, and the ad hoc corporations that operate with fixed funds, e.g., public bond issues. You will want assurance that there'll be money left for you after all the earlier creditors—the excavation men, the carpenters, plumbers, electricians, painters, furniture companies—have been paid off. If you're getting into that kind of heavy water, you should consult your lawyer.

Markets
End-Users

End-users are those who purchase art directly from artists for their own use. They will differ greatly in the quantity and quality of the artwork they want, and in the amount they're able to pay for it. You must identify and contact the person or group that is making the decisions, and these may be limited to or include an owner, architect, interior designer, purchasing agent, committee, department head, or manager.

End-users may be private owners, franchisers, or chains. Private owners may have only one operation or they may control a number of projects with potential for artwork. Franchises may be locally or nationally controlled. In the latter case, you would have to work directly with national or regional headquarters. Chains may be local, e.g., a group of regional supermarkets, or national, e.g., Safeway. Chains represent the opportunity of repeat work obtained through one contact, but the centralized target they present will greatly increase your competition.

It stands to reason that end-users operating in a high income market will be more likely prospects for artwork and will have higher budgets. End-users operating in lower income markets may, however, be more grateful and less demanding, and present a good chance for you to gain experience. They may also be the beneficiaries of subsidiary government or donated financing.

The solvency of end-users will differ. Some (and here new stores and restaurants particularly come to mind) may be so marginal, underfinanced, or incompetent that they fold before they can pay off their creditors. You must be especially careful in your evaluation of these prospects and be sure to get as much money as possible in advance.

In selling to end-users, you can stress your competence; your ability to provide service, especially if you're local; and the value, rather than price of your work.

I'll first discuss contractors and developers in some detail to introduce you to the subject, then briefly list and describe a number of other potential direct buyers.

Contractors and Developers

"Contractor" and "developer" are vague terms that take in everyone from the small general contractor who builds one house a year to the huge corporations which create vast communities. Some contractors and developers specialize in specific types of construction: high-rise apartments or shopping centers, for example. Some plan, design, finance, and operate projects exclusively in-house themselves while others may work entirely under contract to someone else. And there are all manner of combinations in between.

Clearly, some contractors and developers are better prospects than others. For example, a developer building a high-rise condominium in a competitive middle or upper income market might be interested in artwork for the public spaces—the lobbies, corridors, and entrance areas—to set the tone of the building. The type of artwork chosen would depend on what he gauged his market's taste to be—conservative, modern, or middle-of-the-road. The developer would be less interested if his market were not as competitive, if he felt that the taste of the prospective tenants would not justify the expenditure, or if he feared that the artwork might be stolen or vandalized before the building were occupied. Accept the fact that most business people don't put artwork in their projects simply because they love art and want to use it, although for some that is reason enough. Most require a sound economic justification; if they feel they reach their economic goals without art, then your pleas may fall on deaf ears.

If you will be working with developers and other business people, you should understand something about financing. There are two main types of expenses: *capital* and *short term* (also called *current expenses*, or simply, *expenses*). Capital expenses are those which are depreciated over a long term. While a building may be constructed within one year it will be used for a much longer period.

Therefore, its expenses are *capitalized* over various time frames. For example, the shell may be depreciated over 30 years at 1/30th per year; the plumbing and electrical work over twenty; and the painting over five or ten, reflecting their relative useful lives. Short term expenses are those ephemeral items that are used up and depreciated within one year.

In floating a loan for a building, the developer acquires a *construction* loan to cover the building phase which is afterwards converted to a *permanent* loan when the project is completed, after which he either sells, or rents out the building. The rents provide an *operating budget* for ongoing expenses. Money for subsequent *general improvements* (like artwork) or *renovations* must either come from the operating budget or an additional loan.

Private Collectors

It is hard to characterize private collectors, since there are so many types: Mom and Dad who buy an autumn scene for $19.95 at the neighborhood discount store, sharpies out for an investment or a quick killing in the art market, connoisseurs who choose the best, Hirshhorns who purchase entire studios. The most successful collectors have a keen eye and good advice, and are careful students. Some like to meet the artists whose work they buy; others would just as soon not.

If you're doing your own merchandising, keep a record of the people who've bought your work. Notify them when you have a show or put out a new print edition. Periodic open houses at your studio or encouraging visits are another means of maintaining contact, but be sure you have adequate insurance (see Insurance).

Some Other End-Users

Banks and savings and loans: Main offices and important branches of well-established banks are the most likely prospects for artwork; small, neighborhood branches are less so. Some banks actively invest in art and use their walls to display their collections; some others use their walls to display art for sale.

Businesses, corporations, manufacturers, offices: The best prospects are operations that have a positive self image and that deal actively with the public or are concerned with employee morale. Lobbies and executive areas are candidates for prestige art. Manufacturing areas, showrooms, and employees' facilities can be sites for wall graphics and low-budget artwork. Individual offices may either have their decorations assigned by management or be left to the employee's discretion.

Colleges, universities, and schools: Colleges and universities sometimes have reasonable art budgets, especially when augmented by donors. The educational bureaucracy in combination with the resident art faculty can, however, present formidable impediments to outside artists. Schools generally have lower budgets than colleges and universities. While they occasionally employ artists for model school projects, a more frequent source for art is the student body and faculty. Some state and local governments operate art-in-architecture programs that commission artwork for public buildings, which may include educational institutions. (See page 31.)

Country clubs: Country clubs tend to be toney establishments. They may want art for clubrooms, ballrooms, and dining facilities.

Hospitals: Although the trend to humanize hospitals has resulted in the increased specification of artwork, soaring equipment and facility costs may monopolize the funding. Typical art sites include lobbies, corridors, dining facilities, patient rooms, and specialty areas, such as pediatrics.

Hotels and motels: Hotels and motels may be designed locally by the owners or franchisers, by independent specifiers, or by national headquarters. Their art budgets will differ greatly in response to their markets—luxury hotels will need prestige decor; economy motels, cheap reproductions. Typical art sites include lobbies, corridors, meeting rooms, dining facilities, shops, and guest rooms.

Places of entertainment: Places of entertainment, such as theaters, movie houses and sports centers may occasionally desire art for their public areas.

Religious institutions: Religious institutions have been traditional patrons of the arts, although the budgets of individual congregations may be thin. There are artists as well as companies that specialize in producing religious art and artifacts. Should you contribute your work to a religious institution, you can deduct its retail value from your taxes.

Public buildings and institutions: Public buildings and institutions like courthouses, libraries, city halls, zoos, and parks may occasionally use artwork. These may be financed under the regular budget or under special plans, like the National Endowment for the Arts' matching programs or art-in-architecture programs. Commissions may go to local talent or, in the great spirit of boosterism, to ''nationally recognized'' biggies.

Restaurants: Restaurants, like hotels, have varying decorative needs. These may be filled not only with artworks, but also with antiques, herbage, beer mugs, old tools, and fish nets.

Stores: Stores may need decorative signs, wall graphics, and display art. Large stores generally have either in-house display departments or arrangements with graphics shops to handle their routine advertising and display needs, but they may occasionally require outside help for renovations and new stores. You should realize, however, that display and signage are complex, demanding fields that necessitate a high level of professional competence.

Shopping centers: Shopping centers may be either locally or nationally owned. Prestige operations, particularly the large malls, may use banners, wall graphics, and sculpture for their concourse areas, and coordinated decorative signs for their tenants.

Specifiers

Specifiers include interior designers, architects, art consultants, galleries, and management, consulting, or purchasing firms that specify and/or purchase artwork for others. In selling to specifiers you can, as with end-users, stress that you offer competence, service, and value. You may also add that you can reduce their work load by taking on the responsibility of both specifying and supplying their art needs.

Recognize that when they tout your work, especially if it is a prospective commission rather than an existing piece, these professionals are taking what could be a substantial risk if you do not produce up to expectation. Your nonperformance could cost them time, money, prestige, and maybe even their client. When you realize this, you can better understand their reluctance to use art, especially when they've been burned before. Large, prestigious firms with monied clients use well-known artists, not simply because they personally prefer their work (and the people specifying the art may in fact have no feeling for it), but also because they have the budget for it, and established artists are ''safe.'' A corporate vice-president won't catch too much hell if he uses Henry Moore, whose work has been used by many other corporations and who is universally well regarded. Further, if Mr. Moore should act up, everybody is off the hook. The public expects, tolerates, and even savors temperamental behavior from its artists, as long, that is, as they're famous. Smaller firms and individual designers are usually more likely to give unknown artists a break.

In dealing with specifiers you must recognize that they are only *agents for others.* You have to ascertain with what authority they are speaking. On occasion you might be given directions to proceed on a project and even a contract signed by the specifier, without the specifier actually having the sanction of the client. A sticky situation can result. If there is any question, get your instructions in writing and confirm them directly with the client. The client's check should resolve any question about the legitimacy of a contract.

Specifiers usually handle the payment for artwork in one of four ways: (1) The specifier specifies the artwork, and the artist sells to and bills the client directly. This may mean that the artwork is either included in the specifier's budget or that its use is at the client's discretion, in which case the artist may have to deal directly with the client to close the sale. The specifier's time and expenses are either added to his billing for the job or are included in his overall contract. (2) The artist bills the specifier who checks that the work has been done satisfactorily and turns the bill over to the client for payment. (3) The artist sells to the specifier, who marks up the artwork and resells it to the client. In effect the specifier is a retailer or contractor. (4) The artist bills the client directly but includes a hidden markup, which is turned over to the specifier. I find this practice, which is not common, unsavory. Sometimes a *finder's fee*, a commission paid to the specifier for finding the artist a job or a client, is involved. I think this is legitimate from the artist's standpoint if he makes the arrangements openly with a specifier, who then would be, in effect, an agent, but illegitimate if it occurs after the fact. Few professional specifiers will be interested in such a setup, and most would be insulted by its proposal because it would impugn their professional integrity, hamper their freedom of choice, and diminish their primary loyalty to their clients.

Specifiers are sometimes in the same position as elected officials—do they vote their conscience or their constituency? The crunch for the artist comes when he has been working primarily with the specifier, and a difference of opinion arises with the client. Does the specifier support the artist with whom he has been working all along, or does he abandon him and support the client? In practice these disagreements are usually resolved through amicable arbitration, with the specifier serving as a mediator. Occasionally, however, a specifier, through disinterest, a change of mind, or the fear of alienating his client and losing his own job, might try to desert the artist as he would any other supplier who causes trouble. If this happens, a breach of contract dispute may ensue. At such moments good records—memos of phone and personal conferences, signed approvals of your proposals, time sheets, letters of authorization that document the endorsement of your work as it progressed, and so forth—

—pay off.

Architects

Architectural firms come in all sizes from the one-man operation that designs apartment remodels to the mammoth firms with their branch offices that plan airports, office complexes, and whole cities. The larger the firm, the more specialized its employees. A small outfit might consist of an architect and a part-time secretary. The biggest ones have, besides architects, full-time salesmen, accountants, lighting engineers, interior designers, draftsmen, specifiers, landscape architects, graphic designers, mechanical engineers, messengers, and file clerks. Some firms do a little of everything; others specialize in such areas as city planning, institutions, remodeling and restoration, schools, hotels, or shopping centers. Some may never have occasion to specify artwork; others may leave it to their clients' discretion; or subcontract or refer it to an interior design firm; or work with agents, galleries, or art consultants.

Architects differ in their commitment to the use of artwork. Some rare ones are passionate about art, advocate its use wherever possible, and hound their clients to pay for it. Others see their buildings as complete unto themselves; to them, any artistic additions would be superfluous, if not desecrations. While most architects might use art if they could, they will not go so far as to make themselves a nuisance with their clients. (And is this surprising? When have you last defended a new building?)

The initial impulse for a building may be a private exercise, but its realization is a team effort involving many disciplines: engineers, bankers, public officials, carpenters, safety inspectors, plumbers, clients, and electricians. As part of this team you will be asked to collaborate in the joint enterprise. What will constitute reasonable collaboration and what will involve the violation of your integrity, I certainly cannot dictate. I will say that many architectural commissions are unsuccessful, in my opinion, because people have failed to integrate the art with its environment.

As you can see, your potential for success with an architectural firm depends on their attitude, the kind of work they do, the kind of work you do, how they operate, and the timing. For example, if you do large sculpture, you might look for offices that do quality shopping centers, high-rise buildings, or institutional work. Landscape architects are another possibility for outdoor work.

Architecture is part of the cyclical building industry. In recent years as the building boom has slackened, many firms have drastically cut their staffs, and some have even gone out of business. Because of this and the normal job changes, there is a constant flow of personnel between offices, and you may find that entrees and friendships within one firm will gradually lead to an ever-widening circle of acquaintances.

Interior Designers

Interior designers (*never* decorators, a pejorative now only applied to amateurs in funny hats) work with interior spaces, "man's proximate environment." Unlike architecture, there's no licensing or registration control. Like art, anyone can join. The American Society of Interior Designers (ASID), the largest organization of interior designers in the world, has sought licensing to assure professional standards that will help eliminate the gross incompetents and dilettantes who have given their occupation a bad odor in the past.

There are two main divisions of interior design: *contract* (commercial) and *residential*. Many firms specialize in one or the other, and those involved with contract work often further concentrate into such specialties as offices, hotels, hospitals, restaurants, or space planning (the laying out of interior spaces). Interior designers may have their own design studios, or work for other designers, retail or office furnishing stores, architectural firms, industries, or institutions. They may work directly with artists or through galleries, art consultants, reps, showrooms, or mail-order houses.

Interior designers resemble architects, in that they are linked to the cyclical building industry, often participate in team endeavors, and vary in their commitment to the use of art. They tend, however, to specify more art per building, because they are more immediately involved with the building's enrichment. But their unit costs are generally lower, because they award fewer large-scale commissions. In other words, they tend to buy more art but spend less for it. Also their selections may run more to the decorative than the architectural.

In forming an evaluation of interior design firms as prospects, it's helpful to know the character, type, and amount of their work; the size and quality of their staff; and their dollar volume. Unfortunately, there is no national directory of interior design firms that lists such information. The next best thing is the detailed survey of the one hundred top dollar-volume firms that *Interior Design* publishes in its January issue. Also, read the other trade magazines and ask architects, designer's representatives, and other interior designers who's doing what.

Dollar volume is critical, because you are dealing with a fraction of a fraction, the art budget portion (which occurs in only a few jobs anyhow) of the interior design budget for a total building project. In other words, a $5,000,000 building might have a total interiors budget of 10 percent or $500,000. Of that $500,000, $480,000 might go to light fixtures, carpets, furniture, wall coverings, and draperies, and $20,000 to decorations. The $20,000 in turn might be concentrated in one or two major pieces, as in the main lobby of an office building, or dispersed in many prints, posters, and decorative accessories, as in the lobby, restaurant, and guest rooms of a hotel.

A nickel-and-dime firm that does $50,000 worth of offices a year just doesn't produce the same proportion of opportunities as one that processes a steady stream of high-budget hotels, apartments, banks, and office buildings. As I've said before, however, the bigger the prize the more numerous the contestants.

Management, Consulting, and Purchasing Firms

Management, consulting, and purchasing firms offer their services to other companies to help in the operation of their businesses. Some firms give consulting or purchasing assistance only; others provide various combinations of the three. Their help may take the form of space planning, setting up a payroll operation, or ordering supplies.

For example, there are firms that plan and operate hospitals. A community in need of a hospital would contact them for expert advice in fund raising, planning the hospital, purchasing its myriad supplies, and running the hospital when it opens. Similar firms exist to serve other industries, like hotels, motels, and restaurants. Occasionally, such firms specify artwork for their clients and could therefore be a potential market.

Intermediaries: Agents, Art Consultants, and Galleries

Agents

Agents seem to populate the fantasies of artists. After all, the thinking goes, there are agents for authors, actors, and ex-presidents, why not for artists? In fact there are agents for photographers and illustrators who sell to the graphics and advertising industries, and agents for designers who sell to textile and wallpaper houses, but these markets and products are well defined, and the buyers are geographically concentrated in a few centers like New York and Los Angeles.

The circumstances are quite different in the fine arts for many reasons. The art market is geographically dispersed and ill defined. There are potential customers everywhere, but there is little guidance to evaluate them. Intermediaries like galleries are adamant in wanting neither to deal with agents nor to pay the agents' fees. Commissioned art compounds the problem. To make a sale, agents would almost have to know as much as the artists they represent. Early on, the artist would have to appear before the client for an intelligent discussion to proceed.

On the other side, what kind of product would a decent agent want to handle?—one available in sufficient and predictable supply and for which there would be a ready market. Barring that, the agent would expect a regular salary. Multiple editions are the art form that comes closest to meeting his requirements, and it is here—the sale of multiples for a pool of artists—where there might be an opportunity.

What qualities would a decent agent have? He would know the market and the product thoroughly, be industrious, persistent, dependable, honest, sympathetic, and keep good records. A bad agent would be worth less than none at all. He would alienate rather than attract clients.

That settled, many questions still remain: What if the origin of a sale is unclear—the agent makes a call but the sale occurs much later, perhaps after the client sees your art in a show? What of repeat business, where the agent makes the original sale but you deal with the client thereafter? What if you get a good account, then fire the agent? What if the agent dumps you and sells a competitor to your client?

Look for agents through advertisements in trade journals or ask noncompeting reps like carpet or print salespeople if they'd want to take up your line. Remember that good agents must see a profit in it before they'll fool with you. A normal rep's fee is 10 percent.

Art Consultants

Art consultants are a relatively recent introduction to the art field. They have no professional organization, no registration, no licensing. Some are large, efficient businesses; others operate desultorily out of homes. It is hard, therefore, to generalize about them.

From the artist's standpoint, art consultants differ from agents in one key respect: *agents represent the artist; art consultants represent the client.* The art consultant calls on, or is called in by, the same types of clients as the artist: businesses, architects, interior designers—anyone in need of art.

The consultants analyze the clients' requirements, present art selections to them, and then proceed with whatever arrangements have been worked out: purchase, delivery, installation, cataloging, and so forth.

Art consultants are free to obtain their art from the full range of sources: artists directly, galleries, shows. They may solicit slides, visit artists' studios, or deal primarily with favored artists. They may purchase work for inventory, take things on consignment, or specify art for clients.

Unless you enter into some type of exclusive agreement with an art consultant, your business arrangements should be straightforward. You will be dealing with either outright purchases by the consultant or the client, or by consignment or commission, and you would follow standard practices in each instance.

About the only ways for you to locate an art consultant are through hearing or reading about them. You may consider consultants both as additional outlets and as potential competitors. Whereas you offer your clients your work alone, consultants can offer an artistic smorgasbord. Not only is their menu larger, but they set the table, clean up, and take credit cards.

Art Galleries

Art galleries are the traditional places to sell art. The cachet of a good gallery and the services of an industrious dealer can be indispensable in advancing an artist's career. They signal your acceptance into the art world, but by no means do they guarantee a steady income.

Commercial sales galleries, while most familiar, are not the only type of gallery. There are auction galleries like Sotheby's; antique galleries that sell older work; discount galleries that sell paintings on velvet; frame stores that have a sales gallery attached; museum sales and rental galleries; vanity galleries, which charge artists for showing their work; cooperative galleries run by groups of artists, and the increasingly common private galleries operated in private homes or apartments that show

by appointment only. Some galleries are large enough to give several one-person shows at a time; others crowd a few pieces into one small room. Most galleries specialize in particular styles, media, periods, or forms of expression.

Sales galleries ordinarily have a "stable" of one to several dozen artists who receive three-week shows during the regular art season, which falls between October 1 and June 1. Being profit-making organizations, galleries tend to promote those artists whose work sells with regular annual or biannual shows, publicity, and active merchandising. Less marketable artists can expect less frequent and less active exposure—some galleries may stable fifty or more artists who appear in one-person or group shows every five to ten years. A dealer can make more money selling one third-rate Picasso, and make it more easily, than in a season's shows of living artists.

New artists are usually taken on a trial basis. Their work is kept in back and shown to selected clients for their reactions. If the work is well received, the artists may be included in a group show, generally held in the June-through-September off-season. With acceptance, they may hope to enter the stable either immediately or when a vacancy occurs through normal attrition.

No one knows how many legitimate galleries there are in the United States, much less how many living artists have gallery connections. In New York City, there are, perhaps, 550 galleries. Multiplying that figure by an average stable of 24 artists per gallery, we can estimate there are 13,200 artists with current New York representation, a figure—even with an error of 50 percent—that nonetheless gives some feel for the chances of a New York connection.

Evaluate a gallery by asking other artists and by judging the gallery's stable, location, clientele, promotion, advertising, critical connections, physical layout, and mounting of their shows. Do not look for a gallery prematurely, when you're still in school, for example. Wait until you have a body of work to show. Don't attempt big or out-of-town galleries before you know the ropes; start first with the small, local ones. As a rule, the newer and less established the gallery, the more receptive it will be for fresh talent. Don't be put off by galleries not associated with your type of work. Sometimes changes in personnel and philosophy will send galleries into new directions.

The easiest way to contact a gallery is through the front door. A recommendation in advance from an influential person—another dealer, a collector, a museum curator, or a respected artist—can do nothing but help. In fact, some galleries require an introduction. Tuesdays through Fridays, before mid-afternoon, are generally good times to call on them because things are slow. Many galleries are closed Mondays, but some set that day aside for open houses. Avoid busy times like weekends and openings. It's wise, especially if you'll be coming a distance, to make advance arrangements by mail or phone. Take a selection of ten to twenty slides or original art (if it's small), a pocket slide viewer on the off chance the gallery has none, and a resume. *Don't* take friends or family members. Witnesses can make the pain of a refusal more acute for all. Be polite and positive. Once again, you're selling yourself. The dealer will be interested not only in your work, but also in how much of it you will produce, and in your experience and personality. Be prepared to discuss how much money you want for your work. The dealer will tell you what he thinks he can sell it for, and through discussion you should arrive at an acceptable rate structure.

Being rejected (and sad to say, the odds are that you will be) does not mean your work is inferior. The dealer may have bad taste or no room, be insensitive to your type of expression, or have other legitimate or illegitimate reasons. Don't be discouraged. Persevere. If your work has merit, it should eventually find a home.

Enterprising dealers are always scouting new talent. They jury and visit shows and exhibitions, read the magazines and newspapers, and talk with art professionals and collectors. Your chances of recognition are increased by getting your work out on display.

Be understanding of gallery people. They have their own problems. Most have terrific overhead: rent, utilities, insurance, employees, promotion. They may spend years of investment in time and money to establish a market for an artist, only to have the artist take off for another gallery. And galleries get it from both ends—temperamental artists and temperamental clients. Although a few cynical dealers "collect money," I like to think that most are in the business because they believe in it.

The type of arrangement you work out with a gallery will depend on the gallery's policy and on your leverage. The competition for good galleries is so fierce that, unless you have a hot item, you will be negotiating from weakness. If you make too many (or sometimes any) demands, you risk being replaced by someone less troublesome. One artist's group, Artists Equity, advocates that artists represented by recalcitrant dealers bargain collectively, a Pollyanna-ish proposal to me. Most artists, vulnerable and solipsistic, are in no position to engage in confrontation politics. A sharp dealer need only offer the ringleaders a sweeter deal, or drop a few artists, to swiftly quash a revolt.

The business relationship between an artist and a gallery can be very complex, increasing in complexity proportionate to the amount of money at stake. Commissions can range from 25 to 60 percent, depending on the services performed and the expenses involved, with 40 to 50 percent of the sale's price as an average. Some other problems are exclusive rights and the costs of transportation, promotion, and insurance. Several model contracts for artists and dealers have been devised. Examples may be found in: *Art Works*, by Feldman and Weil; *Guide for the Visual Artist*, by Crawford; and *The Artist's Guide to His Market*, by Chamberlain. Others may be obtained from Artists Equity (in a packet which includes one gallery's policy statement) and Lawyers for the Arts Committee, Young Lawyers Section, Philadelphia Bar Association, 423 City Hall Annex, Philadelphia, Pennsylvania, 19107.

The Bay Area Lawyers for the Arts Artist-Gallery Agreement which is reproduced in Crawford, *Guide for the Visual Artist*, covers the following questions:

- Geographical area in which the gallery represents the artist.
- Consignment arrangement: all new works, first choice of new works, minimum number of works to be selected, all new works exclusive of direct studio sales and commissions, or work consigned at separate times.
- Exclusivity of the gallery's representation.
- Transportation cost payment, pick-up and delivery, percent by artist, percent by gallery.
- Verification that title remains with the artist until consigned works are sold.
- Promotion arrangements to be made by gallery.
- Gallery is allowed to discount work by _____ percent.
- Sales commission in percent for each medium, and for studio sales and commissions made directly by the artist.
- Payment schedule for outright, deferred, and installment sales.
- Time limit on approval sales.
- Rental time limit and fees.
- Exhibitions, their frequency, duration, solo or group, control over participation in group shows, cost divisions for exhibitions and other promotional expenses.
- Insurance for loss or damage to _____ percent of retail value.
- Statements of account, their frequency and content.
- Protection of artist's copyright, artist's approval required for all reproductions.
- Artwork not subject to creditors' liens.
- Duration of the agreement and termination arrangements.
- Division of costs for the return of the work on termination of agreement.

Even if you don't have a contract, and many galleries won't use them, you should try to resolve amicably some of the important issues these sample contracts address. Hopefully, you should at least have a written, signed record of your conversation with your dealer, but again, even that may not be obtainable.

The Art Information Center, Inc. (189 Lexington Avenue, New York, NY, 10016) is a nonprofit information clearinghouse run for many years by Betty Chamberlain. The Center, which is open from mid-September to mid-June, sees artists by appointment, looks at their work, and suggests most likely New York gallery possibilities. They also keep a file on about 50,000 living artists with their gallery affiliations, and offer a number of other free services to artists. To learn more about the Center, consult Chamberlain's *The Artist's Guide to His Market.*

Federal Government Markets

Federal programs are not immutable. They reflect the priorities of the public, and the people who support and administer those priorities. Currently, the General Services Administration (GSA) and National Endowment for the Arts (NEA) art programs are doing well. Yet, in the next administration, or next year, circumstances may cause cutbacks or cancellations.

The General Services Administration

The General Services Administration (GSA), sometimes called "the nation's landlord," is responsible for the design, construction, and operation of most of the federal government's buildings with the exception of those of the Department of Defense, Veterans Administration, and various scientific facilities like the National Aeronautics and Space Administration.

The GSA's Art-in-Architecture Program, the nation's largest visual arts program in scope and funding, presently allocates one-half of one percent of the construction or renovation budget of all new, remodeled, or restored buildings for the purchase of works of art integral to the architectural design. The program is subject to the discretion of the Administrator of the GSA, that organization's chief executive, because Congress has never written its mandate into law.

To be considered for the program, contact: Art-in-Architecture Program, General Services Administration, 18th and F Streets, N.W., Washington, D. C., 20405. You will be sent simple instructions for submitting slides.

Because it is long-term, the GSA slide file is the best route for regular consideration, but it is not the only one. Individual members of the selection panel and the project architect can themselves propose artists with whose work they are familiar. Artists can, if they are not registered with the GSA, contact panelists directly, although this is not encouraged.

The program has produced some fine works of art for the nation, but can hardly be considered a source of income for artists. Since its inception in the early sixties to June, 1979, ninety-four works were commissioned, whereas the art-in-architecture office receives perhaps 3,000 applications annually.

In its implementation of the "Living Buildings Program," a recent act of Congress that opened up federal buildings for cooperative public use, the GSA has encouraged individual artists and art organizations to use buildings under GSA management for the display of art and art-related activities. Although there may be some exhibition facilities available in particular buildings, the GSA essentially provides only the space. It is up to the artists to supply their own installation, insurance, display cases (where not available), and the like. For more information and clearance, contact the manager of the federal building under consideration. If you have trouble locating the building manager or any other difficulties, you may contact for assistance: Living Buildings Program, General Services Administration, Washington, D.C., 20405.

Most art items purchased by the GSA (to use the official designation "Class 71–23 Wall Art—to exclude originals") must be selected from an approved GSA Federal Supply Schedule. To be considered, purveyors of art must present the GSA with a catalog containing such information as a price list and maximum and minimum order quantities. When his catalog is accepted, the applicant is considered "under contract" and given a contract number. Being "under contract" only signifies that you are eligible to receive contracts, not that you have been awarded one. The contract list is circulated nationwide. Interested agencies may request a catalog, or the supplier may contact agencies directly. If his catalog is too expensive to give away, a supplier has the option of showing the catalog personally to prospects and leaving only price information behind.

As you may surmise, the paperwork is formidable. Generally, only large-scale vendors of graphic multiples or the most perseverant individuals attempt "getting on schedule." If you wish to take a whirl, contact: General Services Administration, Business Service Center, Washington, D.C., 20405. Your request will produce one mailman carrying approximately one pound of bedtime reading. For help with it you may contact the Washington, D.C., office or one of the other nine regional Business Service Centers, which will provide counseling and assistance. Another source of help in dealing with the federal government, not just the GSA, are the Federal Information Centers located in federal buildings of key cities across the nation.

National Endowment for the Arts (NEA)

The National Endowment for the Arts (NEA) provides money to cities, towns, and other non-federal governmental units, and to universities, nonprofit, tax-exempt private groups, and state arts agencies. This aid supports museums, art publications, exhibits, workshops, and programs. The largest such program is "Works of Art in Public Places" (sometimes confused with the GSA's Art-in-Architecture Program), which furnishes matching grants to participating organizations sponsoring artists or artwork. While artists cannot apply directly to the NEA, they can ask to be considered for planned programs or can lobby for the creation of new projects. Your local arts agency is a good first place to inquire.

The NEA also assists artists individually through its fellowships for painters, sculptors, craftspeople, photographers, printmakers, and art critics; its residence programs for craftspeople, artists, and photographers; and its apprenticeships for craftspeople. Grants range from $1,000 to $10,000 each and are essentially nonrenewable. In 1977, the NEA awarded 98 artists' fellowships, 79 for $7,500 each and 17 for $3,000 each, a total of $663,500.00. There were 3,000 applicants for the fellowships, an acceptance ratio of 30 to 1. Since its inception in 1967, NEA has dispensed $3,710,000 to 754 artists. (If this seems like a lot of money, remember that HEW misplaces more than that on a good day.) The award amounts, total budget, and applicants have all been increasing annually.

For a copy of the *Visual Arts Application Guidelines*, write: National Endowment for the Arts, Mail Stop 606, Washington, D.C., 20506. There are deadlines for each project category, after which you must wait another year for consideration.

Comprehensive Employment and Training Act (CETA)

The Comprehensive Employment and Training Act (CETA), a multi-billion-dollar employment and training program, is divided into eight sections called *Titles*, each of which has a separate goal. Arts-related programs come under: Title I, which provides training and work experience to prepare for future employment; Title II, which provides needed public services in areas of substantial unemployment; Title III, which provides short-term jobs and training for youth and other groups; and Title VI, which provides anti-recession emergency jobs. Legislation now under consideration may change the titles, but the basic provisions will remain the same. Funding for the programs is steady, except for Title VI, which varies in response to unemployment. Presently between one and two percent of the total CETA budget goes to arts-related jobs.

CETA gives money in block grants to "prime sponsors" (state and local governments), which may then subcontract to public or nonprofit organizations for the support of such community programs as wall murals in San Francisco and Baltimore, art workshops in Albany, and the placement of graphic artists with the schools of Tacoma. The prime sponsors are responsible for hiring only. The employing agency must conceive, develop, and implement individual projects with minimal direction from Washington. Questions like ownership of completed artwork and artistic qualifications must be handled at the local level. Artists must meet

standard criteria of unemployment and income status to qualify. The programs are only temporary, designed to help artists get back to work and teach them new job skills. Wages currently vary between $7,000 and $10,000 per year.

To find out what may be available in your area, contact your local agency, or your city or town hall for the number of the regional CETA office, or the U.S. Department of Labor, CETA, 601 D Street, N.W., Washington, D.C., 20213. If there is no suitable CETA program in your area, you can work with appropriate local organizations to design one. You might be its first employee.

NEA provides information and assistance in setting up local programs using non-endowment funds, which includes CETA. Contact NEA's Intergovernmental Affairs Office for more information.

Other Federal Arts Programs

Many other federal agencies have programs that support the arts. Their number, enthusiasm, and funding vary, but the general trend is upward. The Associated Council of the Arts *Cultural Directory* is an excellent introduction. You may supplement it with the *Bulletin on Federal Economic Programs and the Arts*. Both are obtainable from the NEA. The artists' information sources listed in the Bibliography will keep you current on these as well as other opportunities.

State and Local Government Programs

To an increasing extent, state and local governments are enacting legislation to purchase or commission artwork for public buildings and spaces. The plans differ in their administration, preference for local artists, and percentage of funds allocated. Arts groups and periodicals report on new programs as they develop. For information on current programs, contact:

The Mayor's Advisory Committee on Art and Culture, 21 S. Eutaw Street, Baltimore, Maryland, 21201.

Art Coordinator, Metropolitan Dade County Florida, Room 1206, 140 W. Flagler Street, Miami, Florida, 33130.

State Foundation on Culture and Art, 250 S. King Street, Room 310, Honolulu, Hawaii, 96813.

City of Philadelphia Art Commission, 1329 City Hall Annex, Philadelphia, Pennsylvania, 19107.

San Francisco Art Commission, 165 Grove Street, San Francisco, California, 94102.

Seattle Arts Commission, 305 Harrison Street, Seattle, Washington, 98109.

State of Washington—the following have programs: Cities: Yakima, Renton, Wenatchee, Everett, Ballevue; Counties: King, Tacoma-Pierce.

Washington State Arts Commission, 1151 Black Lake Boulevard, Olympia, Washington, 98504.

Museums

Museums are chronically underfinanced. With the exception of a few specialty museums, they have little or no money for buying contemporary art and, like any institution entrusted with public funds, they must follow a set purchasing formula that entails reviews by groups like the staff, acquisition committees, and trustees. Furthermore, museums do not acquire art simply because it appeals to the curators; all acquisitions must conform to the collections' long-range goals.

Each museum has a policy for artists wishing to sell their work. Some museums may be completely disinterested; some may ask that artists mail in slides and other material; others may wish to see actual work. Call or write before taking any action. Do not operate through proxies—curators, like dealers, are turned off by agents and other go-betweens. Given the numbers of artists and the demands on a curator's time, the dreamed-of studio visit that confers the magic touch of stardom is rare indeed.

Donation, despite the inequitable law that allows only the value of the art materials to be taken as a tax deduction, is a route that some artists consider for the prestige of entry into a museum's collection. But even giving your art to a museum is not that easy. True, donation sidesteps the financial hurdle of a purchase price, but it still leaves those of the accession process and the museum's goals. Moreover, as far as the museum is concerned, the costs of acquisition—the staff work, cataloging, and photography—is the same whether artwork is free or purchased.

A museum's exhibitions and their sales and rental galleries are their most realistic resources for artists. As with acquisitions, each museum will have its own policies. Contact your local museums for more information and keep up with exhibition opportunities through artists' periodicals and museum newsletters.

3. Specifying and Purchasing Materials

Specifying Materials

Artwork for public spaces often has different requirements than those for private or museum use. To identify suitable media, materials, and techniques, ask yourself a series of questions.

Whom will you have to satisfy? The hospital administrator, chief surgeon, or the building furnishings committee? What is your client's taste? Will you educate, elevate, reflect, delight, or challenge it?

What public will be using the space? Elite or mass, educated or ignorant, sick or well, lawful or vandal, appreciative or resentful?

What is the function of the space? Is it the president's office, or the employees' lounge, the hotel lobby or the guest rooms, the college library or the dining hall? The president's office may demand dignity and richness, the employees' lounge, budget and zip; the hotel lobby, flamboyance and grandeur; the guest rooms, tranquility and theft resistance.

Will the artwork have any functions? Is it expected to absorb noise, divide space, direct traffic, sell merchandise, instruct, commemorate?

What is the artwork's environment? What is the color, source, intensity, and direction of the *light?* Is it fixed or changing? Daylight adds movement and the drama of shadow, but it can also obscure and dazzle, and fade materials. Light's color and strength affect our perception. For example, cool fluorescents dull warm colors, and vice versa; dimly lit rooms may need bold, contrasty artwork.

Weather is a prime consideration for outdoor art. Pollution, water, sun, wind, and the heating-cooling cycle will limit the life of all coatings and quickly destroy improperly constructed or secured artwork. Check with the property authorities for the acceptable wind tolerance. In Maryland, for example, signs must withstand winds of about 130 m.p.h., well over hurricane force.

How will the artwork be seen? What is the artwork's viewing distance and angle? Will it be seen from close up and afar, and from different angles? Will people walk and ride past it, or sit and contemplate it?

What maintenance will be needed and who will do it? Will the artwork need to be cleaned, periodically refinished, have parts changed? Will special skills be necessary? Will it have to withstand indifferent maintenance personnel with their mops, vacuum cleaners, and scrubbing compounds, or will it demand tender loving care?

Will your artwork be protected? Will the area be supervised? Will your work be accessible or sheltered?

What is your artwork's anticipated useful life? Is it to last for a day, a month, a season, or a year? Until renovation or relocation? For the life of the building or forever?

What is the budget? Does the client want quantity or quality? Does he want it cheap or right?

Some Special Problems

The purchase price is only one component of the cost equation; the price divided by useful life gives a truer idea of the real cost:

$$\frac{\text{Price}}{\text{Useful Life}} = \text{True Cost.}$$

The replacement cost in labor and materials is another consideration.

Soil resistance and easy cleaning are important in areas of heavy traffic, food use, and contact, e.g., walls right above seating. Study the job site for potential problems. Some art forms that attract touching, like sculpture and fiber work, may need special provisions.

Avoid sensitive materials in problem locations or take extra precautions. For example, don't design delicate artwork all the way to the floor of a narrow, busy corridor, where people and equipment will surely destroy it. Start your work above the chair rail height and put paint, tile, carpet, or vinyl below it. Other precautions include physical barriers like railings, low walls, or furniture, and protective shielding with glass, plastic, or applied coatings.

Vandalism ranges all the way from topical improvements with spray paint and markers through structural damage like abrasion, hammering, tearing, bending, and breaking—"creative destruction," one architect called it (but then, Rauschenberg was making art when he erased deKooning's drawing).

We can't prevent determined vandals, but we can take reasonable precautions. Physical barriers, traffic supervision, and guards will help. Avoid large, one-color, sleek surfaces, which, like automobile bodies, are hard to maintain. Use textured and patterned surfaces and those that can be repaired in limited sections. Don't design weak, un-supported parts, such as long arms that can be levered, and avoid working components, such as fountain pipes or machinery that can be jammed or plugged. Strong, resistant materials such as metal alloys, exotic plastics, and tough ceramics are best, but may be too costly.

Neglect invites imitation. Leave one graffito unremoved, and overnight more will join it. Community involvement and pride are critical. People will care for artwork they care for.

Theft occurs in all places, and under the most unexpected circumstances. Like vandalism, it can be minimized by barriers, protective cases, guards, alarms, and secure installations with adhesives and heavy-duty hardware.

Water resistance is a problem for artwork outside, even if it is sheltered, and for any artwork inside if it is in a moisture-laden atmosphere, such as is found in swimming pool, bath, and fountain rooms. Some materials, e.g., nylon, stainless steel, glass, and ceramics are naturally water resistant. Color coatings that are fused to the artwork, e.g., porcelain enamels and ceramic glazes, and colors that are dispersed through it, e.g., colored plastics and clays, will wear much better than surface coatings like paint. Continuous-film coatings deny moisture entry to the interior. Edge grain and inter-faces, particularly where materials with different coefficients of expansion come together, are critical moisture entry points. A good sign man will be familiar with the weather problems in your area.

Ultraviolet light from the sun and most fluorescent tubes fades colors and rots fabrics, especially silk, cotton, most rayons, and nylon. Avoid fugitive colors and suspect fabrics. Rely on reputable manufacturers and read their product information. Screen out the sun with tinted glass, blinds, linings, and barriers. Use ultraviolet screening fluorescents or filters. (See page 153.)

Fire Codes and Officials

In the United States, fire protection requirements are promulgated and enforced at the state and local levels. Therefore, you should review the fire safety requirements of the locale in which you're working. Fire codes are customarily based on those developed by code-writing groups, and the most important code is the sixteen volume code of the National Fire Protection Association (NFPA).

Building codes also contain fire prevention provisions, and are customarily based on the codes of three groups: The Building Officials Conference of America (BOCA), the International Conference of Building Officials (ICBO), and the American Insurance Association (AIA).

Fire officials are involved with a building's construction and with periodic inspections throughout its life. Building inspectors are ordinarily concerned with fire prevention only before the building is occupied. Sometimes the authority of the two may overlap and a jurisdictional conflict may occur. Accordingly, when working on major jobs in new buildings, it's wise to touch base with both. You can identify the appropriate inspectors by asking the building's owners, general contractor, architect, or interior designer; the local governmental division's headquarters; or the nearest fire marshal's office or fire station.

Because there are always so many variables, fire officials determine what's acceptable on a case-by-case basis. Drawing on their experience they consider such factors as the construction of the building, the nature of its occupants, and the fire history of similar structures within the region. It's hard to generalize—what may be approved without question in one jurisdiction might be turned down in the next.

Fire officials inspect buildings periodically according to an established priority. If they should find anything, including artwork, which they suspect may not be flame resistant, they can order it removed until their doubts are satisfied or they may conduct an on-the-spot NFPA Standard 701, Chapter 6 Field Test, which consists of holding a lit match under it for twelve seconds:

6-1 Test Materials.

6-1.1 Test specimens shall be dry and shall be a minimum 1½ inches wide by 4 inches long.

6-1.2 The fire exposure shall be the flame from a common wood kitchen match . . . applied for twelve seconds.

6-3 Test Requirements

6-3.1 During the exposure, flaming shall not spread over the complete length of the sample or in excess of 4 inches from the bottom of the sample (for larger size sample).

6-3.2 There shall be not more than two seconds of afterflame.

6-3.3 Materials which break and drip flaming particles shall be rejected if the materials continue to burn after they reach the floor.

You can avoid this horror by clearing your artwork in advance with the fire official and getting his approval in writing. In addition, you should provide either a certificate of flame resistance, a sample piece, or both.

The NFPA Life Safety Code No. 101

This is the most widely accepted guide. Copies only cost a few dollars. (See Bibliography.) The code divides occupancies into various classifications: places of assembly (theaters, auditoria, dance halls), educational, health care and penal, residential (including hotels and apartments), mercantile, business, industrial and storage. The different occupancies have hierarchies of concern, e.g., the requirements for a hospital or school will be stricter than those for an office or business, and there may be different priorities within the same occupancy according to usage, e.g., a hospital's exitway will be more critical than its doctors' offices. The highest priority is always assigned to exits and exitways which may include lobbies and other areas not especially obvious to the untrained eye. The building's contents and the nature of its operations are also taken into consideration.

A building's *interior finishes* (the exposed interior surfaces including any attached artwork) are rated according to their flamespread and combustibility. There are three classifications in descending fire resistance: *Class A* (0–25 flamespread and combustibility), *Class B* (26–75 flamespread and combustibility), *Class C* (76–200 flamespread and combustibility). A rating over 200 indicates high flammability. Materials are given a corresponding rating which confines their use to the area within their classification. For example, Class A materials are permitted in Class A, B, and C areas; Class B materials are permitted in Class B and C areas; and Class C materials are permitted, with certain exceptions, only in Class C areas. In general, paintings and textiles, unless they are intentionally composed of fire resistant materials, fall in the Class C area and could, therefore, be excluded from Class A and B installations. More about this in a moment.

A sprinkler system advances any area in which it is located one grade. Thus, a Class A area of a sprinklered hospital could tolerate a certain amount of Class B artwork that would not be permitted without sprinklering.

The NFPA uses three principal terms to describe the combustibility of materials:

Fire resistive "refers to properties or designs to resist the effect of any fire to which a material or structure may be expected to be subjected."

Flame resistant, flame retardant "refers to materials, usually decorative which due to chemical treatment or inherent properties do not ignite readily or propagate flaming under small to ·moderate exposure."

Flammable, inflammable "is used to describe a combustible material that ignites very easily, burns intensely, or has a rapid rate of flamespread."

Other common terms are:

Combustible "is used to refer to a material or structure that can burn." It is a relative term: "many materials that will burn under one set of conditions will not burn under others."

Fireproof "has been officially discontinued in NFPA publications . . . *Fireproof* as popularly used is synonymous with *fire resistive* as defined here."

Fire retardant "in general, denotes a substantially lower degree of fire resistance than fire resistive and is often used to refer to materials or structures which are combustible in whole or part, but have been subjected to treatments or have surface coverings to prevent or retard ignition or the spread of fire under the conditions for which they are designed."

It is a specialized vocabulary and the distinctions can be quite important when you deal with fire officials.

General Guidelines

From a fire official's viewpoint there are certain guidelines governing the use of artwork:

1. A reasonable amount of artwork, a painting or two, for example, would probably be allowed in any area of a building regardless of the area's rating.

2. Painting directly on a wall, unless the paint coating is unusually thick, would not be questioned as long as the wall itself passed code.

3. Fabric, and this includes mural canvas and other substrata, attached to a wall is considered an interior finish when that fabric is in excess of 1/28 inch in thickness (according to the NFPA Life Safety Code) and could, therefore, alter the fire rating of the wall.

4. Class C artwork attached to a wall may be considered as "trim" if it does not constitute more than ten percent of the combined wall and ceiling area and thus could be permitted in Class A and B areas.

5. Artworks hanging away from the wall or hanging from the ceiling, banners, for example, are viewed with more concern than artworks attached directly to the wall, for two reasons: hanging art has twice the surface (the front *and* back) exposed to fire, and its elevation increases the danger from falling masses of flaming material which can rapidly spread a fire.

6. Freestanding artworks may be challenged only if they are of a highly flammable material or if they block an egress.

7. Working on location can create a problem if the artist is employing a hazardous technique like welding or if he is using a flammable, pungent substance that smells dangerous, e.g., ether, MEK, or gasoline.

8. Artworks which do not expose a building to fire (those more than, say, twenty feet away) are ordinarily of no concern to the fire official unless they block an egress.

Materials

Metal, glass, stone, clay, plaster, concrete, etc. are traditional materials that are inherently fire resistive and should not be challenged unless they are given a flammable coating.

Wood varies in its flamespread and combustibility according to its species, surface exposure, and surface treatment. Fire retardant paint or varnish can lower it a Class B or even A rating.

A number of manufacturers produce fire retardant paints and varnishes most of which work by *intumescence*. The coating contains tiny particles that, when struck by the heat of a fire, immediately swell into a thick protective layer of insulating foam. Fire retardant paint manufacturers include Sherwin Williams, Baltimore Paint and Chemical, Hanline, Benjamin Moore, O'Brien, PPG, and Pratt and Lambert. Look for their addresses and other names in *Thomas' Register of American Manufacturers.*

Plastics have a bad name among many fire officials because of their adverse fire experience with them. Also, plastics are manufactured in confusing variety, yield erratic test results, and, in many instances, produce poisonous smoke. Your proposal for their extensive use, especially in Class A or B areas, may prompt official opposition.

Fire resistive or inherently flameproof fabrics include fiberglass, metals, and asbestos.

Flame retardant and flame resistant fabrics include Nomex, sarans, wool, treated silk fabrics, and thermoplastics like polyesters and olefins. Thermoplastic fabrics may initially resist ignition, but once they catch fire they tend to melt in a shower of burning particles.

Flammable fabrics include untreated cotton, linen, rayon, and acetate.

Fabrics can be treated with a durable flame retardant finish. For example, Kiesling-Hess (KH), a leading finisher, offers several different processes. KH can treat most fabrics, even velvets, with no appreciable change except for some slight shrinkage. They issue flame resistance certificates for the materials they treat; tell them in which jurisdiction your fabrics will be used. Write KH for a guide booklet with prices. (See Sources.)

There are fire retardant sprays and dips on the market but Mr. Richard R. Hess, president of KH, says this about them: "Our experience has been that fire retardant sprays and dips, while useful in some areas, are normally not suitable to pass Federal, State and Municipal Fire Codes. They normally are applicable to cotton fabrics only."

While it is primarily the client's responsibility to satisfy the fire requirements within his own building, artists should identify and avoid potential problems or at least bring them to the client's attention. Should a fire official reject your artwork, even if the fault is not your own, your client may be reluctant to pay you for something he cannot use.

4. Pricing

Pricing is not a science but a mixture of elements, some reducible to fact, others not. These elements include: what *you* think you're worth, what *others* think you're worth, what you've *been* charging, what your *competition* charges, and what your *costs* are.

Review your finances periodically to see if you're making enough money and adjust your prices accordingly. "But," you may say, "I'm charging as much as I can now, no one will pay me any more." Answer: Raise your prices imperceptibly over time. Identify unprofitable items and either raise their prices or eliminate them. Change your clients to those who'll pay more. Reduce your overhead. Change your product.

I discuss in this chapter two phases of pricing: first, pricing completed artwork, a relatively easy process, then estimating, an often complex process.

Pricing Completed Artwork

The chief determinant in pricing completed artwork is the market—the demand for your work and the price of your competition. One good way to get a feel for your market is to keep your prices low when you start out and gradually raise them until you meet a *resistance point*, a point where people either stop buying your work or start considering competitive sources. If you begin with your prices too high, you may never develop a market. You won't know if your problem is price or product.

Some art experts feel that you should never drop your prices—to do so indicates irresolution and a weakness in the demand for your work. That might be, but many artists prefer to give a painting a good home for $100 than keep it themselves for $125. There are no hard and fast rules. If you don't have an active market (and few artists do) and if you make your adjustments quietly, price variations should go unnoticed. Once you settle on a price structure, try to be consistent.

Dealers, who should know their market and what work like yours should sell for, can give you pricing guidance. You may be happy to find they value your work more highly than you do, or you may be dismayed that they think it less salable. If you think their estimates are unreasonable, frankly discuss your reservations to see if you can arrive at a more acceptable figure.

Do some comparative shopping to determine the prices of your competition. Visit galleries and shows, talk with collectors and other artists. The art world is notorious for misquoting prices, in all directions, ostensibly paid for work. You want the true prices of *actual* sales, not a lot of gossip.

You can stimulate the market for your work by promotional activities like favorable publicity, prizes, exhibitions in prestigious shows, commissions, and open houses in your studio.

Artists who don't have a regular gallery, or whose gallery doesn't have exclusive rights to their work, often worry if they should standardize their prices; if they should charge the same amount whether they're selling from their studio, a gallery, their hometown, or someplace distant. First, talk to your dealer if you have one. Some may want you to charge the same amount for your personal sales as they do with their commission added. This is justifiable from their standpoint; they don't want you to undercut their sales. But, if they've only taken a piece or two of yours, or if they are not actively promoting you, you may deserve a more equitable arrangement. Other dealers may not care what you do outside their galleries. Of course, if your gallery has exclusive rights, you cannot sell through any other channel.

Pricing Your Time

You will need to price your time in order to bill clients for it and to compute estimates. The easiest method is to charge according to the competition. If you cannot find anyone to compare yourself with, you can use as a guide the rates of design professionals who customarily charge by the hour, e.g., graphic designers, architects, and interior designers. Adjust your rates according to whether you think your services merit more or less money, and refine them through market feedback.

Invaluable are the Comparative Cost Studies run by *Signs of the Times* magazine since 1948. (See Bibliography.) This monthly series describes an actual project, then lists a sequence of estimates, which include material and labor costs, derived from voluntary submittals of participating firms around the country. The data are supplemented by an analysis and some of the correspondent's more pungent remarks.

The second method involves some schizophrenia (which shouldn't be difficult for most artists).

You must think of yourself as an employee (of yourself) and decide how much money you'd like to earn in a year. Divide that figure by the number of hours you work to obtain your base hourly rate. Example: You want to earn $100 per week or $5,200 per year. You work the normal 40-hour week for 52 weeks per year (allow yourself two weeks paid vacation) which equals 2,080 hours. Your salary of $5,200 divided by 2,080 hours equals $2.50 per hour. You will take a loss, however, if you charge your clients $2.50 an hour, because you have ignored your profit and overhead, and the sad fact that your employee (you) will spend perhaps half his 40-hour week nonproductively. (Time yourself to see what I mean.) You, as the employer of yourself, have to provide proper working conditions and equipment for your employee (you) and are entitled to a reasonable profit. Therefore, you must mark up your employee's (your) wages. The amount of your markup will depend on the nature of your business, volume, profit margin, and overhead. Accurately defining overhead, those fixed costs that cannot be charged off directly to a specific client, just about requires a full-time bookkeeper, since you must consider liability insurance, utilities, studio rent, office supplies, renovation, equipment, promotion, selling, vehicles, telephone, etc.

You can bypass the overhead calculation by using a standard markup, such as 2½ ×, a widely accepted figure. If you have a lower overhead than most small businesses, 2½ × should yield more than an adequate profit and give you a margin you can trim to become more competitive.

To use it, again think of your wage of $100 per week. Add the fixed costs of FICA of $5.85, federal and state unemployment of $3.20 (see Chapter 15), and employee benefits like medical insurance (which we'll put at $10 per week) and divide the total, $119.05, by 40 hours per week for an adjusted hourly wage of $2.98. Factor the $2.98 by 2½ for a total of $7.45, the hourly fee you, as an employer, will charge clients to make your $2.50 an hour wages as an employee, plus a reasonable profit as an employer.

Here are your calculations stated as a formula:

$$\text{Hourly Desired Net Wages} = \frac{\text{Annual Desired Net Wages (Desired weekly net} \times \text{52 weeks/year)}}{\text{2,080 hours (40 hours/week} \times \text{52 weeks/year)}}$$

$$\$2.50/\text{hour} = \frac{\$100 \times 52}{2,080}$$

corr gal 40 page 39

$$\text{Hourly Gross Fee} = \frac{2\frac{1}{2} \text{ Standard Markup (Desired weekly net} + \text{FICA} + \text{Federal and State Unemployment} + \text{Medical Insurance)}}{40 \text{ hours/week}}$$

$$\$7.45 = \frac{2\frac{1}{2} \ (\$100 + \$5.85 + \$3.20 + \$10.00)}{40}$$

At the end of a trial period, review your figures to see if your markup needs fine tuning.

Speculation and Exploratories

Ideally, no artists should have to work on speculation. As the Society of Photographer and Artist Representatives (SPAR) policy statement puts it, "Speculative work places the gamble—the investment of time, effort, and overhead—totally on the talent while the client makes no commitment either to the talent or to the project." Don't confuse *speculation* where the potential client *asks* you to produce something on the chance that he might buy it with *free-lance work* where you produce work either under contract or in the expectation that you will sell it to a buyer. Many industries—fabric design, greeting cards, and cartooning, for example—operate on a free-lance basis and, for that matter, all self-actuated fine arts can be called free lance.

Unfortunately, some clients, and this includes many federal agencies, require that your proposal be accepted before they give you a contract or any money, and some will not pay for the proposal phase separately.

At times your own clients may also invite you to bid on a project for which there is no alternative to speculation. The decision to speculate is not easy, and each case should be determined on its own merits.

Estimating

Estimating the cost of future artwork is usually much more difficult than pricing completed artwork, because your costs are unknown. Since estimates can be so very time-consuming, first ask yourself some questions:

1. Do you want the job? Do you need the work, or are you too busy?

2. Is it a real project or just dreamland?

3. What are your chances of getting the job? Are you the sole bidder, or are others being considered? Have you been asked in good faith, or are you being used for a cross estimate?

4. Will the job enhance your portfolio, or is it money only?

5. Is it a chance to expand into new markets or new technical areas?

6. Is the client a pain, or one you'd like to work with?

7. Is the client a good pay, or will you have to squeeze the money out of him?

8. What is the ratio of the estimated time to the value of the job? Will it take you two days to estimate a $100 job?

9. When will the contract be let? Bids that drag on and need to be recalculated periodically eat up your time and profits.

Let's look at some considerations in estimating:

Leverage.

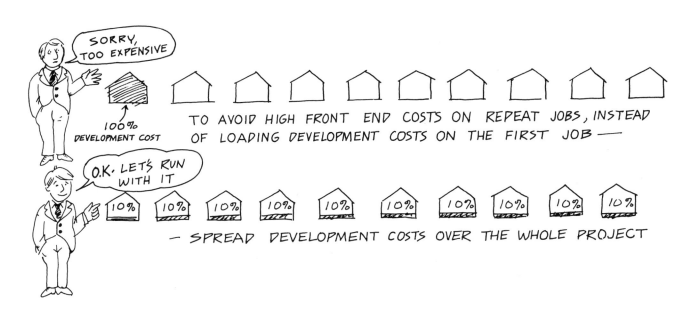

Spread development costs over an entire project.

Leverage

Your bargaining position is proportionate to the uniqueness of your talent, the demand for your services, the crucialness of the artwork to a project, and the eagerness of the client.

Example: An interior designer's proposal for the flagship restaurant of an expensive resort hotel hinges on a large mural view of the resort's harbor in bygone days. The client is captivated with the proposal, likes your work, and wants you to start right away to meet his opening. You have excellent leverage to bargain a good price. If the mural were less important, the client less eager, or the talents required less unique, you'd have less leverage.

Nonmonetary Goals

Sometimes you may want to cut your prices or even take a loss for nonmonetary reasons, e.g., to break into a new market, make new contacts, learn new skills, or secure a new client. But cutting prices to get a new client can backfire if the client only accepts you on the misapprehension that your introductory low figure is your normal price, and expects such prices in the future. Incidentally, some people habitually entice suppliers to give low prices with the lure of future work, which seldom or never materializes. Be on your guard for these.

Costs of the Artwork Relative to the Cost of the Total Project

The cost of artwork is ordinarily tied to the total cost of the larger project of which it forms a part. A $20,000 mural specified for a $200,000 restaurant would most probably be rejected out of hand; 10 percent of the budget would be disproportionate. Conversely, the same $20,000 mural for the main lobby of a $20,000,000 hotel might not be expensive enough. Pricing it at $50,000 might actually make it more saleable.

Rush Orders

The four main reasons for rush orders are: procrastination, scheduling foul-ups, clients who routinely hustle their suppliers with phony opening dates, and authentic crash deadlines. The first three are common; the last, rare. We execute orders on a first-contract-received basis and, in the case of conflict, give preference to regular clients. We also expedite regular clients' *legitimate* rush orders at no extra charge. Otherwise, we tell them that we will work over-time, but charge one and one-half to three times our normal fee as compensation. Invariably, they decide that they're not really in such a hurry.

Repeats

If you're certain a design will be repeated for several projects, you can spread your high front-end development costs for the design over the total number of jobs, rather than load it entirely on the first one.

Example: The Alfred E. Packer chain hires you to design and do a prototype for the remodeling of twenty of their restaurants. Normally, you would bill the prototype store for your design, materials, and execution time. You would then charge the subsequent stores for your materials and execution time, plus a residual for the use of your designs. However, the high start-up cost may jeopardize the whole scheme. One solution is to treat the prototype as a subsequent store. Charge the prototype for time and materials; then add one-twentieth of your design time and hold that price over the twenty stores with an adjustment for inflation.

In practice, a client can seldom guarantee your designs or work over a specific number of stores. If that's the case, you have two options: (1) divide the design cost over the minimum number of anticipated jobs and charge that fraction on the first job, or (2) charge an elevated, but not entire cost, for the prototype and charge a descending fee for subsequent jobs until you get your development cost back, then charge a fair residual thereafter.

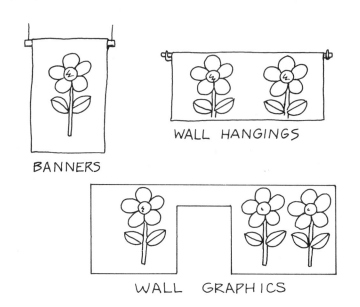

Repeating designs can save time and money.

HAND REPEAT PROCESSES TEND TO BE SIMPLER TO SET UP AND THEIR SAVINGS ARE GENERALLY REALIZED QUICKLY, AFTER WHICH THERE IS NO APPRECIABLE FURTHER SAVINGS.

MECHANICAL REPEAT PROCESSES TEND TO BE HARDER TO SET UP. ONCE THE FRONT END EXPENSES ARE ABSORBED, THE COSTS QUICKLY DIMINISH UNTIL A PLATEAU IS REACHED.

Repeating processes can save set-up, pattern-making, learning, materials, and paperwork costs.

Repeating designs within a single project can also save time and money. For example, we once designed a wall hanging, banners, and supergraphics for a manufacturer. By using the same motifs throughout, we achieved both greater unity and greater economy.

Repeating processes can save set-up, pattern-making, learning, materials, and paperwork costs. We can distinguish two processes, *hand repeats*, e.g., painting, hand weaving or welding; and *mechanical repeats*, e.g., silk screening, machine weaving, and casting. Hand-repeat processes tend to be simpler to set up, and their savings are generally realized quickly, after which there are no appreciable further savings. Mechanical repeat processes tend to be harder to set up. Once the front-end expenses are absorbed, however, the costs quickly diminish until a plateau is reached. In other words, it's ordinarily cheaper to paint *three* pictures than to silkscreen them; it's ordinarily cheaper to screen *thirty* pictures than to paint them. Somewhere between three and thirty is the point where the economy of screening overtakes painting.

Base your choice of a process on cost, and also on your style, preference, and expertise; on the final appearance of the art; on the availability of labor, supplies, and equipment; and on the amount of supervision required.

Preparing an Estimate

There are two quick estimating methods: pricing by *market* and pricing by *area*.

Pricing by market: If you received a certain amount of money for a piece in the past, then (with adjustments for size, inflation, and the change in the demand for your work) you should expect a similar price in future. Your competition can depress your prices, but, on the other hand, competing firms with higher costs than your own can actually allow you to raise your prices, if you stay lean and mean.

Pricing by area is a correlate of pricing by market. If last month you sold ten three-by-five-foot banners at one hundred dollars each and made a satisfactory profit, all things being equal, you could charge the same this month. All things *must* be equal, however. Consider variables like inflation since the last job, if you can use repeats, the current availability of materials and labor, and the nature of the new client (jobs for new clients always take much more time) to see if you must adjust your figures.

Another thing that can throw off area pricing is the *ratio of the number of items in the job to the job's total area*—the greater the number of pieces in proportion to the total area, the more it should cost you to do a job. Example: Twenty-five paintings, two-by-two-feet each, equal one hundred square feet. Four paintings, five-by-five-feet each, also equal one hundred square feet. The fifty paintings will take considerably more time than the four because of the additional design and handling time, paperwork, and surface and edge preparation. Ordinarily, maximum profit results from the lowest design/square foot ratio. Case study II at the end of this chapter illustrates this principle.

A *base area price* permits considerable flexibility. You can raise the base price by (1) *increasing the complexity* (adding more design and more detail); (2) *increasing the handwork* (weaving instead of applique, high polish instead of rough sanding); and (3) *increasing the cost of the materials* (silk instead of polyester, brass instead of steel, gold-leaf frames instead of sprayed bronze). Conversely, you can lower the price by decreasing the complexity, handwork, and material costs.

A HIGH RATIO OF ITEMS TO TOTAL AREA, E.G. 25/ 2'x 2'= 100 ¢ ....

WILL ORDINARILY REQUIRE MUCH MORE TIME THAN A LOW RATIO, E.G. 4/ 5'x 5' = 100 ¢

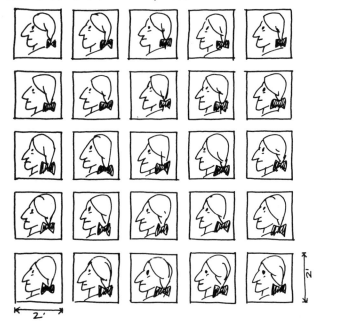

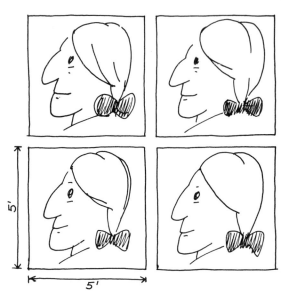

BECAUSE OF ADDITIONAL DESIGN AND HANDLING TIME, PAPERWORK, AND SURFACE AND EDGE PREPARATION. Consider the ratio of the number of items in the job to its total area.

YOU CAN RAISE YOUR PRICE BY:
① INCREASING THE COMPLEXITY —

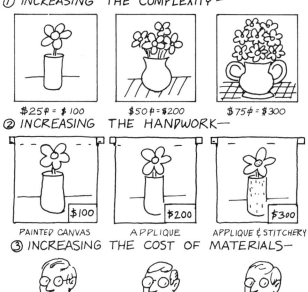

$25¢ = $100 $50¢ = $200 $75¢ = $300

② INCREASING THE HANDWORK —

PAINTED CANVAS $100   APPLIQUE $200   APPLIQUE & STITCHERY $300

③ INCREASING THE COST OF MATERIALS —

PLASTER $500   PLASTIC $1000   BRONZE $2000

You can raise your base price by increasing complexity, handwork, and/or the cost of materials.

More Elaborate Estimates

Full estimates are a combination of labor, experience, and guesstimation, and, as is true for any other contractor, accuracy can spell the difference between success and failure. Many firms, incidentally, charge a fee to prepare complex estimates for speculative projects.

Five major components of elaborate estimates are time, materials, equipment, subcontracting, and expenses.

Time

It's difficult to estimate your time in advance, especially if it's for unfamiliar work and unfamiliar clients. Always estimate on the high side to offset the time you'll inevitably lose on such unpredictables as the weather, people not showing up or performing as expected, equipment failure, late deliveries, misdeliveries, damaged goods, etc. The instances you over-estimate will help make up for the numerous times you don't. Your accuracy should improve with practice.

You can, if you wish, distinguish between *professional time*, e.g., painting a picture, and *nonprofessional time*, e.g., packaging that picture, and charge your clients at different rates. Or, you may feel that your time is the same no matter what you're doing and charge one flat rate.

In preparing your professional time estimate consider:

- *Number and size of the artwork:* It's usually quicker to do one large piece than several small ones of the same aggregate area.
- *Repeats:* A repeatable composition saves design and execution time.
- *Complexity:* A three-stripe design should take less time than a thirty-stripe design.
- *Number of colors:* A three-color design should take less time than a thirty-color design.
- *Details:* A house with no windows will take less time than a house with twenty multipaned windows.
- *Tolerance:* A generalized sailing ship will take less research and time to paint than an accurate portrait of the *Bonhomme Richard* for the curator of the Naval Academy Museum.
- *Presentation format:* Will the client accept roughs and loose drawings or must everything be tight and formal?
- *Nature of the client:* How much preliminary work and consultations are required? Is the client easy to work with and accessible, or will he drive you up the wall?
- *Materials:* Will the materials be unfamiliar or unusually difficult to work with? If they're unfamiliar, will you absorb your learning time as the normal cost of doing business, charge it entirely to the client, or take an in-between position?
- *Supervision:* How much time will you have to spend supervising your employees and subcontractors? Will you have to visit the subcontractors' workplaces and the job site with them?
- *Employees' time:* Estimate the number of employee hours. If you'll charge a unit fee, distinguish among the different skill levels involved. Remember that you must factor your employee's time.
- *Travel time:* You have several options for charging travel time, i.e., time spent in going to see the client, inspecting supplies, visiting job sites, and the like. Some people charge full time both ways, some charge one way only, some charge a reduced rate, and others don't charge at all. If travel time will be consequential, determine your policy.

Don't forget your time spent selling the job, estimating, preparing your contract, packing, shipping, delivering, and so forth. These are integral and should be charged for.

Materials

In preparing your materials estimate consider:

- *Availability:* Are the materials readily available, unfamiliar, or unusual? Will the supplier have to special-order or fabricate them? Will the materials be delivered to you, or will you have to pick them up? Will you have to inspect them anytime prior to delivery?
- *Suppliers:* If you are at all unfamiliar with

the materials, discuss the job with a competent supplier and get his recommendations as to best method, materials, and techniques. Rely on his knowledge. Orders are easiest given over the phone; have them read back to you so you can check their accuracy. Put all complicated and special orders in writing to avoid expensive mistakes—you cannot return cut-to-order materials.

Equipment

In preparing the estimate for your equipment consider:

● *New equipment:* Will the job require that you purchase new equipment? If so, will it be for one job only, or will you be able to amortize it? If it's for one job only, it is an expense chargeable to that job; if it can be amortized, it becomes overhead, although you can charge a certain percentage to that first use.

● *Abnormal wear and tear:* Will the job cause abnormal wear and tear to your equipment? If so, you may want to prorate the equipment and charge the difference to the job.

● *Special rentals:* Will there be any special equipment rentals for scaffolds, tools, forms, vehicles, and the like? Often it's more desirable to rent, rather than purchase, infrequently used equipment that you can't satisfactorily charge to a client. Use a reputable agency to ensure that your reservation is honored and that the equipment will be well maintained and in good working order.

Subcontracting

Consider if you'll supply your subcontractors with their materials or if they'll supply their own. Mark up a sub's cost to you based on your involvement, i.e., how much time it'll take you to plan and supervise his work. If you'll need an extraordinary amount of your own time in proportion to the sub's time (if you'll have to prepare a full set of patterns, for example) you may want to list your time separately. A widely used mark up for subcontractor's costs is 100 percent.

Expenses

Expenses is a catch-all category for those odds and ends not picked up elsewhere: long-distance phone calls, extraordinary travel, living costs at the job site, like meals and overnight lodging, parking, mailing, and shipping.

Markups

Now that you've itemized all your costs, you must mark them up to reflect your involvement in specifying, purchasing, supervising, handling, or storing them. Time is normally listed either already factored, or it is factored separately.

You can factor your other costs—materials, equipment, expenses, and subcontracting—by charging your time, a markup, or a combination of the two. You can use a standard *pass-through markup* (so called because the items are passed through your books) of 15 to 25 percent for routine raw materials like wood, canvas, and paint that you incorporate into your artwork. Charge a higher markup for small orders, a lower markup for large orders. Special-order items should reflect the extra amount of time spent ordering them.

Example: You order one hundred board feet of white pine at $100 for a sculpture. You only have to calculate the amount, place the order, accept delivery, and pay for it. You can therefore place a pass-through markup of, say, 25 percent on the lumber, and charge the client $125. If you were ordering 1,000 board feet, you might mark up the lumber correspondingly less.

Example: It takes essentially the same involvement to order a $10 or $100 picture frame. A pass-through markup is inadequate for the cheap frame but might be adequate for the more expensive one. A *wholesale markup* of 40 to 60 percent, or a *full retail markup* of 100 percent or more might be a fairer reflection of your involvement. Doubling your cost of the $10 frame might not even be adequate if you have to measure, order, pick up, and install it, whereas a 100-percent markup of the $100 frame might be unreasonable. Unless you work with many frames (so the differences even out) you might be better off simply charging your time and expenses on a per-frame basis. Note again the advantages of quantity sales. Your costs for ordering twenty $10 frames are essentially the same as for ordering one, but your profit is much greater.

You can also use market rates as a guide.

Example: You've subcontracted a sign painter at $7 an hour to paint some graphics on a store's window. Since your involvement is minimal, you had planned to mark up his fee 50 percent and bill your client $10.50 per hour. When the sign painter tells you the going rate is $15.00 for similar work, you realize that you can double his time to $14.00 per hour, thus undercutting the market by a dollar, and still make $3.50 more than you anticipated.

Task Analysis Estimates

Estimation through task analysis, an increasingly common procedure in architecture, is based on the premise that any job is logically reducible to its components. The architect (1) discusses the project with his client and establishes a program, (2) breaks down the project into its constituent tasks, (3) charts the tasks and assigns man hours and other costs to each, and (4) adds up the tasks to determine the total cost of the job.

The architect then reviews the job with his client and explains what is to be accomplished and at what price. The client clearly sees where his money is going and has the options of withdrawing at any level or omitting nonessential tasks. (Case Study I, which follows later, was done by task analysis.)

It is a rational replacement for marking up purchases, especially when the purchases are infrequent, because it candidly recognizes your time involvement.

Example: A client wants a mural for his country club. After studying the job, you make this proposal:

Design

8 Rough designs, 6 hours @ $25/hr.[1]	$ 150.00
3 Comprehensive designs, 3 hours @ $25/hr.	75.00
1 Final design, 8 hours @ $25/hr.	200.00

Mural

Artist, 40 hours @ $25/hr.	$1,000.00
Assistant, 20 hours @ $10/hr.[2]	200.00
Canvas and paint[3]	125.00
Paperhanger to attach canvas,[4] 3 hours @ $15/hr.	45.00
Scaffold[5]	75.00

Photography

Five 8 × 10 color enlargements[6]	250.00
Total	$2,120.00

[1] You've entered your time already marked up—$10.00/hr. net × 2½ = $25.00/hr.

[2] $4.00/hr. your cost × 2½ = $10.00/hr.

[3] $100.00 your cost times 25% pass-through markup.

[4] $7.50/hr. your cost × 100% standard markup for subs.

[5] $50.00 your cost × 50% markup to cover your oversight and responsibility.

[6] $165.00 your cost × 50% markup = $247.50, rounded to $250.00.

The client finds the proposal too high; he decides he can afford no more than $1,700 at present. Going through the estimate with you, the client decides he can do without the photographs right now (−$250), supply the scaffold from another of his buildings (−$75), will only need one-half the rough designs to choose from (−$75) and only two comprehensive designs (−$25). He has saved $425.00, which reduces the estimate to $1,695.00, a figure he can live with.

Estimating Case Studies

Some actual case studies will make estimating clearer. The following examples illustrate a range of job problems and types.

Case Study I: A Clear-Cut Estimate: Signs for a High-Medium Income Suburban Shopping Center

Given: A series of lamp poles in the exterior mall area of a high-medium income suburban shopping center requires 2½′ × 6′ decorative panels. Redwood is used throughout the mall area; vandalism is a minor consideration.

Procedure: The first estimate is for routed redwood. Because of the panels' size and the possibility of warping, I relied on my lumber supplier for construction specifications and for fabrication. Since the job was for a good client on a modest budget, and since I was supplied with the outline specs for the panels, I used minimal markups. The actual number of panels needed was uncertain; I used ten for my estimate, a convenient figure which could be easily adjusted.

Routed Redwood	My Cost Each	My Price Each
8/4″ clear, all heart redwood, splined and exterior glued[1]	$100.00	$115.00[1]
Design, 4½ hours @ $30.00/hr.[2] = $135 divided by 10 panels		13.50[2]
Routing, 4 hrs. @ $16.00/hr.[3]	32.00	64.00[3]
Total, pre tax	$132.00	$192.50

[1] Each panel is marked up a minimal 15 percent, an aggregate markup of $150, enough to cover my time and expense.

[2] A typical rate for simple design work.

[3] I calculate that the routing will take from three to four hours. To be safe I take the higher figure and design the job to take no longer. A 100-percent markup is standard under the circumstances. If my time estimate is high, the markup will turn out to be greater, if it is low, it will be less.

Case Study II. An Unprofitable Job: Four Painted Banners

It's difficult to turn down a job after you've made a well-received proposal to a prestigious firm. One of the designers of such a firm asked us to do four painted banners measuring a total of twenty-eight square feet for a fast-food restaurant, a typical low-budget client. Assuming it would be a cheap-'n-cheerful job, we bid $420.00, which came out to $15/sq. ft. The designer came back with $300 ($10.71/sq. ft.), take it or leave it. Gambling that it might lead to more work with both clients or even become a prototype for a chain, we reluctantly accepted.

It was a bad gamble. The job proved more demanding than anticipated. It required extra conferences; special finishes; a fuzzy fabric, which took three times longer to paint than the slick cloth we estimated for and which necessitated fully rendered patterns because we couldn't clean our mistakes off the material. What's more, we were given a rush deadline, which meant repeated long-distance phone calls and hand deliveries. Here's how it worked out:

Our time:	
Conferences	3¾ hrs.
Designs	6
Patterns	8
Purchasing materials	2½
Painting	17½
Supervising sewing	1½
Grommeting	1½
Total time	40¾ hours

Our cost:	
Fabric	$57.76
Sewing	25.00
Phone	6.00
Poles	5.00
Total cost	$93.76

That comes to $5.06/hr. gross before subtracting overhead and profit.

Analysis: For the job to be profitable, we would have had to charge $45/sq. ft., which was out of the question. A slick-surfaced, nonabsorbent fabric would have saved about four hours in patternmaking and nine hours in execution.

To illustrate the economies of materials and scale, if we had used slick fabric and quadrupled the banners' size from 28 to 112 sq. ft., we would, I estimate, have only increased the patternmaking time from 4 to 7 hours and the painting time from 8½ to 20 hours, a total of 40¼ hours. The costs would probably have risen to $159 for fabric, $65 for sewing, and $10 for poles, a total of $317.76. Our time at a straight $30/hr. would equal $1,207.50, and our costs, variously marked up, another $638.50. Adding the time and all the costs together and dividing the sum by the number of square feet yields $16.50/sq. ft., a profitable figure for the job had it been quadrupled in size. Whereas, the comparable cost of $15/sq. ft. that we originally bid on, and clearly the $10.71/sq. ft. that we received, were not.

5. Contracts and Purchase Orders

"If good fences make good neighbors, good contracts make good business partners."

Richard Wincor, *Contracts in Plain English*

Contracts

A contract is an agreement between two or more parties that is enforceable in a court of law. It disciplines the expectations of both parties. To be binding, it should be signed and dated by all participants, and something of value should be exchanged between them, e.g., an artwork for money. Contracts may be as simple as a scrap of paper recording an understanding, or as complex as a several-hundred-page document framed to protect public commissions against artists. Sometimes the agreement may be only verbal, which, although technically equal to a written agreement, provides no supportive hard evidence. Contract law is very complex. Always go over any contract, particularly the first of a kind, with a lawyer so you can understand what you're committing yourself to.

During your professional career, you may encounter contracts presented by agents, galleries, businesses, and government agencies. These are often printed forms with blanks for the inclusion of specific terms.

Occasionally you may need to prepare a contract for a client. Many professional art organizations provide sample contracts for their members, and other contracts are available in books and magazines. You can also buy standard business contracts from a stationer and, if you wish, imprint them with your letterhead. My criticism of these contracts is that they are too cumbersome and arcane for the average situation, and they do not lend themselves to adaptation.

I present here two sample agreements for commissioned work. The first is simple, the second a more detailed expansion. They are called agreements, to sidestep the forbidding word "contract," but the distinction is only semantic. Both follow a letter format. They are intended as guidelines only; no sample could possibly cover all situations. Adjust them to suit the occasion.

Don't overload your contracts. Piling on clauses can raise remote chimeras, and, rather than avoiding controversy, they might actually add fuel for dispute. The bedrock of any agreement is the fundamental goodwill of the participants and their shared interest in reaching common goals. Without that, *any* contract is essentially worthless.

Sample Letter of Agreement I

(Date)
(To)
Dear _____:
I agree to (design, execute, fabricate, design and execute, etc.)[1] for (client, installation, user, etc.)[1] (as per our conversation, understanding, submitted designs, etc.)[1] the following:

(quantity, dimensions, description of artwork, unit costs, total item costs, etc.)[1]

$_____

Sales Tax[2] $_____

TOTAL $_____

F.O.B._____,[3] packing extra.[4]
This agreement good for _____ days, after which time it may be withdrawn if not accepted.[5]
All work executed under this agreement is protected by copyright. All reproduction rights in all media are reserved by the artist.[6]
All agreements contingent upon strikes, accidents, or other delays beyond the artist's control.[7]

_____
(Artist's name)   Date

_____[8]
                         Date

[1] Insert appropriate word or words.

[2] Leave out in cases where sales tax does not apply or replace with "Plus sales tax."

[3] Free on Board (F.O.B.) means the buyer accepts the responsibility and pays the freight from your point of shipment which could be a studio, mill, foundry, etc.

[4] Packing can be a significant expense at times, and you should alert the client that it is his responsibility.

[5] Never offer a proposal without a time limit. Inflation or changes in supply could demolish your profits. Customary time limits range from ten to ninety days. If you must stipulate a longer period, factor in a margin to cover inflation. If the client remains interested after the time limit expires, you have the option of renegotiating the contract at a different price.

[6] This serves notice to your client that he is not to pirate your work for his room theme, menu cover, Christmas cards, business logo, or T-shirts without your consent (and compensation). (See Chapter 14.)

[7] This clause is optional but protects you against delays beyond your control.

[8] You may type in a name and title if you're sure who'll sign. Try to establish that the signator has the "capacity to contract," i.e., that he has the legal authority to make commitments for a client.

Sample Agreement I Filled In:

February 30, 1985
Captain Robert Martin
The P-38 Disco
Gotham
Dear Captain Martin:
I agree to design and paint for your establishment, as per our conversation, the following:

1 24″ × 36″ painting entitled "Airboy" in a 2½″ #B12 gold leaf frame for	$300.00
Sales Tax	15.00
TOTAL	$315.00

F.O.B. my studio, packing extra.
This agreement is good for 30 days, after which time it may be withdrawn if not accepted.
All work executed under this agreement is protected by copyright. All reproduction rights in all media are reserved by me.
me.

_____
Raoul Elstir   Date

_____
Captain Robert Martin   Date

Sample Letter of Agreement II

(Date)
(To)
Dear:
I agree to (design, paint, fabricate, design and fabricate, etc.) for (client, installation, user, etc.) (as per our conversation, understanding, approved designs, etc.) the following:

(quantity, dimensions, description of the artwork, unit costs, total item costs).[1]
Schedule:[2]
Work shall be submitted in _____ stages:
(1) Rough designs: _____ or more rough designs due _____ days after my receipt of this approved agreement.

(2) Comprehensive designs:_____ or more comprehensive designs due _____ days after approval of rough designs.

(3) Finished designs: One finished design (model) (per item) due _____ days after approval of comprehensive designs.

(4) Final art: Final art due _____ days after approval of finished designs.

Installation will take place within _____ days after (approval of, completion of, payment for)[3] final art. I will make every effort to honor these deadlines, which are estimates only, but will not be held responsible for any damages arising from the failure to deliver by these dates. I will notify the client of any delays as they occur or are anticipated.[4]

Payment:[5]

_____ % upon approval of this agreement[6]
$_____

_____ % upon approval of rough designs
$_____

_____ % upon approval of comprehensive designs $_____

_____ % upon approval of final designs
$_____

_____ % upon (approval, completion, shipment, delivery, installation,[7] of final art $_____

$_____   Total
$_____   Sales Tax
$_____   TOTAL[8]

F.O.B. _____, packing extra[9]
Terms: _____ % _____, net _____.[10]
Installation[11] $ _____ permit fees extra.[12]
This agreement good for _____ days after which time it may be withdrawn if not accepted.[13]
All work executed under this agreement is protected by copyright. All reproduction rights in all media are reserved by the artist.[13]
All agreements are contingent upon strikes, accidents, or other delays beyond my control.[13]

Additional Clauses:[14]
This agreement may be terminated by the client without further obligation on either party after the completion and payment for any of the above stages, inclusive. The artist will retain his work up to the final stage.[15] _____ shall serve as sole and final approving authority for all work executed under this agreement.[16]

All preparatory artwork and models shall remain the property of the artist (unless otherwise noted).[17]

Any alteration in the final art by the approving authority after approval of the final design will be executed only upon written instruction and will, if entailing extra costs, be billed extra.[18]

Client will carry normal and necessary insurance.[19]

Not responsible for structural or other damage due to artwork's weight, size, or design. Not responsible for damage to hidden, or unmarked conduits, pipes, raceways, etc.[20]

Additional expense caused by nonconformance to blueprint specifications at the installation site will be billed extra. Client must submit field dimensions.[21]

The client agrees to save and hold harmless the artist from all claims arising from this work.[22]

_____   _____
(Artist's name)   Date

Accepted: (The above prices, specifications, and conditions are satisfactory and are hereby accepted. You are authorized to do the work as specified. Payment will be made as outlined above.)[23]

_____   [24] _____

---

[1] Insert appropriate word or words.

[2] This schedule divides the work into natural increments, gives the client a time line, and alerts him that orderly progress depends upon his timely approvals. Of course, you can alter the schedule, leaving out or adding stages. If you don't want to be tied down to deadlines, omit or generalize the dates. You can also add information like "in a scale of 1/2" = 1'," "color pencil on tracing paper. . . . "

[3] These are fine shades of meaning. Where and when will "approval" occur? In your shop, at a foundry, before installation, after installation? Be specific in order to avoid misunderstandings. "Completion" means that you can bill as soon as you complete your work. It doesn't mean the client will pay you then; he might hold off until it is approved, installed, or some other time that better suits him. "Shipment" means you can bill as soon as the work is shipped. "Delivery" means you can bill as soon as the client accepts delivery. This is potentially clumsy because of delays en route, in acceptance, or in your notification, but many clients prefer it because they have the goods before they pay. "Installation" means you can bill after the work is installed. This assures the client that a work custom-designed for a specific environment performs as promised, but construction and other delays can postpone your payment far longer than you'd wish. Installation could be specified in greater detail or covered under a separate contract.

[4] This clause protects you against damage claims from not delivering your work on time, e.g., an installation crew has to make a special return trip to put up your artwork, thus running over the budget, and the client wants you to pay the difference. Include it if you're uncomfortable with your work schedule or if you feel that you may be held financially accountable for delays.

[5] Like the work schedule, you can alter the payment schedule as needed. Adapt your schedule to reflect the time and money in each part. An example of a schedule long on the construction end would be (after the design is approved) beginning construction, one-half construction, completion of construction, etc. In general the smaller the job, the more abbreviated the schedule.

[6] The initial payment is a tangible indication of the client's good faith. It should accompany the counter-signed agreement or not be far behind. You may wish to delay starting work until you receive the initial payment. After this first installment you will be working in advance of payment. In the case of a doubtful client, you can try delaying each subsequent completion until he's paid for the previous installment.

[7] As with note 3, these are fine but important shades of meaning. For example, "approval" means that the work must be approved before installation can take place. "Completion" means you're free to install as soon as the work is finished. "Payment" means you won't install until paid.

[8] The final billing should account for all expenses like taxes, packing and shipping, permits, and add-ons. These expenses, if known in advance, may be apportioned over the entire schedule.

[9] See Agreement I, notes 3 and 4.

[10] The discount terms allow for prompt payment within so many days, after which the net (full) payment is due. For example, 2 percent 20 days, net 30 days means a 2 percent discount is allowed for payment within 20 days and the net within 30 days. The discount should be related to the interest you would gain if you had the money to use, and also the potential aggravation it may save. Commonly, you add the discount in advance to the total figure—the discounted total is the price you *actually* mean to receive, the gross figure, in other words, is your actual price plus the discount. In this way the incentive does not come out of your pocket.

[11] As discussed in Chapter 25, installation can be tricky. Clauses 24 and 25 cover some aspects of it. A separate agreement at times may be useful.

Additional installation sample clauses include:

"Primary electrical feeder or service, plumbing and/or water service where required must be provided by purchaser at installation location where connection will be made to unit by installation crew."

"The installation site will be freely accessible during the designated installation period and will be clear of obstructions, workmen, and all else that might impede the installation activity."

"An OSHA approved, two-man, movable scaffold erectable to installation height will be in place at the installation site for the installation crew's exclusive use during the entire installation period."

[12] Permit fees may be necessary for some outdoor work. They can be expensive and time consuming. It's easier for you if the client can handle them.

[13] See Agreement I, notes 5–7.

[14] The following clauses are *optional*.

[15] Use this termination clause when the client is uncertain about the end product. It allows him to ease gently into a project while holding to an escape clause which he can exercise after payment of the last completed stage if he is dissatisfied. It is rarely exerted in practice.

[16] This clause is very useful where more than one client, particularly a committee, is involved. Authority is vested exclusively in the sole approving authority and in theory you need satisfy only him. A client may still balk at paying for work the sole approving authority approves which doesn't please him as well.

[17] Occasionally a party to a project may want to keep your preliminary work. You, however, may prefer to keep it for your portfolio or for your retrospective. This clause says that your price assumes your retention.

[18] This protects somewhat against the client who requests changes to the final art after he approves the final design. The requests may be reasonable or not, according to the exactness of the final design and the nature and degree of the changes. Clearly, any large scale, unanticipated change which adds expense should be paid for by the client, although he may claim that the change is due to your error or omission.

[19] This assures that the client will have necessary insurance coverage.

[20] This absolves you from responsibility for your artwork cracking or pulling down a wall, collapsing a support, or causing similar damage; and from installers inadvertently breaking hidden structures.

[21] Covers situations where an object has been designed for a site, the construction of which deviates from specifications. Use it where a lot of contractors are involved and acountability may be obscure.

[22] This transfers the liability for your completed work to the client who may then assume it under his own liability policy. It's useful for artwork like sculpture or hanging signs where continued liability might be a problem for you. (See Insurance, pages 89–90.)

[23] This clause spells out the responsibilities of acceptance.

[24] See Agreement I, note 8.

Purchase Orders

Purchase orders (P.O.'s) are unilateral contracts. You accept the P.O. by producing the items requested. You are under no constraint, other than self interest, to perform—you may ignore the P.O. if you choose. Often, as with the federal government, there will not be a divided payment schedule; one fixed price will cover the whole job. Preparatory work, therefore, must either be handled by a separate P.O. or done on speculation. Besides their simplicity, P.O.'s have another advantage for purchasers: they usually don't mention deposits. Negotiate for one if you can before beginning work.

The P.O. may contain such information as:

Purchase order number: The number assigned to that P.O. Use it in all your correspondence.

Shipping instructions: It may be "best way," "supplier's vehicle," "UPS," "Air Freight,"... whatever is requested or has been agreed upon.

Ship to: Where you're requested to ship the items.

Bill to: Where you're to send your bill.

Vendor: Your name and address.

F.O.B. point: It may be "vendor's shop," "destination," "warehouse," etc.

Delivery date: the date the delivery is expected. It may include such phrases as "no later than," or "not before" to delimit the delivery period.

Discount terms or payment terms: Notes the discount you allow, if any.

Description of items (s): May list such headings as: item number, quantity, description, unit cost, total cost.

Buyer: Person who requests the order.

Authorized signature: Signature of the person who authorizes the purchase.

A quantity of instructions, terms, conditions, and provisions may appear, often in fine or light print, on the front or back of a purchase order. Look these over carefully; they are in effect the terms of your contract. They may include: how to identify your shipment, when title passes, rejection of a shipment for nonconformance, billing instructions, warranty and insurance requirements, etc. As has been said, your production of the goods is your effective acceptance of a contract, so you should know what you're agreeing to. In the event of difficulty, you can be sure your client's lawyer will.

You can issue your own purchase orders to suppliers and subcontractors. You can buy standard P.O. books and forms (and have these imprinted with your name) or have a printer make them up for you.

6. *Scheduling*

You can make a project board covered in Mylar to keep track of your jobs. List them in a vertical left-hand column and list calendar divisions across the top. Mark in each project horizontally, and, if you wish, divide the project into phases like: design, ordering, construction, painting, delivery. A glance at the chart tells you what stage each job is in or should be in, at any given moment.

You may hear, incidentally, of the "fast track" scheduling system, which some volume operators like engineers, contractors, and architects use. "Fast track" coordinates the phases of a big job to let them proceed simultaneously as much as possible.

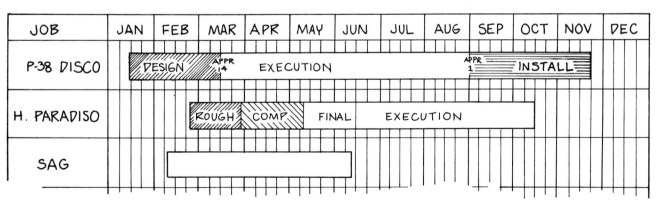

JOB	JAN	FEB	MAR	APR	MAY	JUN	JUL	AUG	SEP	OCT	NOV	DEC
P-38 DISCO	DESIGN		APPR 14	EXECUTION					APPR 1	INSTALL		
H. PARADISO			ROUGH	COMP	FINAL	EXECUTION						
SAG												

Project board.

P.O.# B-7340 L HOTEL PARADISO LOBBY
1 EA. PUB SIGN, DOUBLE FACED, 30" x 36"
#2 WHITE PINE, DISTRESSED & ANTIQUED
BLUEPRINT L-23. DUE SEPT 19, 1980
TONY GREEN, DESIGNER   22 LBS.
EST: 4 HRS CONST. 12 HRS PTG. $20 MTL.
ACTUAL: 3¾ ", 14   "   , $14 "
                    COST   # 350.00

Record individual parts of large jobs on separate loose-leaf pages.

Scheduling Large Jobs

It's a good idea to keep all the information for large, complicated jobs in a loose-leaf binder. Place your order forms, receipts, and correspondence up front. Make sure you have memos on all decisions, with the critical ones approved in writing. Allocate a separate page for each piece of art and record thereon such information as: identifying number (either the client's, taken from the contract, or one you've given it); client's name; location within the building; quantity; time estimate for execution; blueprint reference; due date; description (subject matter, style, materials, finish, dimensions, price, weight); designer or contact for the job; unit price; total. You can also include your construction drawing if you have to build anything. These sheets will form the basis for your shipping list.

You can use other sheets for components like frames or shipping containers to record their cost and the date they were ordered and received. You can also have a check sheet to note each piece as you complete it.

When you finish the job, remove your paperwork from the notebook, weed it out as necessary, and store it in a report cover. It, and a slide taken of each unique piece, will be your permanent record of that job. You will need these records if your art is lost, damaged, or stolen, and you must make either an insurance claim or a duplicate. Also, the information will be there at hand for estimating and creating similar work in the future.

Time Sheets

Employees in many big offices keep *time sheets:* chronicles of what they have done, for whom, and for how long each day. Time sheets can be useful for you, too. They serve as a comparison between estimated and actual time, as a record for billing clients by the hour, and as an account for your employee's time. Should you have a dispute with a client over your fees, time sheets provide hard evidence in court.

			NAME _____		WEEK OF _____									
Day	Job No.	Client	Description	9	10	11	12	1	2	3	4	5		O T.

A time sheet—fill in the blocks for a time record (O T. stands for overtime).

7. Identifying Yourself

At some point in your career you may need stationary and perhaps identifying material such as a business card. If your contacts are limited, you can get by with stock stationary from a printer, stationer, or mail-order house. Rubber stamping, offsetting, typing, or screening it yourself are even cheaper. But if you expect to deal with people like architects, interior designers, and businessmen who handle superior visual material every day, or if you're engaged in attracting the public's attention in an increasingly competitive marketplace, you cannot afford an unprofessional appearance. Also, you may need printed stationary to establish your credibility with manufacturers and wholesalers. A corny card will stigmatize you at once as an amateur.

Graphic Designers

Unless you're adept with print, see a graphic designer. You can ask a faculty member, student, or graduate of the nearest art school. Better yet, seek out a working member of the profession. Ask around, track down the creator of work you've admired, look in graphics publications, which include designer's credits, like *Illustrators Annual* or *CA*, or walk into a designer's office and ask to see his portfolio. Don't be put off by established designers or

what you presume to be their high fees. Experienced people are often more approachable than beginners, because money may no longer be their primary object. Your design can present a refreshing challenge, new direction, or just plain fun, as long, that is, as you cooperate by not being demanding and by giving them a free hand. They may accept your art or some other service as full or partial payment. Your job may form a desirable addition to a less recognized designer's portfolio, and, although he may be more in need of money, he, too, may be willing to barter.

Printers

Before you're too far along, get some guidance from a printer on costs and on his technical capabilities. You may locate a printer via your knowledge of his work, his satisfied customers, or your designer. If your designer is not overseeing the printing, give first nod to someone nearby. You'll be seeing a lot of your printer before your job's done, and you'll probably need him for occasional repeat business.

Press time is a printer's major expense; he wants to keep his presses as busy as possible. He can save you money, if you are willing to be flexible, by fitting your job into a hole in his schedule, by ganging it up with another job, or by running it behind the same color ink to save a wash-up charge. Have the printer explain his operations if you're unfamiliar with them. Not only will it be educational for you, but it may suggest new techniques and further money-saving approaches. Ask him, too, about bartering. He may want some art or help with his business, e.g., illustrations for his publications.

Logotypes

The logotype (logo) is a distinctive way of writing your name. It may be as simple as a unique color, shape, or typeface, or as complex as the identity program of a major corporation. Don't strain for a novel graphic symbol. There are already so many around that it's tough to come up with one that has any meaning. Don't turn your logo into a gallery for the display of your artwork. It can be heavy handed and can typecast you.

Letterheads

The letterhead is a sheet of stationary containing your logo, your full business name, address, phone number with area code, plus any additional necessary information not listed elsewhere. Don't design your letterhead by itself. Judge it with a complete, signed letter typed under it.

Be sensitive to the characters of the different typefaces: clean, forthright Helvetica; bookish, scholarly Baskerville; traditional, dependable Caslon; bold, uncompromising Futura; romantic, giddy Desdemona; goofy, laid-back Baby Teeth. If you're really good, you may want to design your own typeface. In any case, select one that accords with the image you wish to project, but avoid the currently fashionable faces, which date rapidly.

When choosing printer's type, keep in mind your typewriter's type style and size so it will coordinate. Align your printing with your intended letter margins. Use standard (8 1/2- by 11-inch) paper if your correspondence is primarily for business; the smaller (7 1/4- by 10 1/2-inch) monarch size, if primarily for personal use.

Use the same paper for the second sheet as the first; don't try to save a few pennies by switching to a cheaper stock. Don't reproduce the letterhead on the second sheet. Repeat the logo, either the same size or smaller, but eliminate the factual information. If you must conserve money, leave the second blank, but match the paper.

Envelopes

Envelopes come in the same stock as the letterheads; match them. Standard-size paper takes either a number-ten or number-nine envelope. Monarch paper takes a monarch envelope. Place the logo and address, omitting the phone number, on the front left side or on the back flap.

Envelopes can be printed unassembled and then glued up after printing, which permits more design flexibility but is more expensive, or they may be printed assembled. Because no two assembled envelopes are exactly alike, don't specify printing too close to the edge. The variation between

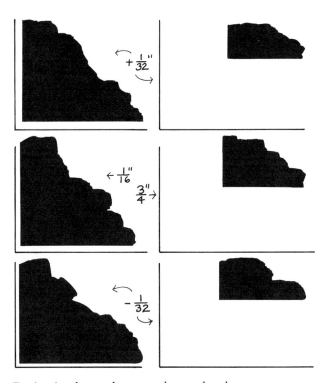

Don't print the envelopes too close to the edge.

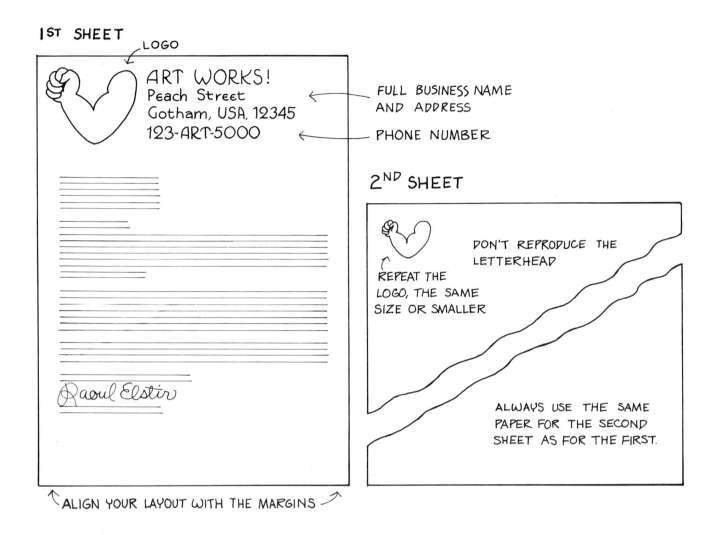

1ST SHEET

LOGO

ART WORKS!
Peach Street
Gotham, USA, 12345
123-ART-5000

FULL BUSINESS NAME AND ADDRESS

PHONE NUMBER

Raoul Elstir

ALIGN YOUR LAYOUT WITH THE MARGINS

2ND SHEET

DON'T REPRODUCE THE LETTERHEAD

REPEAT THE LOGO, THE SAME SIZE OR SMALLER

ALWAYS USE THE SAME PAPER FOR THE SECOND SHEET AS FOR THE FIRST.

PLACE THE LOGO AND ADDRESS ON THE FRONT UPPER LEFT OR ON THE FLAP. OMIT THE PHONE NUMBER.

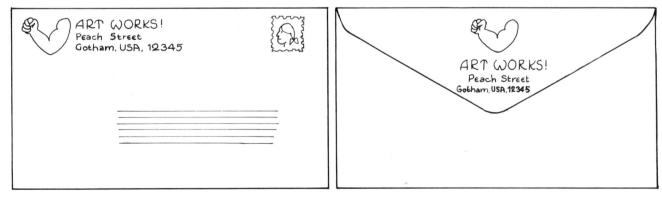

ART WORKS!
Peach Street
Gotham, USA, 12345

ART WORKS!
Peach Street
Gotham, USA, 12345

Letterheads and envelopes.

envelopes, combined with the action of the press, prevents tight tolerances. A deviation unnoticeable in a two-inch border becomes glaring in one only one sixty-fourth of an inch wide.

Business Cards

More latitude is customary in business cards. They may either match the letterhead and envelope or be thicker, thinner, folded over or cut out. Business cards are usually sized to fit a wallet, but because artist's cards are most often kept in three-by five-inch file boxes, they can be as large as that. Making them any bigger may create an annoying storage problem for the recipient. The more cards you order, the cheaper the unit cost, and the cheaper the unit cost, the more you'll be inclined to give away. Since that's what cards are for, order a lot at a time, say one thousand.

Other Printed Material

Any other printed material you need—labels, news releases, purchase orders, packing slips, invoices—should form an ensemble. When you design invoices and similar printed materials that require typing, coordinate the spacing of the printing with the spacing of your typewriter. If you don't, you'll need to adjust your roller constantly as you proceed. To use your letterhead as an invoice, cut off the bottom third and fold the remainder over once.

Color

Colors, like type, convey moods; select appropriate ones. Again, as with type, be wary of what's "in" this year, lest you be "out" the next. Work with color samples the same size as the printing you'll be specifying. A vivid red that sings out in a two- by two-inch square will look almost black reduced to eight-point type. Also, the color and texture of the paper as seen through the ink or lying next to it will affect your perception of the ink's color.

The new two-color and four-color presses have substantially reduced the costs of multicolor printing, thus giving designers greater flexibility. Check to see if your printer has such a press.

You can choose your colors from the PMS (Pantone Matching System) book, which most printers own. Given the PMS code for a color, any printer

THEY MAY MATCH YOUR LETTER-
HEAD AND BE STANDARD SIZE

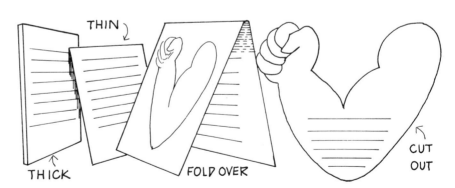

Business cards.

with a copy can read out the corresponding mixing directions. Unfortunately, that doesn't mean the match will be exact. Differences due to the aging of the PMS books and inks, batch variances, humidity, paper stock, lighting, and human judgment will always prevent a perfect agreement.

Screening is a method of regulating ink intensity, expressed in percent, by printing through a spaced screen of dots. It yields tonal variations within one run of ink, but in practice the results are difficult to forecast precisely. *Gain*, caused by the interaction of the press, ink, and humidity, makes the dots flow in a somewhat unpredictable fashion. What seemed perfect on a PMS screening guide may come out a little darker or lighter.

Paper

First check to see what papers your printer carries; special orders can take time and always cost more. As you thought about your paper when you considered ink, so must you think about your ink when considering paper. Again, relate the paper's color and texture to your logo and business image. A laid finish, for example, may confuse a detailed logo, large areas of ink, or embossing. Wove, a smoother finish, might be a better choice.

Consider also how you will correct typing errors. Correction papers like Ko-Rec-Type and correction fluids come in a limited color range, which will be further limited by the selection available at your stationer. There are companies that match correction fluids to paper, but these fluids cost more and cannot be stocked in quantity because their highly volatile solvent evaporates rapidly.

A twenty-five-percent rag paper, twenty to twenty-four pounds in weight should suffice. Ask the printer to feed the paper so the watermark reads correctly, not so much because papers are one sided, although a few are, but because it's plain dumb to hold a letterhead up to the light and find it's printed backwards. The envelope should match the letterhead stock and should be heavy enough not to be seen through.

Embossing

If your logo suggests it, consider embossing. While more expensive, it adds panache, exudes an aura of accomplishment, and can be a better investment than adding more colors. Blind embossing (embossing without an ink overprint) is often the most effective method. It adds a felicitous sculptural dimension that might otherwise be confused by an overlay of ink.

The effect of paper texture.

TEXTURED PAPER CAN CONFUSE:

DETAILED LOGOS

LARGE AREAS OF INK

EMBOSS- INGS

a

Paul Davis
Rector Street
Sag Harbor
New York, 11963

Letterheads of (a) Herb Lubalin,
(b) Paul Davis, (c) Milton Glaser,
(d) Richard and Roberta Hyman.
(Reproduced with permission)

Paul Davis
Rector Street
Sag Harbor
New York, 11963

b

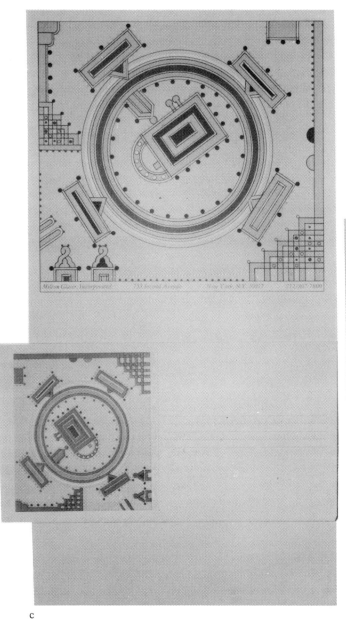

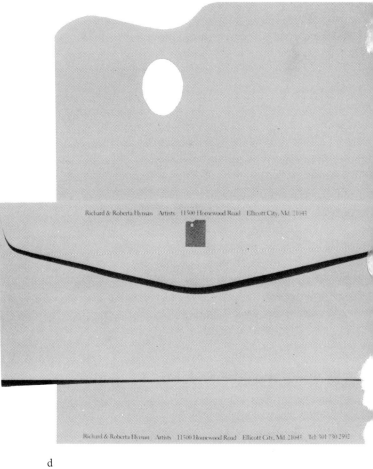

c

d

8. Promotion

Promotion means spreading the word about yourself through direct contacts, shows, and the news media. It can increase your market sales and prices.

Portfolios

Your portfolio, a collection of material to show your prospects, is an indication of your work style. It should be attractive and logical. You can use actual work, such as neatly presented paintings, drawings, prints, roughs, models, and working drawings, as well as photographs or slides. Location shots show how your work looks and integrates with a real setting and proves you've been professionally accepted. Use at least 5- by 8-inch glossy photos, custom printed for best results. (See Chapter 22.)

Binders are convenient for protecting and displaying your material. They are inexpensive and flexible—you can readily add, subtract, and shuffle their contents. They have, however, three major drawbacks: only a few people can examine them at one time; if not designed imaginatively, they will look commonplace; and their sheet protectors scratch easily and glare. Binders come in a wide variety of sizes, styles, and coverings: multi-ring, easel, flexible cover, vinyl, cloth, and leather. Sheet protectors come in various weights and finishes of Mylar, acetate, and vinyl. Plan to replace them before they get shabby. You must match multi-ring sheet protectors to your binder; the number and spacing of the rings is not standardized.

You can individualize a binder by screening your logo on it or by covering it with fabric. If you're considering giving binders to clients, investigate having a custom bindery print your name and logo for you. If you can meet the bindery's minimum, custom binders are not much more than the stock variety.

You can also mat or mount your photographs on foamboard or mat board, and cover them with adhesive-back mylar or acetate. The identifying copy can be presstype, hand lettering, print, or photostats. Use different-colored mats to distinguish your media and styles. Trim the edges of the boards clean with a mat knife if they fray.

Alternatively, you can design a box to hold your photos. It can be made of metal, wood, Plexiglas, hardboard, or cardboard; covered and lined with fabric, leather, or vinyl; and screened, painted, stamped, carved, or etched. It can open from the top or side, and have a hinge, handle, strap, or tie. A box is unusual. Its contents can be added or removed, grouped or selected, displayed or handed around. But a box has a finite capacity and may be difficult to construct. Also, the photos kept in a box can get soiled or tired, lost or misplaced.

Carrying Cases

Carrying cases come in many materials, sizes, and styles. The smaller sizes, called attaché or catalog cases, are handy to carry around all day. For larger art, you'll need an artist's portfolio (the term "portfolio" also means the portfolio's contents), which comes in various materials, sizes, and styles. Art stores, if they don't carry them, will order portfolios for you, or you can have one custom made by a leather worker. Hard-sided portfolios protect artwork better, but they are heavier and will not expand with a load. Soft-sided ones expand, but they are less protective. The construction of commercial portfolios often does not match their high price tag; be sure to inspect the one you're interested in carefully, especially its hardware and finishes.

Besides art, you can carry other things with you: a flat scale ruler, tape measure, extra brochures, story boards, give-aways, samples of fabrics, finishes, and paints.

Slide Viewers

There are three basic types of slide viewers: hand-held viewers, internal projectors, and slide projectors.

Hand-held viewers, which are small and cheap, accept one slide at a time. They may be either externally illuminated by holding them up to the light, or internally illuminated with bulbs and batteries. They're handy for impromptu use, as when you catch someone out of his office and want to show him one or two slides, but they're far too limited for regular presentations.

Internal projectors are at least of three types. The cheapest are the small viewers that have about a 4- by 4-inch screen and cost under twenty dollars or so. While too large to carry around in your pocket like the hand-held viewer, they're still not big enough for presentations. The second type is a folding case that contains a simple projector, which bounces an image off a mirror onto the rear of a frosted screen, that measures about 10 by 12 inches. These are quite portable and give a reasonably good image that several people can see together, but they require a darkened room. The third type is a standard slide projector coupled together with a small screen. They're rather large and heavy, but once they're set up, their bright, crisp image and their easy control (manual, remote, or automatic) have made them favorites for trade shows.

(a) Hand-held viewer, (b) open, illuminated viewer, (c) folding projector.

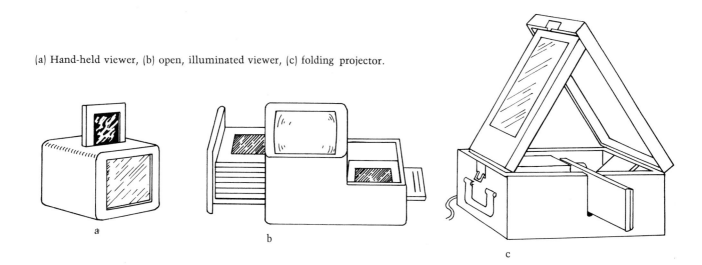

a

b

c

Slide projectors are best for showing work to a number of people, but you should determine in advance that the client has the proper facilities—either a regular projection room or a darkenable room with either a white wall or a portable screen. Don't rely on other people's equipment; take your own projector, an extension cord, and an extra bulb. Run through your slides the night before to make sure that they're in order, and get to your meeting early enough to set up. Slide projectors are easy to operate and have large, brilliant images, and the remote controls let you face an audience, but they are cumbersome to carry around and set up, need darkness, and are sometimes prone to mechanical failure. Kodak's Carousel is the most widely used machine and is relatively foolproof. Remote control and automatic focusing free you from having to stand by the projector and fiddle with it.

Brochures

You should have descriptive printed material that you can send to prospects or leave behind after a presentation. It should match your logo and letterhead in tone and content. There are many possi-

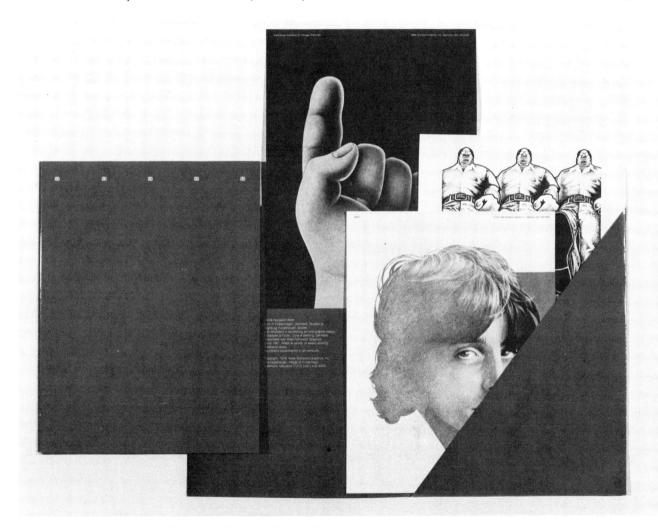

Adler-Schwartz Graphics, Inc. brochure. (Courtesy Bente and Joel Adler)

ble brochure formats—single sheets, foldovers, booklets; many possible enclosures—binders, boxes, covers, folders; and many possible binding methods—spiral, glue, post and screw, staple. Get ideas by talking with a printer or graphic designer and by looking over other brochures at a large crafts show or in the files of an interior designer or architect. An easily amended format, such as confining transitory information to a slip-in sheet, will minimize reprinting. Your brochure can present three main types of information: business description, biography, and client list.

A page from our brochure.

Your business description should include:
● Services: Your business—its history, the kind of work you do and how you do it, e.g., commissions, direct sales, limited editions, consignment, etc., and salient reasons for working with you.
● Media: Types, techniques, scale, materials.
● Fees: Specific prices or your price rationale, e.g., time and materials, if you will work within a fixed budget, if you will prepare a budget, your deposit requirements.
● Installation: Terms and circumstances.
● Shipping: "F.O.B. our studio, packing and shipping extra." or "Unless instructions are given, we will ship by best way."

Your biography if you wish to use it may include: names and descriptions of the members of the firm, including their education, degrees, and academic honors; work experience; and professional achievements—shows, publicity, publications, lectures, and honors.

Your client list may be organized by client type, e.g., hotel, institutional, museum, private collector, or hospital; or by client name. It may include detailed project descriptions such as: names, locations, sizes, media, dates, architects, and interior designers.

Illustrations are very helpful in a brochure. A prospect can immediately see the quality and nature of your work, and later, when he is leafing through his files, illustrations will jog his memory better than the printed page alone. Include a representative selection, or you can be incorrectly typecast. Color is best, but full-color printing is expensive. Black-and-white printing, color photocopies, photos, or slides are alternatives. Identify illustrations with their name, location, medium, size, and date. Add your letterhead information to all that are loose.

A page from our presentation binder.

1., 2. Sports panels. Capitol Centre, Largo, MD. 1976. Acrylic on wood, 2½' x 3', 3' x 3¼'.
3. Murals. Giant Food Inc., Owen Brown, MD. 1978. Acrylic and oil on canvas, 5½' x 5½',
5½' x 30'.

Richard & Roberta Hyman Artists 11500 Homewood Road Ellicott City, Md. 21043 Tel: 301 730-2592

If you are interested in high volume and mail orders, you may want futher information about *terms:* "20 days 1%, 30 days net"; *credit:* requirements for opening an account; credit, bank, or trade references; *stock accessories:* stock frames, mounts, bases, with descriptions, prices, and how to order; *claims:* "all claims must be made with the shipper"; *returns:* "returns on stock items only at _____ % handling charge, no returns on custom work"; etc.

Make your brochure succinct; people don't want to wade through a lush verbal thicket. I have watched many clients read ours. They skim the business description to see how we work and to be assured that we follow familiar business practices. They may check our biography out of curiosity and even comment on our academic background, but they always examine our client list.

I have also observed prospects' reactions to our portfolio. Some pore over it, asking thoughtful questions; others fan through distractedly as if they were in a doctor's waiting room flipping through an old copy of *Today's Health.* Few are interested in press clippings (except when they are from prestigious national publications), working drawings, or presentations unless they relate to some job they have in mind. Most want to see either our actual work or photographs of it, especially those shot on location. Again, they tend to be most interested in our work that pertains to their current projects.

A portfolio is ordinarily essential to landing jobs, but at the same time, it can predetermine the commissions you'll receive. Most clients are more likely to say, "Hey, I like that. Give me five of them in green." than "Come up with a fresh new solution for the project I'm going to show you." You may, of course, want to repeat yourself ("exploring an image" is a kinder term), but if you think another solution more appropriate, you'll have to provide some suasion.

Resumes

If you are looking for a job, or need background information for shows or the media, you will want a resume of your education and your professional qualifications and experiences. The brochure is a tool for selling your *art;* the resume is a tool for selling *yourself.* You can have one resume, or several, slanting each for a particular audience. Thus, a resume for a job might stress work experience, detailing employment, clients, and projects, whereas one for a gallery might omit non-art-related activities and emphasize shows, collections, and honors. For guidance look at publications like *Who's Who in American Art,* or an exhibition catalog, or contact the College Art Association.

An inclusive resume format could list *name and address; education*—college art school, or other educational experience, including courses of study, famous instructors, degrees with dates, honors, and scholarships; *work experience*—employers (list yourself if self-employed), addresses, dates of employment, job descriptions, special projects and responsibilities, and clients; *professional experience*—shows, collections, commissions, honors, memberships, lectures, seminars, and publications.

Presentations

While it is far better to make your presentations in person, it isn't always possible. You can as an alternative send slides, an album of photos, or, if unavoidable, original artwork. Identify each item and keep a good record of what you have sent. For slides, you may wish to type a separate identification list keyed to numbers on the slides to supplement the slide titles. You may want your material to stay on file with important prospects, or you may (and this is especially true of original art and valuable photos) want it promptly returned. While most people are reasonably conscientious, some are careless, and getting material back without offending a prospect can be a real problem. Fabric houses, for instance, when they send out expensive samples, may include a cover letter containing such wording as, "This material is sent for your consideration. I would appreciate your returning it within _____ days. If I do not hear from you by the end of that period, I will assume that you wish to retain it for your permanent files and will send an invoice (you may wish to include a dollar figure)." If this is too strong for starters, you may wish to rephrase the sentiments and dispatch them with a bill after the second attempt to get your work back.

Insure valuable material with the post office, and if you want to be cautious, request either a "return receipt," which will notify you that the package was received or "restricted delivery," a return receipt that a specific individual must sign.

Publicity

Publicity is public notice communicated through the press, electronic media, and word of mouth. Most people feel publicity is more objective than advertising, since it comes from a source other than yourself. What's more, it's free. Unfortunately, you may have little or no control over what's being said about you, and publicity seldom "droppeth as the gentle rain from heaven." You have to work at it.

If you can identify your potential market, then the task of reaching it with the best message becomes easier. Say, for instance, that you want to work with architects. A small appreciative article about your work in *Progressive Architecture* will do you more good than a splash in the local newspaper—which architects may not see or trust. Again, if you've completed a commission for a bank and would like to attract similar work, a photograph in a banking magazine would probably be more effective than one in an interior design magazine. Once you select your medium and your audience, the more carefully you tailor your copy and the more accurately you target the editor, the more likely your material will be used.

Another potential source of publicity is tie-ins with enlightened manufacturers. If you're using a new product, or an old product in a new way, it doesn't hurt to contact the manufacturer and suggest the publicity possibilities. They might provide you with materials with which to experiment or use you and your work in their advertisements.

News Releases

You transmit your information to the news media via a news (press) release, which should follow a standard format. Start with a "lead," which answers the questions, "Who, What, When, Where, and How," and follow with your most important attention-getting material first, then the explanatory details in descending order of magnitude. You do this not only to attract the editors' interest but also to protect the most important information, because if your copy doesn't fit, it will be cut starting at the bottom. Avoid fancy rhetoric. Be concrete, factual, clear, and direct. Allow enough time for its use. Daily newspapers may only need a day or two advance notice, but weeklies can use a week and monthlies a month or more.

Place your name and address at the top of the release. Either use your letterhead, a blank sheet, or a special news release form, which you can have printed. Type neatly, allowing 1½-inch margins below your name and address, and on the left and right, to give the editor room for notations. Head the release with, "FOR MORE INFORMATION CONTACT:" and list the name, address, and phone number of the contact. Lined up to the right, type the date, and underneath the release time, either "FOR IMMEDIATE RELEASE," if it's to be used right away, or "FOR RELEASE" and state the later release date. Leave a space and type your headline in caps. Leave another space and follow with your copy typed double- or triple-spaced. If you need more than one page, type "MORE" at the bottom of each page except the last, where you type "END." At the top left of each page after the first, type "ADD . . .," filling in the number of the page in addition to one. Thus page two is "ADD ONE," page three is "ADD TWO," etc. Opposite ADD . . . type the contact's name in caps. If you send the release to more than one person or department within the same organization, note on the release to whom you've sent the other copies. You may include a cover letter to explain the release's significance.

Example:

ART WORKS!
Peach Street
Gotham, U.S.A. 12345
FOR MORE INFORMATION   February 29, 1979
CONTACT: FOR IMMEDIATE
Raoul Elstir   RELEASE

The NBA announced today that Raoul Elstir, internationally known artist and long-time resident of Gotham, was awarded an NBA grant of $25,000 for his proposed ''Railwork.'' In ''Railwork,'' Mr. Elstir will direct the painting of the Gotham Reservoir railing in his own shade of Elstir green, an electrifying pastel tone.

Gotham will match the NBA grant. Its mayor, Michael Henchard, says, ''We couldn't be more delighted. Plans are already underway to add 'Railwork' to our town seal. This is a great day for Gotham!''

ADD ONE   RAOUL ELSTIR

Since 1968, Mr. Elstir has devoted all the time he can spare from his duties as Professor of Art at Academy Swinburne, to painting his beloved city. Starting with a small Cape Cod in the exact center of town, he has thus far painted 324 houses in his trademark, Elstir green. Seen from the air, the houses form a tremendous spiral superimposed on the motley background of Gotham.

Mr. Elstir says about his work, ''I wanted to articulate spatial and textural interfaces on an environmentally hylomorphistic scale. I like to think I've succeeded.''

END

Photographs should be 5- by 7-inch or 8- by 10-inch black-and-white glossies. Submitting both vertical and horizontal shots will give the editor more latitude in setting up his page. Caption each photo with a brief identification and explanation typed on a separate sheet of paper, and tape the sheet behind the photo so the caption is visible underneath. Flap the photo to protect it.

You can keep your publicity items in a scrapbook or portfolio and mail reprints to clients.

Media Tips

Newspapers: Contact the editor most appropriate to your subject. For example, contact the art editor for a straight story, such as an exhibit or opening; the home editor, if the story is about your studio or an installation in a client's home; the business or real estate editor, for a business installation; or the food editor, for a restaurant.

Magazines: You should also match the right magazine to your purpose. Distinguish between general-interest magazines like *House Beautiful* or *Vogue;* regional magazines like *Yankee* or *Washingtonian;* trade magazines like *Frozen Food Age* or *Supermarketing;* professional design magazines like *Interiors* or *Progressive Architecture;* art magazines like *Art in America* or *Art News;* and business magazines like *Fortune* or *Business Week.*

Radio and TV: You have a number of choices: news assignment editors, personalities, local public-interest shows, talk shows. If you have a newsworthy story, you can offer it as an exclusive to the most desirable radio or TV station, emphasizing the visual angle if you are seeking TV exposure. If your story warrants, you can issue it as a general release to all the stations. Follow up in a few days with a call to see if it's being used.

Original Writing

Original writing is a means of attaining status with your peers and clients. Again, match the subject to the publication. Example: You've just installed banners for a new children's hospital. It was a challenging job, and you'd like to tell about it—the problems you faced, how you solved them, the reactions to your work by the staff and patients. You could approach a hospital, interiors, or crafts magazine, each from a different angle. The hospital magazine might appreciate a story on the therapeutic climate your work helped to create, that it was funded by patrons' donations, and how you designed it for low maintenance. An interiors magazine might like that information plus details on how you approached the challenge from a design standpoint. The crafts magazine might like a touch of the foregoing, but with more emphasis on your solutions of the technical problems that you faced.

Submit an inquiry to the editor with an outline of your proposed article and explain how you would implement it. Include a self addressed stamped envelope. If you haven't heard from him within three weeks, write or call and find out why. If your proposal is rejected and you still think it worthwhile, contact another magazine. Do not submit the same article to more than one magazine at a time.

Mailers and Freebies

Mailers such as calendars, announcements, and cards help clients remember you. They should be fresh, imaginative, low-pressure, and fun. They may mark occasions like moving, New Year's, or Valentine's Day; the acquisition of a new piece of equipment, like a printing press or kiln; or just be for the hell of it. If your mailers are regular and amusing, clients will look forward to them (and to you when you call). Magazines like *Graphics* and *CA* are good idea sources.

Even better than mailers are freebies, such as models or designs from a shared project, or artwork, like prints, miniature banners or paintings. People treasure and display these long after they've chucked out everything else.

Advertising

Advertising is generally of two types: *specific*, to promote an event like a show or a print edition; and *general*, to let people know you're out there. To be most effective, advertising should be shaped for a selected audience and transmitted through the optimum conduit—direct mail, newspaper, magazine, broadcast, signboard, or handout. Again, study top publications for guidance.

Advertising is expensive, especially through national media. There is not only the initial cost to consider, but you may also need follow-up material for inquiries. In view of the expense, except for well-defined, immediate goals, your money will be more productively placed elsewhere.

9. The Office

You need a place to keep your records and transact your business. It can be as simple as a shoebox and a card table, or as fancy as a separate office with a conference room. Your life style, work volume, finances, and operations will determine your set-up.

Usually a corner of the studio is most convenient for an office. You'll not need a separate phone, and your job information will be there as you work. However, it is easier to maintain order and cleanliness in a separate office, and your employees (if you have any) will have less access to your private files.

Equipment

You'll need some basic equipment. A stationer's catalog will provide suggestions. You can purchase much of your equipment second hand in good condition.

A typewriter, preferably an electric, which will handle more carbons and provide neater copy, is just about essential. An inexpensive electric portable will suffice unless you do a lot of typing. Rebuilt office typewriters can also be good investments. You can keep your machine on a typewriter stand or on a desk or table, or you can store it on a shelf and take it out when needed.

You can start out keeping your files in card-board storage files or in corrugated cartons, but as you accumulate them, you'll be much better off with a metal file cabinet. A four-drawer, heavy-gauge, legal-width (15-plus inches) file with roller-suspended drawers is most serviceable. Four drawers often cost no more than two, and you'll always find use for the extra space. The legal width will let you keep your designs in the file folder with your papers, and the rollers and heavy-gauge steel will assure long life and smooth sliding. Files can be expensive even at a used office furniture house; look for a lawyer who's retiring.

You'll benefit from an adding machine to balance your checkbook and ledger, and a calculator to figure area estimates and percentages. The two functions are combined in a printing calculator.

A telephone is, of course, essential. Some people like answer machines. You can use them when you're working and don't want to be disturbed, or when you're out.

Supplies

In addition to your stationery, you will want blank paper, carbon paper, and extra envelopes. A good selection for envelopes is: 3 5/8 by 6 1/2 inches (check size), 4 1/2 by 9 3/8 inches (letter size), 9 by 12 inches (unfolded letter size), and an oversize like 11 1/2 by 14 1/2 inches. Larger envelopes can be made from wrapping paper. You can return address the envelopes with a custom rubber stamp, printed labels, by hand, or by typewriter.

Keep your clients' and suppliers' names and addresses separately either on index cards in card file boxes or on a rotary card file. You can alphabetize them by name, or group them alphabetically by type, e.g., Clients—local, Clients—out of town; Architects; Carpenters; Art Supplies; Lumber; etc. You may note on the cards data like visits and results, prices for materials, directions, quality of service, and employees' names.

Other odds and ends include: an appointment book—for appointments and also for recording long-distance calls for tax-deduction purposes; forms—purchase orders, statements, speed letters; gummed mailing labels—*Fragile*, *Third Class*, *Do Not Bend*; pens, pencils, rubber bands, paper clips, a standard size stapler; a postal scale for weighing letters and a package scale with at least a fifty-pound capacity.

Reference Materials

You will accumulate catalogs and samples. Shelve or file the catalogs either by subject or alphabetically. Store your samples in shoe boxes, cabinets, or shelves, or hang them on the wall. Weed them out periodically. You'll also want a reference library of technical, research, and source books, and a clipping file for inspiration.

Services

One thing I've craved but have never been able to justify is a secretary to type my letters and disentangle my prose. The joy of saying "Take a letter Ms. Nims . . ." surely ranks with having a Xerox copier and a car phone.

You may consider a secretarial service, somebody to come in periodically, or taking a typing course. Part-time secretarial service can involve a lot of travelling back and forth, not having your work done when you want it, and not knowing where things have been filed. When I do my own filing, at least I know where I haven't put my records.

10. Bookkeeping

You can, through reading, taking courses, and asking others, operate a business without the aid of an accountant, but you'll be like the man who doctors himself: You'll never be certain you're doing right until you get sick.

An accountant can analyze your business, organize it properly, and set up a bookkeeping system. He can oversee your affairs at regular intervals, provide ongoing, up-to-date advice, help with your taxes, forestall and assist with audits, show legitimate ways to avoid the unnecessary payment of taxes, and help prevent costly or even disastrous errors.

As when locating any other professional assistance, ask people you trust. Look for an accountant who has experience with artists or people in related fields, or at least with small businesses, and who is philosophically compatible with you. Accountants tend to specialize, as do other professionals, so that someone regularly handling corporate, institutional, or insurance work may not have the experience to give you the best service. You may also find someone who will moonlight from their regular job with a large firm or a government agency. A word of caution—you may want to avoid relatives; their intimate knowledge of your affairs can become a discomfort for you.

An accountant's fees vary according to his expertise and overhead and your geographical area. He may charge either an hourly rate, which will reflect the task and staff involved, or a fixed fee based on his estimate of the probable hours involved plus a little extra as a hedge. He can refine his estimate once he has worked with you and seen how well you keep your records and manage your affairs, and how much demand on his time you make.

He may give you the option of saving money by doing some of the work yourself: by keeping your own books, or by your going to his office rather than his coming to your studio, or by requiring less frequent oversight. He may charge you separately for tax returns and charge extra for setting up your books. Ask (1) if he will renegotiate your fees if you should take over more duties, and (2) how he charges for IRS audits—if they are assumed in his annual fee or if he charges for them by the hour, and if by the hour, at what rate?

An accountant can reduce your taxes through his knowledge of the laws and customs, sometimes in actual excess of his fees (which are a tax-deductible business expense). And, as important, he will give you some peace of mind.

The law requires that you keep business records systematically and accurately, and that the records be available for the inspection of IRS agents for a period of four years in the normal case of records, and forever in the case of fraud. Tax return copies must be kept indefinitely. You should also keep contracts, bank records, accounting records, check disbursements, income records, and information like estimates and research that might be useful again. Weed out routine correspondence, rejected bids, and outdated samples.

Good records reveal your overhead and your profitability—two considerations in raising or lowering your prices. They also make data easier to retrieve and are a defense should a business/hobby challenge arise. (See page 81.)

Accounting Methods

There are three basic accounting systems: *cash*, *accrual*, and *hybrid*, a combination of the first two. All are based on a 365-day year, usually the *calendar year*, which starts on January 1, but sometimes the *fiscal year*, which may start at any other date (July 1 for the federal government). There is always a question about reporting expenses and income for the brief period on either side of the new year. It may be difficult to establish exactly in which year an item is paid or received, allowing some latitude for reporting the item in the more favorable year, i.e., delaying a billing in a successful year so that payment will occur in the next, possibly less successful year, thus reducing the tax base for the successful year. Manipulating entries, i.e., not recording items at the time they were mailed or received so as to willfully place them in more favorable years, is illegal.

Cash is the simplest accounting method, and the one most often used by artists. You record income as you receive it (*actual receipt*) or as an agent, like a gallery, receives it for you (*constructive receipt*). You record expenses as you pay them.

Accrual is a more complicated method. You report income at the time you earn it, rather than when you receive it. You report expenses at the time you incur them, rather than when you pay them. Businesses whose inventories are a material factor must use the accrual system; it helps the IRS control stockpiling to achieve a more favorable tax position. You needn't consider modest amounts of art materials to be used in future work as inventory.

Hybrid systems are a combination of the cash and accrual methods. For example, an artist who keeps a large inventory of materials or unsold artwork might record his expenses as accrual and record his income as cash.

Income

Income is divided into two types for tax purposes: *earned income* and *unearned income*.

Earned income (also called *ordinary income*) is the money you earn from your professional activities, i.e., designing and selling artwork. It is taxed on a sliding scale. *Gross income* is your total income before you deduct anything from it. *Net income* is the amount left after you deduct your expenses.

Unearned income is your income from interest, dividends, capital gains, and so forth. *Capital gains* are income from the sale of capital assets like equipment, real property, and stocks. If you own the capital assets more than one year, you need only pay taxes on forty percent of their capital gains.

Scholarships and fellowships are tax free if they are made primarily to further your education and not as compensation for your services, or "for studies or research primarily for the grantor's benefit." Prizes and awards, whether cash, goods, or services, are taxable except for those like the Nobel or Pulitzer Prizes given in recognition of past accomplishments. (See: *Your Federal Income Tax:* Fellowships and Scholarships, Grants, Prizes and Awards.)

Expenses

Expenses must be "ordinary and necessary" to your business to be deductible. Some expenses: paint, canvas, and nails, for example, are clearly ordinary and necessary; other expenses: a hi-fi set in your studio, entertaining clients, or travel to see an exhibit, are less clear. It's on these judgment-call deductions where you can really benefit from an accountant's advice.

You should document your expenses through cancelled checks, receipts, credit-card sales slips, and similar records. Where documentation might be awkward—taxi fares and phone calls for example—you can keep an expense diary in a notebook or in a special record book you can buy at a stationer's. When entertaining or traveling, note the business reason for the activity, what business was transacted, with whom, and the date and time in either your diary or on the receipt for the expense. Questionable deductions or those disproportionate to your gross income may prompt an audit.

Most of your capital assets, those items not consumed within a short period, e.g., buildings, real estate, furniture, and equipment, can be taken off as an expense (*depreciated*) over the projected useful life of the item. There are many ways to compute depreciation. The general procedure is to consider the initial purchase price, projected use, and *salvage value* (value, if any, at the end of the period of use). Your accountant will select the proper formula.

Separating Business and Personal Finances

Taxes and good management require that you keep business and personal finances apart. Separate and distinct checking accounts—different banks, radically different style checkbooks—will help reduce confusion. Pay by check and obtain receipts for cash to provide easy documentation. Expenses, like vehicles, utilities, and telephone, may be both business and personal. Enter the payment into your books and then divide it into its personal and business components under the proper headings.

Deposit your business income into your business checking account. Make withdrawals for your personal use from your business account and note them in a personal column. You can deposit nonbusiness income (unearned income) into a personal checking account, but be sure to keep a record of it for your taxes by logging the income in a journal as you receive it, and by totaling year-end earnings statements mailed to you.

Sales journal showing totals on a monthly and quarterly basis. The first four columns should equal the last column. Monthly and quarterly totals may be in pencil.

1979		RECEIVED FROM	SALES		SALES TAX		TEACHING		MISC											TOTAL	
Jan	6	Hotel Paradiso	2222	55	89	80														2312	35
	27	La Fountain	74	00																74	00
	30	Academy Swinburne					120	00												120	00
	30	Refund, Designs Unltd.							30	00										30	00
		Total Month	2296	55	89	80	120	00	30	00										2536	35
Feb	7	Ft Knox	630	00																630	00
	15	P-38 Disco	2856	15	144	25														3000	40
	30	Acad. Swinburne					120	00												120	00
		Total Month	3486	15	144	25	120	00												3750	40
Mar	30	Swanko Apts	500	00																500	00
		Acad. Swinburne					120	00												120	00
		Total Month	500	00			120	00												620	00
		Total Quarter	6282	70	234	05	360	00	30	00										6906	75

Taxes

You must pay federal income tax, and in many jurisdictions, state income tax, city income tax, and other forms of business tax. You may also be liable for withholding, sales tax, unemployment, and FICA payments. Your accountant and the various government agencies involved will enlighten you.

Artists have a few occupational tax problems. These include:

Prizes, awards, scholarships, and grants, which were previously discussed on page 77.

Income averaging. Income averaging is a com-

(a) 1980		PAYEE (b)	CH # (c)	CASH (d)		PERSONAL (e)		AUTO (f)		HEAT & LIGHT (g)		PHONE (h)		SUPPLIES (i)		SUBCONTR.		OTHER (j)		
June	1	Visa Credit Card	24	84	40	55	01							5	79			Frames	23	60
	3	Raoul Elstir	25	500	00	500	00													
	3	Flash Auto	26	39	20			39	20											
	7	IRS 2ᴰ Qtr	27	250	00	250	00													
	15	Gas & Electric	28	45	78	22	89			22	89									
	26	Marino Gallery	29	78	43													Frames	78	43
	27	Kelly Movers	30	150	00													Freight	150	00
	28	A & B Phone Co	31	27	55							27	55							
	28	Exxon	32	75	20	49	97	25	23											
	28	Arnold Factory	33	14	50									14	50					
	28	State Sales Tax	34	20	02													Sales Tax	20	02
	28	Bill Daubert	35	118	00											118	00			
	29	Sears	36	54	09	21	87	20	03					12	19					
(k)		(TOTAL)		1457	17	899	74	84	46	22	89	27	55	32	48	118	00		272	05

Cash disbursement ledger showing monthly expenses. Make up column headings to suit your needs.
(a) Date of check, (b) Person or company to whom check is issued, (c) Number of the check in your checkbook, (d) Face amount of the check, (e) Money either paid to yourself (e.g., check #25) or for personal use. Check #24, for example, shows personal component of a credit card charge for both business and personal items, (f) Elstir has two cars, one business and one personal. When he charges fuel and repairs, he notes which auto on the ticket. In this case, $49.57 goes to his personal car, and $25.23 to his business car, (g) Elstir's studio is attached to his home, and equal to it in size. Check #28, therefore, is apportioned 50/50, (h) He has a business phone, which is charged entirely to his business, (i) With more columns in the ledger, supplies could be divided into types, e.g., frames, hardware, art supplies, packing supplies, (j) Other is a catch-all for whatever doesn't fit elsewhere, (k) The total cash disbursement (column d) should equal the total of the other columns (e through j).

1980		PAYEE	CH #	CASH		FEDL. WITHHOLDING		FICA		STATE WITHHOLDING		GROSS SALARY					
June	29	Fawn LaPides	37	84	03	14	50	6	41	4	56	109	50				
June	29	Margalo Byrd	38	68	68	10	20	5	09	3	03	87	00				
		(TOTAL)		142	71	24	70	11	50	7	53	196	50				

If you have employees, you can add a payroll section to your ledger.

ARTIST CLIENT

CONTRACT

CONTRACT

CHECK $

② THE CLIENT KEEPS ONE CONTRACT, COUNTERSIGNS THE OTHER, AND RETURNS IT WITH A DEPOSIT CHECK.

SALES JOURNAL

BANK DEPOSIT SLIP COPY

BANK

① TYPE THREE COPIES OF YOUR CONTRACT, SEND TWO SIGNED COPIES TO THE CLIENT, AND KEEP ONE COPY FOR YOURSELF

CONTRACTS/ PURCHASE ORDERS

③ DEPOSIT THE CHECK IN YOUR BUSINESS CHECKING ACCOUNT. ENTER THE AMOUNT IN YOUR SALES JOURNAL, ATTACH YOUR COPY OF THE BANK DEPOSIT SLIP TO THE CONTRACT, AND PLACE THE PACKET IN YOUR CONTRACTS/PURCHASE ORDERS FILE.

④ WHEN YOU COMPLETE THE JOB, BILL THE CLIENT. ATTACH A COPY OF THE BILL TO THE CONTRACT PACKET AND PLACE IT IN YOUR ACCOUNTS RECEIVABLE FILE.

BILL

COPY

CONTRACT BANK DEPOSIT SLIP COPY

ACCOUNTS RECEIVABLE

CHECK $

SALES JOURNAL

BANK DEPOSIT SLIP COPY

BILL BANK DEPOSIT SLIP COPY

⑤ WHEN THE CLIENT PAYS YOUR BILL, DEPOSIT THE CHECK IN YOUR BUSINESS CHECKING ACCOUNT. ENTER THE AMOUNT IN YOUR SALES JOURNAL, ATTACH YOUR COPY OF THE BANK DEPOSIT SLIP TO THE CONTRACT PACKET, AND PLACE IT IN YOUR ANNUAL ACCOUNTS RECEIVED FILE.

BANK

ANNUAL ACCOUNTS RECEIVED

ACCOUNTS RECEIVED 19___

⑥ AT THE END OF THE YEAR, TRANSFER THE CONTENTS OF YOUR ACCOUNTS RECEIVED FILE TO A PERMANENT ACCOUNTS RECEIVED FILE FOR THAT YEAR.

Our contract/billing/filing system.

plicated tax-saving calculation for averaging out the unusually large income of a current year over the four preceeding years, thus taking advantage of the lower tax rate of those four leaner previous years. Sometimes you can save money by it, and sometimes not. It can only help, never hurt, so see if it applies.

Estimated income tax. The federal government and other jurisdictions require that the self-employed pay taxes quarterly based on either the previous year's income or on their educated guess, made by April 15, of their income for the coming year. If you use the previous year's figure, you will not be penalized or charged interest if you make more money (If you make less, you've just lent Uncle some money interest free). If you don't use last year's income, guess wrong, or guess and earn more than a certain margin, you must pay a penalty on the difference plus interest. You can alter your quarterly payments during the year if the discrepancy becomes apparent.

Gift taxes. You and your spouse can each year give $3,000 in cash or goods, such as artwork, to every member of your family with no tax to either the donor or the recipient.

Business or hobby? The question of whether your artwork is a business or a hobby only arises, as far as the IRS is concerned, when you take a loss—when your expenses exceed your income. A business can show a loss in any one year; a hobby cannot. The principal requirement for a business is that it show a profit for two years out of every five. You can control this to a certain extent by grouping your expenses and income to secure two profitable and three unprofitable years, rather than five marginally unprofitable years. Even if you fail the two-in-five rule, you can still qualify as a business if you display the *intent* of profitability in such ways as keeping good records, using business stationery, and being professionally active, but the chances of qualifying are small. Discuss your circumstances with an accountant.

Barter. Barter—the exchange of goods or service in lieu of money—does not relieve you from your obligation to report the transaction if you operate a business. If you are deducting your expenses for creating your artwork, then whatever you receive in exchange—money, medical care, or a sack of potatoes—is income. You should list in your cash journal the monetary value of the commodity received (it should be equivalent to that of your artwork) and identify its source and nature.

The home studio. A portion of the Tax Reform Act of 1976, devised to curb abuses of offices in the home, makes the deduction of home studios difficult for those whose artwork does not qualify as a separate, bona fide business. To be deductible, according to the law, the studio portion of the home must be used "regularly and exclusively" as a place of business, be the "principal place of business," be "for the convenience of your employer" (who is you if you're self employed), and not be used "both for personal and business purposes." IRS Publication 587, *Business Use of Your Home*, explains the law.

The law can affect artists in several ways:

Artist-teachers, whose "principal place of business" is the classroom, but who maintain a studio as a vital adjunct to their teaching, probably can't deduct their studio unless they can incontrovertibly demonstrate that it is either a requirement of their employment or at the "convenience" of their employer.

You can probably deduct a one-room shared studio/living quarters if it is your principal place of business and if you demarcate the two functions by such means as partitions, railings, painted lines, or curtains.

You cannot deduct your studio if you use it to do work for your employer in the evenings or on weekends. It is not your "principal place of business." You can, however, deduct your studio if you use it to do moonlighting for clients other than your regular employer. It would be the "principal place of business" for your second business.

Using your studio only on weekends or during the evening would qualify as "regular use" if you satisfied the other provisions. Nonregular use might be using the studio once a month or on vacations only.

These distinctions in many instances are not hard and fast, they are judgment calls, but the burden of proof rests on you. Consult an accountant if in doubt.

Death taxes. After death, federal estate taxes and, in many states, an inheritance tax as well, are imposed upon your wordly goods. The personal representative (executor) of your estate must engage a competent appraiser to evaluate your nonliquid assets, e.g., real estate, car, equipment, unsold artwork. The value of your nonliquid assets is added to that of your liquid assets, e.g., stocks, bonds, cash, to arrive at your total taxable estate. Your estate must pay this tax in cash, promptly. The federal government does not take credit cards.

Any competent appraiser should realize that in most cases, only a fraction, if any, of an artist's output is ever sold during his lifetime and that it would be unreasonable to use those scattered prices to evaluate the remainder. If an artist's heirs think the appraisal unfair, they can challenge it in court. They can sell the artwork (which might be necessary to pay the taxes) and submit the sale price, if it is lower than the appraisal, as evidence to support their challenge. Unloading large inventories at one time depresses the market, a fact that should be kept in mind by both assessors and heirs.

Audits

The agents of the IRS have the right to audit any taxpayer's books. A very few are chosen by random computer selection. Most are targeted because of questionable, not necessarily illegal, returns. Given its limited resources, the IRS tends to select those most likely to yield the greatest return for investigative hours; thus, persons in higher brackets are more likely to be selected. In particular, the IRS sets its computers to question deductions that are disproportionate to income. Inflated or unusual deductions (a $5,000.00 trip to Paris, when you're making $10,000.00 a year) as a percent of total income may invite an audit.

Audits are often expensive and always unpleasant. The auditor will want to review all your finances—books, records, tax returns, receipts, savings accounts—everything. He can go back three years for a normal audit and six for a twenty-five percent or more suspected understatement of gross income. Since the returns being examined may already be several years old, you may have to produce records that are five or more years old.

If the auditor visits your workplace, he may improve his time by admiring the little tax-saving crochets you've devised. He can afford to take your time; he's being paid no matter. And you can anticipate that he probably won't go away empty handed. In addition to unpaid taxes plus interest, an audit will cost you your time, your accountant's time, and a great deal of anguish.

Financial Planners

Financial planners assist people in organizing and rationalizing their financial affairs. Lawyers, stock brokers, insurance agents, and accountants see fragments of their clients' financial lives; financial planners see them all. Certified Financial Planners (C.F.P.) have passed examinations given by the College of Financial Planning, assuring a high level of competence.

Financial planners will work with you to make a comprehensive, confidential inventory of your total assets: your real property, stocks, bonds, insurance equity, investments, savings, and personal possessions. You must supply them with such information as: your tax returns, insurance policies, retirement and savings figures, and average income and itemized expenses.

They will help you identify your financial goals, and plan for retirement income, the purchase of land or a house, an estate, or regular travel. They will then devise a strategy incorporating your data with the current legal, tax, and financial environment to pursue those goals, and periodically monitor your progress to keep you on target.

II. Lawyers

You can avoid many legal problems by consulting a lawyer before your difficulties begin. You'll need a lawyer primarily for three reasons:

1. To help set up your business, in particular before you become deeply involved in it or make any binding commitments. Of course, I don't mean every time you paint a picture or sign a check you should clear it with your lawyer, but, until you get your sea legs, when you're involved with a contract that obligates you to perform something or that transfers your rights to someone, have a lawyer explain just what you're getting into. After awhile, your business affairs should form a pattern, and you'll only need to confer when something unfamiliar comes up.

2. For the occasional problems that confront any small-business person: landlord-tenant disagreements, contract disputes, bad debts, and the like. There are a few special problems related to the arts, such as royalties, copyright infringements, invasion of privacy, and obscenity, for example, but these, fortunately, are rare.

3. To defend you. *Absolutely*, see a lawyer if you are threatened with any kind of legal action.

To find a lawyer, ask other people whom you trust, e.g., your banker, insurance agent, or accountant. In most large towns there will be at least one lawyer sympathetic to artists who specializes in working with them. Locate this nonpareil through your local artist's group, museum, or art council. You can also consider, especially for routine problems, legal clinics, which are becoming increasingly common. They keep their fees low by having paralegals do much of the repetitive operations. Inquire, however, if you'll have one person assigned to you for all your work, or if you must take whomever's on duty each time you come in.

Volunteer Lawyers for the Arts (36 West 44th Street, New York, N.Y., 10036) offers free legal counsel to artists and publishes information on the arts and the law. This 300-member organization helps over 500 clients annually with such problems as negotiating and drafting contracts, copyrights, and taxes. Look in the phonebook to see if there's a chapter in your area, ask your local bar association, or, if you have no luck, contact national headquarters. Since the success of any volunteer organization depends on the support of its members, your experience with VLA will hinge on the zeal of its local affiliates. Don't be startled if people prefer to work for money.

One other free resource is Legal Aid, a government-funded legal assistance program for the indigent. It won't assist you with business matters, but you might keep them in mind for help with your personal problems if there's an office in your area, and if you're poor enough to qualify.

Legal fees differ widely, depending on the individual lawyer and your geographical area. They are basically of two kinds: (1) a retainer plus an hourly rate, used mainly for open-ended situations, and (2) a set fee for standard services, such as forming a corporation or writing a will. Unless they're very busy, most lawyers will talk with you free of charge to identify your needs and estimate their fees.

Inasmuch as chronic lack of money is a recognized field mark for artists (and may be the root cause for seeing a lawyer in the first place), propose barter or other imaginative forms of compensation. Lawyers who've worked with artists before should be familiar with this route, and may, in fact, prefer to take it.

12. Banks

You'll need a bank for a checking account, hopefully for a savings account, and possibly for other services, like loans, credit checks, and advice. Commercial banks, which specialize in working with the business community, are the best choice for your business checking account and other business activities. Savings and loan associations, which specialize in residential and commercial mortgages, are a better choice for your savings since they currently pay higher interest rates.

Ask your acquaintances, especially those whose business judgment you respect, for advice on selecting a commercial bank. Consider service first: a bank that will take the time to work with you and give you the help you need, and that will stick with you in periods of tight as well as loose money. A small, local bank may offer more personal assistance; a large metropolitan bank may offer broader facilities and resources. Choosing banks by their interest rates and checking-account terms can be misleading; rates and programs are figured by a complex of methods, and what may seem at first either cheapest or more lucrative often isn't. In any event, the small savings that you may realize by spreading your business around, rather than concentrating it in one or two institutions, will be more than offset by your added travel time, by your increased paperwork and by your not forming an established relationship with a bank and banker.

Establish your banking connection on a personal basis. Your best contact will probably be a commercial loan officer. He should know all aspects of banking—trust, business, estate, consumer loans—as well as commerce in general. Don't settle for a branch bank manager. Some banks station managers at an office for only a brief period. A branch manager may also lack experience and lending authority. Select someone you can trust and with whom you can work comfortably. Don't be shy. Even though you may not amount to much now, a bank officer should be interested in your potential, and in his reputation in working with customers, in his good name in the community, and in the referrals that you might send his way.

A Bank's Services

Having chosen a bank and a compatible bank officer, set up your business checking account. While that's in the works, review your prospects with him. He may have good advice on the market potential of your area, on insurance, and on taxes. He should be able to supply you with the names of accountants and lawyers, direct you to business locations, and assist in establishing credit with new suppliers.

Credit Checks

A bank has many services. They can help make credit checks on your new clients. Ask a new client for the name of his bank (to avoid appearing mistrustful, you may offer to exchange bank references). Have your banker then contact the client's bank for such data as the client's checking account balance (you'll not get specific numbers but round figures like "low five-figure amount"), his borrowing experience, and his length of time as a customer. If you require additional information, such as how promptly the client pays his accounts, your banker may be able to obtain a trade check (which might, for instance, say "pays slowly—90 to 120 days"). Credit information services, of which Dun and Bradstreet (D and B) is the nation's largest, supply reports for their subscribers on other businesses that include such information as history of the company and its principal managers, how it pays its bills, the number of employees, financial statements, and physical descriptions. D and B's services cost at least a thousand dollars a year.

Certified Checks, Cashier's Checks, and Bank Wires

There are two other types of checks in addition to regular business checks: *certified checks* and *cashier's checks*. These checks may be required from you as payment by new or distant creditors with whom you have not yet established credit and who are, therefore, uncertain of your ability to pay.

A *certified check* is a check the bank stamps (certifies) to indicate that the money has been transferred from your account to a special account awaiting presentation of the check. When the check is paid it will not be retained by the bank; you should request a copy for your files.

A *cashier's check* is a check that a bank writes in your behalf in exchange for money that you give it.

Use a *bank wire* when you must move money fast, as when you need goods shipped immediately from a new supplier. For a small charge, your bank will transfer money via telegraph from your account to a customer's account in another bank. If he knows your voice, your banker may be willing to make the transaction on telephone authorization alone.

Borrowing Money

We're all familiar with the J. P. Morgan image of the banker—tough, tight-fisted, and conservative—who only lends money when he's absolutely certain you don't need it. Be assured when you go for a loan you won't be seeing J. P. or, most likely, any of his descendants. What you will see is a salaried employee responsible for soundly investing the money that others like yourself have entrusted to his bank. This employee is evaluated on the success of his lending record, and, furthermore, in many banks he will also be responsible for loan collections. He may, thus, have the onerous duty of liquidating the assets of those very businesses to which he has loaned money, an unpleasantness he'd certainly like to avoid. On top of that, he knows that eight out of ten businesses in the United States fail within their first three years. Is it any wonder, then, that bankers are cautious?

Before you ask for a loan, do your homework. The loan officer may ask you to fill out a loan evaluation form and question you carefully on such topics as why you need the money, your cash flow, and your prospects. He may approve the loan, or he may reject it for any number of reasons. For example, he may feel that you have good ideas but lack experience. If that's the case, he may suggest that you work awhile in your own or related fields to gain business skills and contacts with potential clients. Or, loan money may be tight because of the current economic conditions. Or, he may think artists are a poor risk.

Don't be discouraged too easily. Reevaluate your presentation—perhaps you were emphasizing the wrong points, not selling your assets strongly enough, or were lacking vital information—and try your luck with another loan officer at another bank. If you do no better, your local Small Business Administration (SBA) or Arts Council may have some advice.

There are three basic types of loans: *working-capital loans* (short-term loans), *term loans*, and *mortgage loans.*

Working-capital loans normally are granted for periods of from 90 to 180 days and cover short-term needs and temporary cash shortages. For example, you have a large contract that you will collect on in four months, but the expenses for it are due now, and you can defer them no longer. A working-capital loan will cover you, sometimes with the contract assigned as collateral. At the same time, your loan office may help you head off such crises in the future by assisting you in planning your cash flow.

Term loans run from one to ten years to cover equipment, furniture, and fixtures. If you're renting, term loans may include leasehold improvements. The bank will seek to secure their money in several ways. Ordinarily, they will mandate that you personally guarantee the loan. They may also require liens on your inventory, your accounts receivable, and the equipment purchased with the loan money, as well as a second mortgage. Finally,

the bank may want to see periodic financial statements to keep track of their investment and make sure that you're monitoring your business conscientiously.

If you cannot provide collateral to the bank's satisfaction, the S.B.A. is authorized to guarantee up to 90 percent of a loan to small businesses not to exceed $350,000. Your loan officer will assist you in filling out an application and will send it to the S.B.A., which customarily follows his recommendation. The S.B.A. can be accommodating, e.g., it can offer deferred participation to cover a period beyond the bank's normal loan period.

A *mortgage loan* is for purchasing *real* (land and buildings thereon) property. A commercial bank will make mortgages of up to 10 to 15 years for business-property purchase only. A savings and loan association can lend mortgage money for up to 20 to 30 years for residences or residence-studio combinations. Payments are monthly. The longer the payback period the lower the monthly payment, but the higher the interest rate and the total amount of interest paid.

13. Insurance

Art is a risky business, not simply in the sense of making a living or in taking audacious aesthetic gambles, but in the dangers that you or your work might pose to the persons or property of other people. A salesman who injures himself in your studio could sue you for all you own (which may not seem much until you start adding it up), or a disastrous fire could destroy a major job and leave you without a source of income. For a price, known as a premium, insurance companies will share risks with you.

Your insurance budget is finite; calamities are not. It is essential, therefore, to gain the optimum protection for every insurance dollar. You must ponder the cost/benefit ratios in each instance and choose the best response. Your options include: (1) insuring yourself fully, especially for primary activities with bankrupting potential; (2) insuring yourself until the expense is no longer commensurate with the risk; (3) insuring yourself only beyond a certain threshold (a deductible policy); (4) not insuring yourself against remote risks or for rare activities; (5) discontinuing or refusing uninsured activities; (6) transferring liability through a "hold harmless" or similar agreement.

There are many types of insurance: life, health, liability, income protection, workmen's compensation, vehicle, rain, shipping, dwelling, and property. Some special terms include:

Blanket Policy: A policy that covers several different items listed in the policy.

Endorsement: An alteration attached to a policy. *Rider:* Another name for an endorsement, especially used in bonding and personal accident policies.

Floater Policy: A policy written on movable, as opposed to fixed, property.

Schedule: The list of properties covered by a policy.

Self Insurance: The setting aside of money by an individual or organization to meet his or its losses.

Umbrella: A broad-form liability policy providing high-limit excess coverage.

Agents

The surest way to locate a good insurance agent is through the recommendation of someone whose judgment you trust, e.g., your lawyer, banker, or accountant. Interview a prospective agent to assess his qualifications: if he will devote adequate time and interest to you; if he will sell you what's best for you, rather than what is easiest and most profitable for him; and if he is sufficiently familiar with and sympathetic to your line of work.

There are two categories of agents: the company agent, who works for and sells the policies of one company exclusively, and the independent agent, who can select from the policies of a number of companies. Since your requirements will probably be diverse, the independent may be the better choice. The initial C.P.C.U. (Chartered Property and Casualty Underwriter) indicates the agent has passed a rigorous series of qualifying exams and assures a high level of competence.

Agents may further be grouped into generalists who sell all kinds of insurance and specialists who sell only one or a few related kinds. In theory, generalists should enjoy the advantages of a good working knowledge of the whole of insurance, and should view their client's needs in their entirety. In practice, few generalists have the comprehensive knowledge and experience to compete with a good selection of specialists. A generalist may, through using the services of specialist colleagues, however, offer the advantages of both in one person.

Go over your business operations thoroughly with your agent. Do not assume that he knows more about your affairs than you do; bring potential problems to his attention. Do not conceal information. Your policies will be based on your ''representations'' (factual assertions). Should your representations prove false or misleading, your policies can be cancelled and your claims denied.

The rest of this chapter will suggest topics for your review. Learn to see unfamiliar situations from an insurance angle before you commit yourself to them. Contact your agent when alterations occur which might require changes in your coverage, and check regularly every year or two for reappraisals necessitated by inflation.

Claims

There are two divisions of claims—those made *against the insured*, e.g., personal or liability damages; and those the insured makes *against the insurance company*, e.g., property replacement.

In the first type of claim, those against you, it's impossible to estimate the exact nature and amount of a potential claim until the damage occurs. You can't tell what injuries a delivery man who slips on your newly washed floor will sustain until after he actually falls. It could be a sprained ankle, but then again, it might be a broken back. You can know this much, however: Awards have been rapidly soaring into the millions of dollars. Inadequate liability insurance can be ruinous. Companies have responded to the problem of escalating claims with *umbrella policies*, which, for affordable premiums, give protection over and above basic liability policies.

In the second type of claim, those made by you against your insurance company for the replacement of lost, stolen, or damaged goods, it's possible to accurately estimate the value of the goods insured, but you must provide the company with documentation. With life insurance, for example, prima facie evidence is usually straightforward—the insured is either dead or he isn't. With artwork, the evidence may be difficult to substantiate, but you must nevertheless provide it. Remember, the burden of proof is not on your insurance company· it is on you. More about this in a moment.

Insuring the Studio

Your insurance agent thinks of your studio as three entities: (1) property, (2) improvements and betterments, (3) contents and stock.

1. If your studio is part of, or attached to your house, you can insure it by adding a business use endorsement to your homeowner's policy. If your studio is part of, or attached to your apartment, you can insure it by adding a business use endorsement to your tenant's policy. If your studio is entirely separate from your dwelling, you must insure it with a separate policy.

2. Substantial improvements and betterments to your studio, e.g., built-ins, attached furniture, shelving, must be added to your policy if you want them covered.

3. Contents, e.g., *equipment*, like easels, drafting tables, machinery, and *supplies*, like paint, paper, and canvas, are included in your general

policy. Keep an inventory of the more valuable items in case of loss. Should your purchases exceed your coverage, you should increase your policy. Your contents and stock are *not* insured outside your studio unless you take out a specific rider or separate policy.

Stock, i.e., artwork, must be listed on your policy to be insured. Documentation for property, improvements and betterments, and contents is relatively easy through receipts, property assessments, and photographs. Documentation for artwork is more difficult and has three aspects—*quantity, value,* and *state of completion.*

Document *quantity* by systematically inventorying artwork as you create it. Photographs of your work are good, especially if keyed to a log. Example: Photo # 232—*Man and Dog*, oil on canvas, unframed, 16″ x 20″, completed June 1978. Rack 3, slot 27.

Document *valuation* through contracts and sales records. Valuation is linked to a work's condition and state of completion. If there is no established market value for your artwork, valuation will be quite difficult.

It's tough enough for *us* to tell when our own work is completed, what then can we expect of a claims adjustor? Establish a work's *state of completion* through photos, inventories, and time logs, which record the hours spent per piece. The delivery dates on contracts can give guidance for a work's presumed state of completion. It can be argued, for example, that a job is approximately half completed when its contracted period is half run.

You can take out policies to insure individual projects, particularly where their loss would be more than you'd care to risk, e.g., a long-term job with high material costs. Such policies may contain guidelines for recording completions as they occur.

Liability

The standard homeowner's and tenant's policy *excludes* business pursuits. Your risk is not simply the obvious one of clients' visits, but that of anyone remotely connected with your art business—the delivery man, salesperson, bill collector, or casual guest. Have your agent endorse your homeowner's or tenant's policy for your studio. If your studio is separate, you will need a separate liability policy.

Most liability policies exclude coverage of those things considered under your "care, custody, or control." Thus, your policy will probably not insure other people's possessions left in your studio with you. Don't, for example, take up framing or picture conservation, or store someone's valuable paintings, without first checking with your agent. He may suggest a *bailee's* policy to protect you.

Insuring Employees

Employees must, by law, be insured against injuries sustained on the job. Most states have a dual workman's compensation insurance system, whereby the state serves as an insurer of the last resort to supplement the policies of private companies. A few states have monopolistic systems, wherein only the state may provide insurance. Ask your agent for details.

For liability insurance, employees may be endorsed onto your own policy. Review their activities with your agent. You will probably be charged higher rates if your employees must work outside your studio, making deliveries or installations. Given the rate difference, you may conclude that it's not economically justifiable from an insurance standpoint to have them engage in marginal outside activities. You may wish to insure only yourself or, say, one employee for outside work, or relegate such work entirely to subcontractors.

Optional group insurance for employees includes health, life, and disability. Since these are discretionary, and the money for them will in part come from employees' wages, they may be elected in conference with your agent and employees.

Insuring Subcontractors

Whenever you've contracted a subcontractor for whom liability insurance may be needed, an installation for example, ask for a description and certificate of his liability insurance. If his coverage is inadequate, you have the options of: suggesting that he increase it, taking out a rider on your policy to cover yourself, refusing to contract with him, or contracting with him and accepting the risk.

Even if a subcontractor under contract to you is insured for liability damage, in the event of a lawsuit *you* may very well be named as a codefendant, particularly if the subcontractor's insurance is insufficient for the alleged damages. *Independent Contractor's Coverage* will protect you against such a possibility.

Vehicles

Be sure you and your employees have personal and property liability insurance for all owned, nonowned, hired, or other vehicles used in your business. Before you give your car to the kid who works for you one afternoon a week to run into town for some nails, consider if you have proper insurance. If he knocks someone down, you may be held responsible. An *Employer's Non-Ownership Auto Liability Policy* will provide protection for anyone who uses a vehicle in your business.

Your medical insurance (which surely you already have) will cover you for your personal injuries sustained while driving on business.

Insuring You and Your Artwork Outside Your Studio

A policy that insures artwork in your studio will *not* protect that artwork once it is removed from the premises. Your work while it is in transit, whether in your own vehicle or any other vehicle, is *not* insured unless you have *shipping insurance*. Discuss your shipping requirements with your agent. He will propose a policy based on such considerations as: number of shipments, average and maximum values, replaceability, and packing procedures. Policies can cover fire, theft, vandalism, and damage in your vehicle or with a common carrier.

There are various types of shipping insurance policies:

Annual Transportation Floater Policy: A policy the rate for which is predicated on the approximate number, average value, and maximum value of shipments within a year. The amount of coverage per loss is set at the estimated value of any one shipment. An annual policy will be cheaper than the aggregate cost of individual floater policies for that same year.

Per Shipment Transportation Floater Policy: A policy taken out to cover a single shipment. It is useful when a shipment is of extraordinary value and/or when its loss might be disastrous.

Common carriers (UPS, air freight, motor freight) always offer some form of shipping insurance. Their policies may be inadequate for several reasons. They may be based on weight alone, making a five-pound painting equal in insurability to five pounds of birdseed. They may insure only the value of component materials—a $1,000.00 painting may only be insurable for the $50.00 value of its frame and canvas. They may have a ceiling that is too low, or not cover artwork that is "unique," i.e., irreplaceable. Finally, common carriers cannot insure against "acts of God" (windstorm, earthquake, fire). The carriers may also prove hard to collect from, and may even have gone out of business before your claim can be settled.

A Personal Shipping Policy will cover over and above the maximum of a common carrier and will insure against acts of God. Even so, you may decide that the policies of carefully selected carriers will be adequate for your shipping needs and you will not require the additional expense of your own policy.

Your property insurance policy may not cover your artwork away from your studio, i.e., on loan, exhibit, or consignment to individuals, galleries, dealers, shops, or museums. Check with your agent.

Installation

A personal transportation policy and/or a common carrier policy will insure artwork that is to be installed, while it is in transit. Once accepted by the purchaser, the artwork is *his* responsibility unless you are to install it, in which case *you* will again resume responsibility at the time of the installation. If you deliver the artwork, the responsibility remains with you until the purchaser signs for it, which may not occur until installation is completed. Thus, if you deliver a work that must be stored until you install it at a later time, you should have the purchaser or his representative sign for it, or have it covered by your own policy.

Your general liability policy may not protect you against some forms of property damage that can occur during installations. You'll recall that when I discussed studio insurance I mentioned that anything placed under your "care, custody, and control" was generally excluded from coverage. The same holds true for working on location. You may be held personally responsible for your artwork and for the installation site under your jurisdiction. What, however, constitutes your jurisdiction is often quite ambiguous and may be interpreted differently by different insurance companies. Damage or theft during the installation period further complicates matters and may lead to your claiming negligence on the property owner's part, and he, on yours.

You can purchase a rider to your liability policy to insure your artwork during its installation, but you may have no luck insuring yourself against damage to the site. Should you engage a subcontractor to install your work, have him accept responsibilty for it in writing.

Your general-liability policy may not insure you or your employees for other work on location, like painting a mural on a wall, touching up installation damage, or supervising subcontractors. Check with your agent. Make sure your subs have insurance and give you certificates for it. In addition, your general-liability policy also may not cover you for work-related activities outside the studio, like selling, conferences, lecturing, buying supplies, study, and research. Check with your agent. You may need an *Off-Premises Rider*, which will cover you for all outside activities.

Liability for Your Artwork

You are potentially liable for an indefinite period for injuries or damages caused by your negligent workmanship. For example, you, as manufacturer, installer, or owner may be sued if a child hurts himself playing on a sculpture that you have lent for exhibition; or if a sign that you installed blows down in a wind and hits a pedestrian; or if a piece of your construction in a hotel breaks off and smashes a lamp.

A *Completed Operations Coverage* rider to your general-liability policy will protect you once a job is completed, but, of course, you'll have to keep it up to assure coverage.

Another option is to ask the client to sign a *hold harmless agreement* such as: [client] agree(s) to save and hold harmless [you] from any and all claims arising out of [job or contract description].

Hold harmless agreements transfer the liability from you, the creator, to the purchaser, who assumes the responsibility thereafter. Some clients may refuse to consider such an agreement, because they may see no merit in taking an added risk. Others may have no objections, or stipulate a warranty period after which they will assume the liability. A lot will depend on the nature of the job and the relationship between you and your client.

A *Product Liability Policy* will protect you against claims arising from your ostensible negligence in producing a useful product. If, for example, someone scalds himself when the handle of a cup you've made snaps off, or if someone injures himself when a chair you've crafted collapses, you could be sued for negligence. In addition to insurance, careful construction and labelling your products against unreasonable uses will help protect you against such claims.

14. Copyright of the Visual Arts

On January 1, 1978, the new Copyright Act of 1976 came into effect, the first extensive revision of the copyright law since the original Act of 1909. The law's purpose is to encourage creativity by protecting the fruits of that creativity from unauthorized copying. Since the Act is so new, court interpretations have not yet refined and clarified it. Therefore, when Marybeth Peters, Chief of the Information and Reference Division of the Copyright Office, explained the law to me, she was more tentative than she would be, say five or ten years from now. What follows is the best current interpretation. You may use it with confidence, but recognize that there may be some subsequent minor refinements.

What the Copyright Protects

The Copyright Act of 1976 defines a work of the visual arts as "pictorial, graphic, or sculptural works" including "two-dimensional and three-dimensional works of fine, graphic, applied art, photographs, prints, and art reproductions, maps, globes, charts, technical drawings, diagrams, and models."

According to the Act, the copyright is automatically created and becomes the artist's property as soon as his work is "fixed"—"is sufficiently permanent or stable to permit it to be perceived, reproduced, or otherwise communicated for a period of more than transitory duration." The copyright lasts for the life of the artist plus fifty years and remains with the artist even after he sells the physical artwork (the "material object" in the Act). The copyright does not transfer to the purchaser unless through a written conveyance.

What Can Be Protected by Copyright?

Quoting Ms. Peters' *General Guide to the Copyright Act of 1976*, court decisions have established that:

The work must . . . be fixed in some tangible form from which the work can be reproduced. The work must be a product of original creative authorship. . . . [It] must be original in the sense that the author produced it by his own intellectual effort, as distinguished from merely copying a preexisting work. There is no requirement of novelty, ingenuity or esthetic merit. [It] must represent an appreciable amount of creative authorship.

Unless there is a written agreement to the contrary, artists do not retain the copyright to works that they execute for an employer during their regular working hours as the normal result of their employment. Such work constitutes "work made for hire" as defined in the Act, and under a work made for hire arrangement, the employer buys all the rights to the work done in his behalf by his employees, including the copyright.

In some instances, the employer/employee relationship may be construed to include work done on commission. To avoid any controversy, if you're working on commission, always include a clause in your contract stating that you retain the copyright to all work you produce under the terms of the commission. By the same token, beware of phrases like "work for hire" or similar language in contracts presented to you. Such clauses establish an employer/employee relationship, and the contractor will own the copyright.

Fair Use

The doctrine of "fair use" as specified in the Act permits use of copyright material for " . . . purposes such as criticism, comment, news reporting, teaching, scholarship, or research." There are no hard and fast determinants for "fair use." The Act says that consideration should include: if the use is for profit or for education; the nature of the work; how much is reproduced proportionate to the whole; and the effect upon the work's value or market.

For example, it would be fair use to illustrate an article on an artist with a photograph of one of her paintings. It would probably be a copyright infringement to use that same photograph to illustrate an unrelated article in a commercial magazine for which an artist would normally be hired.

Copyright Notice

The copyright notice should consist of:

1. The symbol ©, the word "Copyright," or the abbreviation "Copr.";

2. The name of the owner of the copyright, or an abbreviation by which the name can be recognized, or a generally known alternative designation of the owner;

3. The year the work was first "published." Under the Act, the date may be omitted "where a pictorial, graphic, or sculptural work with accompanying text matter, if any, is reproduced in or on a greeting card, postcard, stationary, jewelry, dolls, toys or any useful articles."

Examples: © Raoul Elstir, 1980; Copr. 1980 Raoul Elstir; Copyright R. Elstir 1980.

It should be placed "in such manner and location as to give reasonable notice of the claim of copyright." According to the Copyright Office's proposed implementation of the Act, examples of placement include, for two-dimensional work: "a notice fixed directly or by means of a label cemented, sewn, or otherwise permanently secured to the front or back of the copies, or to any backing, mounting, matting, framing, or other material to which the copies [i.e., artwork] are permanently attached or in which they are permanently housed . . ."

For three-dimensional artwork "a notice affixed directly or by means of a label cemented, sewn, or otherwise permanently secured to any visible portion of the work, or to any base, mounting, framing, or other material on which the copies [i.e., artwork] are permanently attached or in which they are permanently housed," For artwork that by virtue of size or physical characteristics cannot be permanently labelled directly, jewelry for example, "a notice is acceptable if it appears on a tag that is of durable material and that is attached to the copy with sufficient permanency that it will remain with the copy during the entire time it is passing through its normal channels of commerce."

The notice is required whenever a work is "published," which the law defines as the "distribution of copies . . . of a work to the public by sale or other transfer of ownership, or by rental, lease, or lending. . . . The offering to distribute copies . . . to a group of persons for purposes of further distribution, public performance, or public display." According to Ms. Peters:

Omission of the notice does not automatically forfeit protection and place the work in the public domain. . . . A work published without a notice will still be eligible for statutory protection for at least five years, whether the omission was partial or total, unintentional or deliberate . . . copyright is not lost immediately, but the work will go into the public domain if no effort is made to correct the error and if the work is not registered within five years after copies were published without a notice."

In defining "publication," the House committee that drafted the Act stated:

It is not the committee's intention that such a work [a painting or statue that exists in only one copy] would be regarded as "published" when the single existing copy is sold or offered for sale in the traditional way—for example, through an art dealer, gallery, or auction house. On the other hand, where the work has been made for reproduction in multiple copies—as in the case of fine prints such as lithographs—or where multiple reproductions of the prototype work are offered for purchase by the public—as in the case of castings from a statue or reproductions made from a photograph of a painting—publication would take place at the point when reproduced copies are publicly distributed or when, even if only one copy exists at that point, reproductions are offered for purchase by multiple members of the public.

Considering what could be at stake, it is always prudent to (1) place the copyright notice (e.g., © Raoul Elstir 1980) on all works that leave your studio, particularly those for public display, and (2) definitely place the notice on all multiple-edition works. For presentation drawings or free-lance designs and the like, where casual infringement is a persistent worry, you may want to add a warning to the notice such as: "This work is protected by copyright. All reproduction rights in all media are reserved by the artist (or your name)." A stronger reading is: "This work is protected by copyright. The artist (or your name) retains all rights. Unauthorized use is prohibited, and will be prosecuted to the full extent of the law." Adding the warning to a printed title block will make it look more official.

As the value of the new Act becomes appreciated, artists are increasingly using the notice.

Copyright Registration

Registration is not mandatory, but it is a prerequisite to any infringement suit. To register a copyright, request FORM VA (Application for Copyright Registration for a Work of the Visual Arts) from: United States Copyright Office, Library of Congress, Washington, D.C., 20559. You will receive an application form, which you must fill out and return with a ten dollar fee and a "deposit." The "deposit" may be an actual copy, but in the

visual arts it is often "identifying material"—either mounted slides no smaller than 35mm or photographs that are "not less than 3 by 3 inches and not more than 9 by 12 inches, but preferably 8 by 10 inches." All identifying material must be in the actual and (2) statutory. Actual damages are the of less than three hundred numbered copies may be represented by a slide or photograph. Editions of more than three hundred require an actual copy.

You may register more than one item on your application form for the same ten dollar fee. As of now, these include works "published" together as a unit and, for "unpublished" works (most works of art that are not multiple editions or have not been reproduced), those that are assembled together in an orderly form and have a single identifying title. In other words, you could register a stack of slides at one time for the same fee provided you presented them neatly, titled them individually, and had an overall title for the collection, e.g., "Paintings of Raoul Elstir, January-September 1980."

Infringement

Infringement is the unauthorized use of copyrighted material. The plaintiff (the person who brings the suit) must show that the defendant (the alleged infringer) had (1) access to the work in question, and (2) appropriated the work. According to Ms. Peters, "the key element to show is copying, i.e., that the defendant's work in whole or substantial part copies the plaintiff's work. It is true that the plaintiff has the burden of proving access, but access can be presumed when the similarities are so apparent as to preclude independent creation."

The law provides two types of damages: (1) actual, or (2) statutory. Actual damages are the demonstrable financial loss or harm that the infringement causes. Statutory damages are those fines established by law. Awards usually range between $250 and $10,000 but may rise to $50,000 for willful infringement.

As has been said, registration is a prerequisite to any infringement suit. Registration within three months of first publication or before an infringement begins will allow you, if you win your case, to obtain injunctive relief, reasonable lawyer's fees, and a choice of either actual or statutory damages (which choice may be exercised any time before the court renders its final verdict). Registration, either after the infringement begins or after the work has been published for three months, entitles you to obtain actual damages and injunctive relief only.

If you think your work has been illegally copied, first confront the suspected infringer. Most often you can reach an amicable resolution. You might have been mistaken or the other party may have made an innocent error. If there has been an infringement, you can ask for compensation, withdrawal of the infringement, or both.

If you do not wish to confront the suspected infringer, or if he gives you no satisfaction, you can either drop the matter or have a lawyer assess your allegations. If you go to court, you may assume that the defendant will plead fair use, innocence of intent, non-access to your material, and so forth. Unless there is a lot involved and you have a strong case, you will be best off settling the matter personally or with the help of a lawyer out of court.

Debasement

The Copyright Act includes no protection against the debasement (distortion, mutilation, or alteration) of a work of art. Proposals are under consideration to add such protection to the Act.

Compulsory Licenses

A compulsory license is a legal device that permits the use of a copyrighted work without the consent of the copyright owner, provided that certain conditions of the law are met and compensation on the terms specified in the statute is paid by the user to the copyright owner.

Section 118 of the Copyright Act is a compulsory license that permits noncommercial broadcasters to use published, copyrighted art works. The use is regulated by the Copyright Royalty Tribunal, which has established rates that vary from $10 to $60 per use.

V.A.G.A.

A nonprofit organization has recently been founded as the visual arts counterpart of ASCAP (the American Society of Composers, Authors, and Publishers) to police the unauthorized reproduction of artists' work by the periodical, book, poster, and specialty publishing industries. Their task is large and their fees are small. For more information contact: Visual Artists and Galleries Association, Inc, (V.A.G.A.), Suite 1535, One World Trade Center, New York, New York, 10048.

In Sum

1. The copyright is created automatically, concomitant with the creation of the artwork. It remains the property of the artist for life plus fifty years unless formally transferred in writing.

2. Copyright does not extend to mechanical and utilitarian aspects of creations nor "works in which the creative authorship is too slight to be worthy of protection."

3. The copyright for artwork created as the normal result of an artist's working for an employer belongs to the employer, not the artist. Because this "work made for hire" provision of the Act may be interpreted to include commissioned art, always state that you retain the copyright in any contract covering commissioned art.

4. "Fair use" permits the use of copyrighted material for purposes such as criticism, comment, news reporting, teaching, scholarship, or research.

5. Affix the copyright notice to all work that leaves your studio, especially multiple editions.

6. Registration is not mandatory, but it is a prerequisite for any infringement suit. Registration before an infringement begins allows significant legal advantages.

15. Employees

Hiring another human being is a personal passage that can affect people in strange and unpredictable ways. It can turn rabid Marxists into hard-nosed capitalists, nice guys into tyrants.

Before we go any further, let's distinguish between employees and subcontractors. An *employee* is a person who works for another person or business for pay. The employer provides the employee with direction, workspace, tools, equipment, and materials. He sets the wages and the hours, and keeps a pay record. He hires, and, if need be, fires the employee. He deducts from the employee's salary federal withholding tax, federal and state unemployment insurance, and FICA (Federal Insurance Compensation Act), which he must match.

In contrast, the *subcontractor* (sub) sets his price by the job, provides his own supplies and tools, works his own hours, carries his own insurance, and renders his own bill. The distinction is clear if you think about it, and the folks at IRS and Social Security often do. In fact, they are quite touchy about people willfully confusing the two in order to avoid deducting expenses and paperwork.

Do You Need Them?

Employees can save you time and let you earn more net income. You're putting in the same hour whether you spend it painting a portrait or priming a canvas. If you have someone to prime the canvas for you, you will have more time to paint portraits. Employees can perform jobs for which you haven't the skills or abilities, like carpentry or heavy lifting. They can do jobs you may not want to do like cleaning up, polishing, or framing.

Employees can also cost you time and money. They can abuse your equipment and materials—one used my chisel, honed to a razor edge, to pry off a paint-can lid. They can require extra facilities, like an additional bathroom, lunch area, or parking space. They require tedious paperwork and payments to tax collectors and bookkeepers. They can steal from you, not only small tools, a petty annoyance, but also clients. (I came in unexpectedly to find one employee perusing my files during her lunch hour. When confronted, she sweetly replied, "I didn't think you'd mind.") Employees require supervision, sometimes constant. They can be undependable. They probably won't share your commitment to your work. They can quit in the middle of crash projects, just as you've gotten them trained enough to be useful, or take off when the fancy strikes. Finally, there's the loss of your privacy, not a problem if you're running a store, but possibly acute if you're sharing a studio.

Analyze your jobs. Some, like design, color, material selection, and work that requires your personal "handwriting" only you can do. It is the expression of your unique intelligence and talents. Others, like foundry work, cabinetry, or lithography, may be beyond your skills, strength, experience, or equipment. For these tasks you must either hire employees or subcontractors. The jobs that remain—packing, priming, tracing, painting backgrounds, polishing—you have the option of either doing yourself or giving to subcontractors or employees.

Choose to hire employees rather than subcontractors when you want to keep the work in your own shop for greater convenience, control, and time and cost saving, and when there's enough benefit to offset the paperwork. Choose subcontractors over employees for skills or equipment that would be otherwise unobtainable, where an operation would be undesirable or impractical in your studio, when it would be easier, cheaper, quicker, or more convenient than doing it yourself or with employees, and when you don't wish the commitment of employees.

You have no alternative to hiring employees if you're involved in retailing or production, have a heavy workload, or need someone to come in and do simple chores.

Whether to hire people full- or part-time is another consideration. You can have more control over full-time employees, since you are their sole source of income. You can hope to train them and have some continuity, but it obligates you to the pressure of providing enough work to keep them busy. You can hire people by the project, if the project will last long enough, but again you will lose the training time. Part-time employees relieve you of work pressure, but you have much less control over them. They're best for semi-skilled labor.

Sources of Employees

Find employees through recommendations of friends, relatives, and other artists. Additional sources are advertisements in trade publications or the newspapers; community bulletin boards; suppliers; art and vocational schools, and colleges and their placement bureaus and faculties. For part-time employees, add to the list places like fire houses and police stations where people work odd hours.

Make up a job description and assign priorities to skills, e.g., power tools, selling, and design; and to character traits, e.g., honesty, competence, reliability, and industry. The higher the skill level, the wider you must throw your net. You can find someone at the local high school to pack boxes; you may have to advertise in a national trade journal for a metal finisher.

A word about art students. Your first impulse may be to go to an art school for assistants. You assume art students will be motivated, skilled, informed, and in need of money. Unfortunately, you may find them indolent, arrogant, and ignorant—with an elevated opinion of themselves and a lowly opinion of you. You'll want them to prime panels so you can do the artwork. They'll want *you* to prime the panels so *they* can do the artwork.

Hiring

Other than for casual labor, you should conduct serious interviews with your prospective employees. Evaluate their qualifications. Ask to see their work, especially of the kind they will be doing for you. Ask for references and check them carefully.

You should have a definite idea of the going wage and what you are prepared to pay. You may determine this by asking people with comparable employees in similar positions. Allow for age, experience, skill level and, if part-time, you may wish to compensate for the greater relative time lost in travel.

Train new employees adequately and be patient with them until they learn the ropes. You can set a trial period in which you may evaluate one another.

It is expensive to train new employees, and we hate to lose them, but it is even more expensive holding on to people who are marginally productive.

Paperwork

You must withhold for each employee (1) federal withholding tax, (2) F.I.C.A. (Social Security), (3) federal and state unemployment, and (4) state withholding tax.

1. Employers must withhold their employee's federal income tax and send it either directly or through a bank to the federal government at the end of the year. Contact the Internal Revenue Service (IRS) for a table of deductions. They are in the phone book under "United States Government, Internal Revenue Service, Federal Tax Information and Assistance." In areas where there is no local office, a toll-free 800 number is listed.

2. Federal Insurance Compensation Act (FICA or Social Security) is a life insurance and old-age pension plan maintained by the federal government through compulsory employer payments. Employers deduct an amount based on government tables from their employee's wages, match it with an equal sum, and send the combination to the IRS by the week or by the quarter, depending upon the dollars accumulated. Obtain forms from the IRS (see address above).

3. Unemployment insurance is gathered by the federal and state governments for compensation to unemployed workers, usually paid by the week, during all or part of their unemployment. The employer pays federal unemployment based on his employees' salaries at times and rates prescribed by the IRS. A deductible credit is given for state employment paid on time. Contact the IRS for forms. State unemployment, credit for which is deductible from the federal payment, is also based on employees' salaries. Contact your state's information, labor, or unemployment department for information and forms.

4. Some states and local governments also require that employers withhold taxes from employees' salaries. Contact the income tax department of your state and local government for information and forms.

In addition to the above compulsory payments, employers may wish to offer full-time employees life, health, and other forms of insurance, profit-sharing and pension plans, uniforms, use of a vehicle, and other fringe benefits.

Example

Based on current rates, the paycheck for an employee earning $100 in the state of Maryland would look like:

Wages		$100
	Federal Withholding	(10.00)
	FICA	(5.85)
	State Withholding	(4.15)
Total Take-Home Pay		$ 80.00

The employer would pay in addition to the $100 wages:

	FICA (matching contribution)	$5.85
	Federal Unemployment	.50
	State Unemployment	2.70
	Total Contribution	$9.05

Thus, the employer is actually paying out $109.05 per week, plus his own or his bookkeeper's considerable time for processing the paperwork.

16. Subcontracting

A *contractor* is a person or a business that agrees to perform services or furnish supplies at a fixed, or contract, rate. A *subcontractor* is a person or business that agrees to perform services or furnish supplies to a contractor.

You may find that subcontractors in the manual trades (and even those in visual areas, like sign painters) who have had no real contact with artists, apart from the fanciful tales in the popular media, will at first be uncomfortable working with you, especially if you're young, inexperienced, or, if they're male, female. They may suspect that you're unreliable, putting everybody on, and, while you're at it, making a killing.

The best way I've found to gain subcontractors' confidence is to treat them as you would have yourself be treated. Respect their skill; regard their advice; be dependable and fair. Subs may not understand your art (and will delight in telling you so), but I can't think of a decent one who didn't appreciate craftsmanship no matter what its guise. I personally value praise from a fellow mechanic—a carpenter, paperhanger, or sign man—more than from an art critic. Finally, and as important as anything, don't play games with a subcontractor's money. Pay promptly and properly.

If you aren't familiar with a prospective sub, ask him for references of people or businesses that he's worked for and the names of his bank, insurance agent, and suppliers. You may then ask his previous employers about his skill and reliability and, if you wish, visit the jobs and inspect his workmanship. You may check his insurance coverage with his agent and his credit with his bank and suppliers. After all, you don't want to pay off a sub for a job that involves considerable materials, only to find that he's not been settling with his suppliers. If the suppliers can't squeeze their money from him, they may next turn to you. If you're really concerned about this possibility, while the job is still in progress, call his principal suppliers shortly after you've made each payment to the sub to confirm that he's been keeping up. In especially uncertain situations, you may want to make your checks out to the sub and his supplier conjointly. The sub may not be pleased, but you wouldn't be doing it without justification.

The arrangements you make with a sub will depend on your relationship and the size and nature of the job. Small, uncomplicated jobs with subs whom you trust are customarily consummated verbally or, at most, with a few written notes. Have a general advance idea of what you think is a reasonable price or what you can afford to pay. After a little friendly horse trading, you should then be able to arrive at a mutually satisfactory figure. If his price is either too high or too low, go over his calculations with him to see which of you misunderstood the conditions. Never take advantage of a sub who makes a bid that you know to be unreasonably low. It's not only dishonest, but also bad business for two reasons: He will neither work for you again, nor will his colleagues who find out about it; and, once he realizes he's been had, he'll try to reduce his losses by cutting corners to the detriment of your job.

Artistic projects are often hard to define. If a sub must give a firm quote, he will usually inflate it to protect himself. One alternative is to agree on a maximum figure, but have him keep track of his time and materials. Should his time and materials total less than the maximum figure, you can pay time and materials instead, or negotiate the difference.

On large jobs, do a careful *take off* (cost analysis) to get a clear idea of what you expect to pay, get three to five estimates from subs of comparable quality, choose the low bidder, and draw up a contract to record your understanding. The contract can state such things as: the scope of the work; the total price, terms, and payment schedule; the insurance requirements; that all materials must be approved by you; that changes are only to be made with your written consent; that the sub is to be responsible for damage to other work at the job site; and that he furnish suppliers' receipts on request. You would be wise to consult a lawyer or have a lawyer experienced in this area draw up your contract.

Hold back ten percent of each *draw* (contract payment) to insure that the sub will come back after the job is completed to make good any unsatisfactory work. Should the sub prove uncooperative, as sometimes happens, you'll have enough money for a replacement to correct the mistakes. Of course, you will have conscientiously monitored the work all along to catch any obvious deficiencies.

Take nothing for granted, especially the first time you work with a sub. A detail that's crucial for you may not be apparent to him, and things of which you're ignorant may be critical to his calculations of prices and performances. In advance, go through the project with him from stem to stern and then, as necessary, make detailed working drawings and full patterns if anything needs to be fabricated. Provide specifications for finishes, colors, materials, edge treatments, protective coatings, installation hardware, and whatever else that you can think of. The more explicit you are, the less likely he'll make mistakes.

17. Architectural Blueprint Reading

The blueprint process is actually obsolete, having been replaced by positive blue or black line prints, but the name remains as a generic term for architectural drawings. Blueprints may at first seem complicated, but with a little experience they'll be no more difficult to read than a road map. In most cases you need only be concerned with the visible surfaces and not the deeper mysteries of the mechanical and technical functions of buildings.

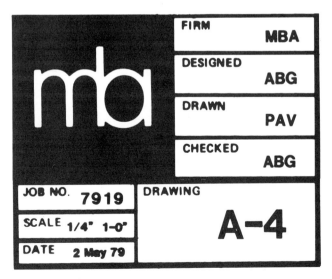

Title block. (Courtesy Mark Beck Assocs.)

First, locate the *title block*, which is usually in the lower right-hand corner of the blueprint. It contains such information as the client's name; type or name of the building; its location; the name of the architects; the name of the draftsman; the date; the identification number of the drawing stated as a number in a full set of drawings, e.g., 3 of 24; and the scale, either stated or listed as "noted," which means that the individual views depicted are scaled separately. Even when the scale is stated in the title block, variations may occur on some of the views. Therefore, check each view to make sure there are no scale changes, and, if in doubt confirm the dimensions with an architect's scale.

Four *views* may be illustrated on a blueprint: (1) the *plan*, (2) the *elevation*, (3) the *section*, and (4) the *detail*.

1. The *plan* is a horizontal or bird's-eye view usually drawn to 1/8″ = 1′ or 1/4″ = 1′ (or even smaller if necessary). There are four types of plans: *site*, *floor*, *ceiling*, and *roof*.

The *site plan* places the building, usually illustrated by a *roof plan*, in its setting. Sometimes the engineer's scale, e.g., 1″ = 20′ or 1″ = 30′, is used instead of the architect's scale. An arrow or similar device will indicate north. The site plan may also show walks, streets, vegetation, and con-

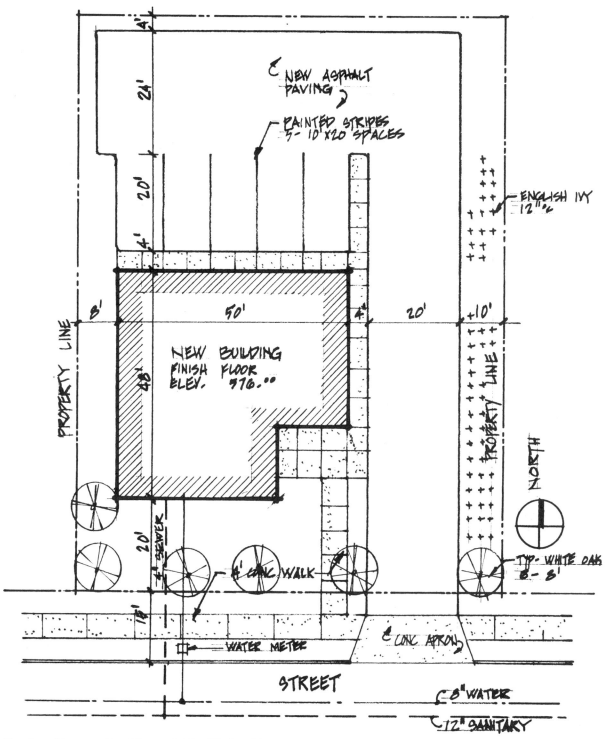

Site plan. (Courtesy Alan Glass and Allen Hitchcock)

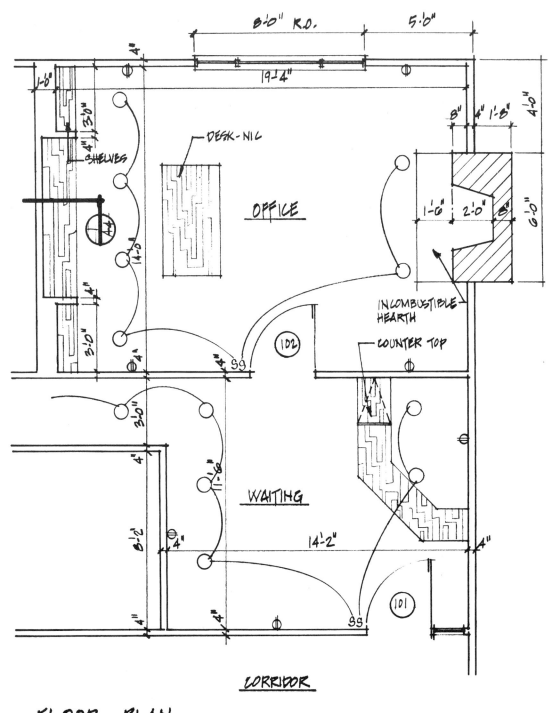

FLOOR PLAN
SCALE ¼" = 1'0"

Floor plan. (Courtesy Alan Glass and Allen Hitchcock)

tour lines. Site plans are important if you are working outside—for example, siting a sculpture with respect to buildings and topography—or inside if you want to know the views out the windows, traffic flow patterns, and general ambience.

The *floor plan* shows the building as if sliced through horizontally about four feet above the floor. It reveals critical elements like doors, windows, walls, and partitions both above and below the slice. The floor plan is important for placing objects like sculpture on the floor, measuring walls for murals or paintings, and determining sight lines, traffic patterns, and light effects.

The *ceiling plan* (usually called the *reflected ceiling plan*), which is seldom shown, is the mirror image of the ceiling as seen from the floor. It may be important if you are hanging objects like banners or if you want to know such ceiling information as skylighting and lighting fixtures.

The *roof plan*, also infrequently shown, is a straight view down on the building and is often combined with the site plan. It will be important if you are placing artwork on a roof, deck, balcony, or courtyard.

2. *Elevations* may be either exterior or interior. *Exterior elevations* are views of the outside of the building as you face it. They are usually labeled by compass orientation, e.g., south elevation (the side of the building facing south), or by site orientation, e.g., street entrance, parking-lot entrance. *Interior elevations* are views of the individual inside walls of the building as you face them. They are usually labeled either by main-entrance orientation, e.g., rear elevation, left elevation; by feature orientation, e.g., fireplace elevation; or by compass orientation, e.g., south elevation. Elevations are important if you're designing murals or supergraphics, laying out paintings on a wall, or considering backgrounds for hangings or sculpture.

3. *Sections*, views of the entire building as if sliced through vertically from the roof through the foundation, can be of various types. *Design sections* are architectural views to clarify the prominent interior spaces. Design sections are important if you are designing or locating your work in a building and want a feel for its interior spaces. *Construction sections* illustrate, for the benefit of contractors, construction details like insulation, foundations, and stairs. Construction sections can be important if you're designing work for an alcove and want to know the sight lines and lighting fixtures, or if you're installing on a wall and want to know its composition. *Site sections* show the building and its site together, sliced through. *Perspective sections* are design sections with perspective added to them. They are rarely encountered and are never found on working drawings.

4. *Details* are just that, details of parts of the building too complicated to show adequately on the other drawings. They may be of plans, elevations, or sections, and may not be specifically identified as details. Details should be located under, or with, the detail title and are usually at a larger scale: 3/4", 1/2", 3"—whatever enlargement is necessary.

The complete set of documents prepared by the architect for his client's interaction with a contractor are called *contract documents.* They include, in addition to the drawings portion just described, written information. For the artist, the most important parts of this written information are the *schedules* and the *specifications.*

Schedules (here meaning "list" not "time") define required qualities and installation methods. Examples are paint schedules, which list the paints needed for a job, or finish schedules which list the finishes such as siding, wall covering, and flooring.

Specifications (specs) describe "what" and "how many." They provide data not included in the drawings, e.g., construction procedures, types and quantities of materials, and installation methods. Schedules and specs are intended for contractors and suppliers, and you, as a contractor, may need them for information about wall coverings, paints, flooring, and other materials that you may either have to provide or work with.

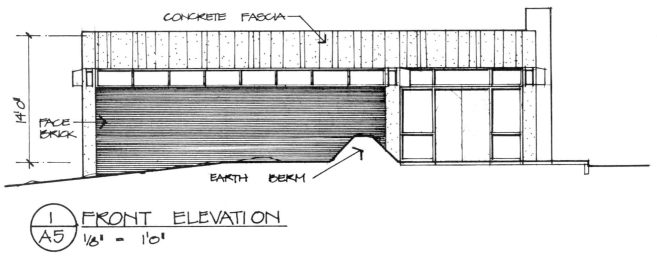

CONCRETE FASCIA

14'0"

FACE BRICK

EARTH BERM

1/A5 FRONT ELEVATION
1/8" = 1'0"

Exterior elevation. (Courtesy Alan Glass and Allen Hitchcock)

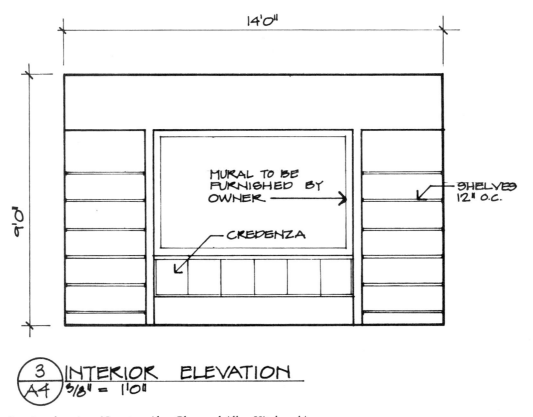

14'0"

9'0"

MURAL TO BE FURNISHED BY OWNER

SHELVES 12" O.C.

CREDENZA

3/A4 INTERIOR ELEVATION
3/8" = 1'0"

Interior elevation. (Courtesy Alan Glass and Allen Hitchcock)

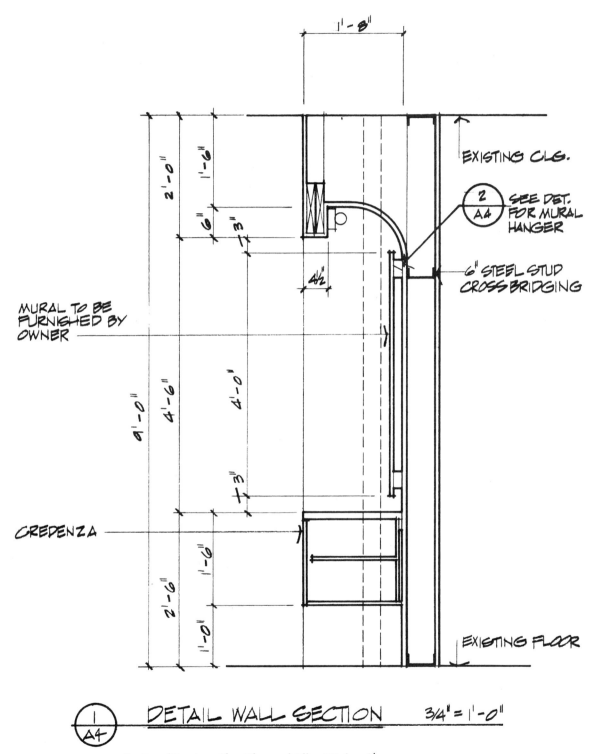

1'-8"

EXISTING CLG.

2'-0"

1'-6"

6"

3"

4½"

2 / A4 SEE DET. FOR MURAL HANGER

6" STEEL STUD CROSS BRIDGING

MURAL TO BE FURNISHED BY OWNER

9'-0"

4'-6"

4'-0"

3"

CREDENZA

2'-6"

1'-6"

1'-0"

EXISTING FLOOR

1 / A4 DETAIL WALL SECTION   3/4" = 1'-0"

Section. (Courtesy Alan Glass and Allen Hitchcock)

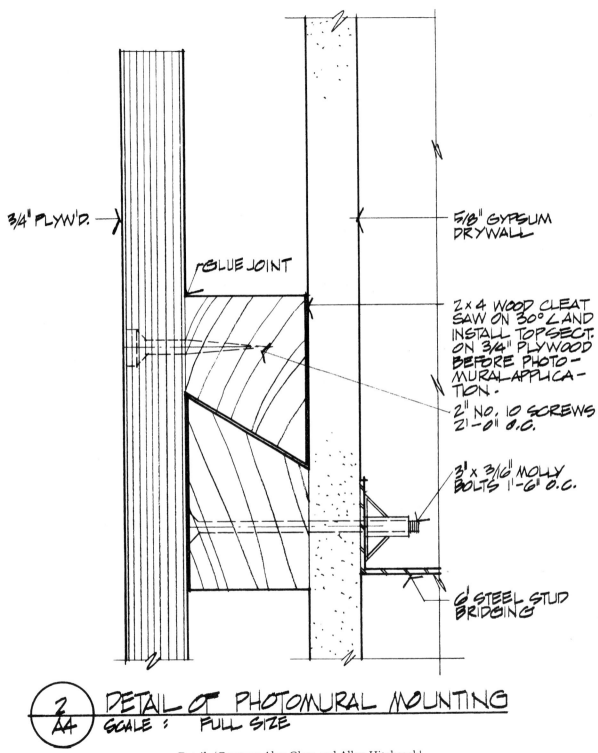

3/4" PLYW'D.

GLUE JOINT

5/8" GYPSUM DRYWALL

2 x 4 WOOD CLEAT SAW ON 30° ∠ AND INSTALL TOP SECT. ON 3/4" PLYWOOD BEFORE PHOTO-MURAL APPLICATION.

2" NO. 10 SCREWS 2'-0" O.C.

3' x 3/16" MOLLY BOLTS 1'-6" O.C.

6" STEEL STUD BRIDGING

2/A4 DETAIL OF PHOTOMURAL MOUNTING
SCALE: FULL SIZE

Detail. (Courtesy Alan Glass and Allen Hitchcock)

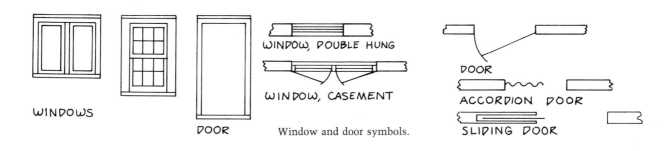

Window and door symbols.

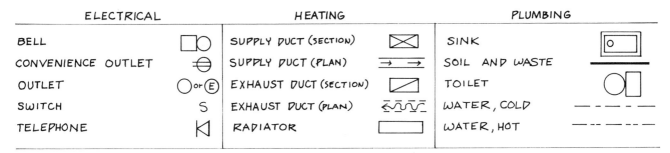

Electrical, heating, and plumbing symbols.

Material symbols.

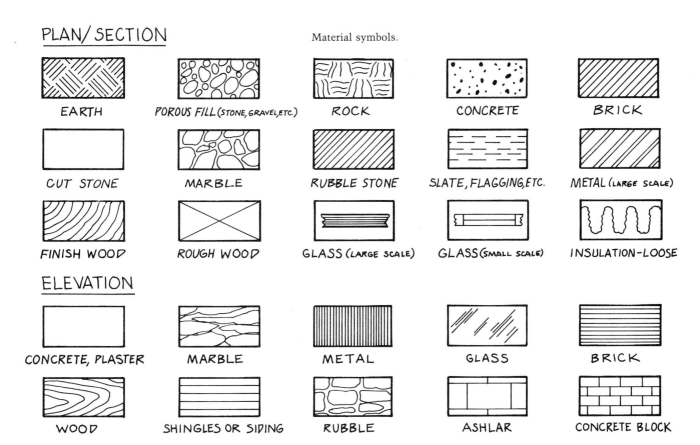

HEAVY SOLID LINES DEFINE THE MAIN OUTLINES OF A BUILDING, ITS WALLS, COLUMNS, DECKS, ETC.

LIGHT SOLID LINES DEFINE SECONDARY ELEMENTS LIKE DOORS, FURNITURE, AND WINDOWS. THEY MAY ALSO BE:

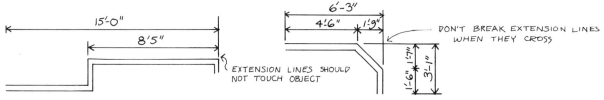

DIMENSION LINES ILLUSTRATE THE EXTENSION AND DIRECTION OF A DIMENSION. PLACE THE DIMENSION ABOVE THE LINE OR BREAK THE LINE FOR THE DIMENSION.

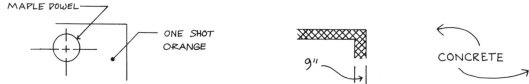

EXTENSION LINES EXTEND LINES ON A VIEW FOR DIMENSIONING PURPOSES.

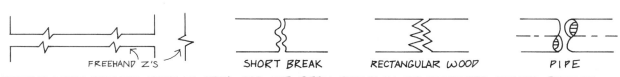

LEADER LINES CONNECT A DIMENSION LINE, DETAIL, OR SYMBOL TO THE INTENDED PLACE ON THE DRAWING. THEY SHOULD END IN ARROWS (OR DOTS IF THEY END ON A SURFACE) MAY BE STRAIGHT OR CURVED, AND IF STRAIGHT ARE USUALLY DRAWN AT A 60° ANGLE. DON'T USE LONG LEADERS, NEARLY HORIZONTAL OR VERTICAL LEADERS, OR CROSSING LEADERS.

BREAK LINES INDICATE THAT AN AREA HAS NOT BEEN SHOWN IN ITS ENTIRETY, EITHER BECAUSE SPACE DOESN'T PERMIT, OR BECAUSE IT WOULD BE UNECESSARILY CONFUSING OR TEDIOUS TO DO SO.

HIDDEN LINES SHOW THINGS ABOVE THE AREA SHOWN ON THE DRAWING.

BOUNDARY LINES SHOW BOUNDARY OR PROPERTY LINES.

Lines.

18. Architectural Drafting

You should know the rudiments of drafting to produce professional-quality presentations. Written instruction can only be introductory; you should increase your knowledge through a short course in a trade school or community college, or through working with an architect or draftsperson.

Materials, equipment, and techniques are constantly changing. You should stay up to date by occasionally visiting supply stores, reading catalogs, and talking shop. Cheap equipment is seldom a good investment. Quality tools are not only a pleasure to use, but also they're more accurate, dependable, and last much longer.

Materials and Equipment

Drafting Tables

Any smooth surface that's large enough will do for drafting: a drawing table, a flush door or tabletop set on saw horses, or a pair of two-drawer file cabinets. If you use a T-square, the left edge of the drafting surface must be true, or a metal angle should be attached to it. Manufactured drafting tables come in many sizes, designs, materials, and

A homemade drafting table/file cabinet/bookcase combination utilizing a hollow drafting platform cum bookcase made of 3/4″ plywood attached to two, two-drawer file cabinets.

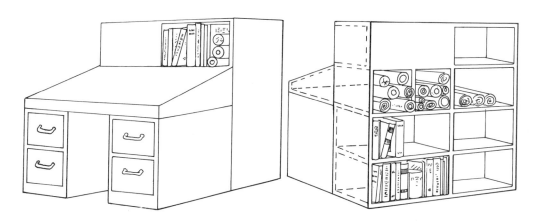

costs. The drafting surface on all of these can be adjusted to a comfortable working angle. When shopping for a drafting table, consider such features as electrical outlets, the size of the board and its ease of adjustment, the table's overall construction and finish, and the number and usefulness of drawers and other storage space. The cheaper tables are essentially a movable top on tall legs; you can utilize the waste space under them with improvised shelves, tubes, boxes, and drawers. Used drafting tables are often available from people retiring or trading up, or you may find them at auction sales or used office furniture stores. Check the newspaper or yellow pages, or look out for architectural, engineering, contracting, or development firms that are consolidating or going out of business.

You can work directly on the drafting-table surface, but covers are easier to use and maintain.

Vinyl mats: Smooth, stain-resistant, non-glare, resilient, and expensive, vinyl mats are sold in standard board sizes, by the roll, and by the foot. While most draftspeople consider vinyl the optimum available work surface, some complain that it is too resilient and that it telegraphs imperfections underneath.

Linoleum: Battleship or countertop linoleum is smooth, tough, and monochrome. Unfortunately, it has not been manufactured in several years, and there is nothing comparable available—all current linoleums and vinyls have at least some surface texture. You may still be able to find a piece, but stocks are rapidly dwindling.

Plastic Laminates: Plastic laminates like Formica or Micarta are smooth and durable, and come in white or light colors, but present a surface that is too hard for most people.

Plasticized Paper: Smooth, slick, and inexpensive, plasticized paper comes in rolls, either plain or printed with a grid. It stains, delaminates, and wears, especially at the edges, and must be replaced periodically.

Illustration Board: Cheap and quick, for temporary use. Dense boards work best.

Drafting and Measuring Tools

T-squares, in lengths from 18 to 60 inches, come in plastic, wood, or metal and combinations thereof. Metal edges are handy for cutting against. Plastic edges are transparent, so you can see your drawing through them, but they are too soft for use as cutting straightedges. T-squares are portable and cheap, but they have several disadvantages: They rely on a true table edge, they become increasingly unreliable as you work out toward their end, and, because you have to steady the T-square with one hand, they are awkward to use with triangles and other drafting aids. Parallel rules and drafting machines have largely replaced T-squares, except for work away from the board. In any edge used for inking, look for a raised or beveled edge, which will prevent ink from spreading by capillary action.

The *Parallel rule*, available in sizes from 30 to 96 inches long with plastic or steel edges, is a straightedge that rides on wires secured to the top and bottom edges of the drawing board. Once adjusted, it will remain parallel and is easy to use with triangles and other drafting aids. Keep the underside and the drawing surface clean or the rule will drag dirt along as it goes. To help, you can place two narrow strips of matboard inside the wire at both sides to raise the rule off your drawing.

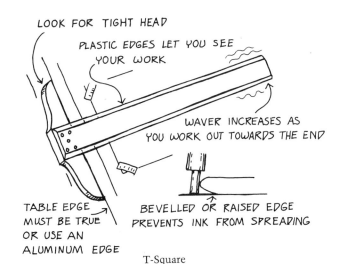

LOOK FOR TIGHT HEAD

PLASTIC EDGES LET YOU SEE YOUR WORK

WAVER INCREASES AS YOU WORK OUT TOWARDS THE END

TABLE EDGE MUST BE TRUE OR USE AN ALUMINUM EDGE

BEVELLED OR RAISED EDGE PREVENTS INK FROM SPREADING

T-Square

The parallel rule is the best combination of cost and convenience, a great improvement over the T-square. Its main disadvantage besides dragging dirt is that equipment on the board interferes with its operation.

The *drafting machine*, a movable-arm mechanism that attaches to the board, combines the functions of straightedge, triangle, scales, and protractor in one unit. It is accurate and convenient but expensive, and because it's short you must draw long lines in steps.

Triangles, used to draw vertical and angled lines, come in metal or clear plastic, in various sizes and weights, and in either 30–60–90 degrees (called 30–60) or 45–45–90 degrees (called 45). Buy one of each, with the 30–60 two inches longer on the perpendicular than the 45. You can raise the edges of triangles and other drafting aids with drafting tape, or stick on Smudge-Bans to keep ink from running underneath. The adjustable triangle, which combines the functions of the protractor and the triangle, can be adjusted to any angle and then locked in place. Cast acrylic triangles, which are individually machined and finished, are more expensive than the injection molded ones, but they are more accurate.

Flexible curves are adjustable 12- to 36-inch-long plastic strips with a metal core that can be temporarily bent to shape for drawing irregular curves. Splines are more expensive and more controllable 24- to 60-inch-long flexible plastic curves that are held in place with lead weights.

A *French curve* is a flat plastic drafting guide composed of several scroll-like curves. It comes in many different patterns. To use it, freehand the curve first, then draw it in using selected portions of the French curve.

Plastic templates—guides for drawing and inking—are available in a wide range of sizes and shapes, including geometrics: circles, ovals, ellipses, squares, and standard symbols, like furniture, landscape, and arrows. They are quick, accurate, and convenient.

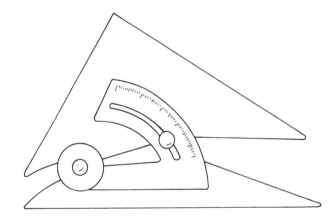

Adjustable triangle.

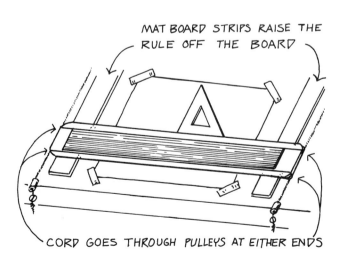

MAT BOARD STRIPS RAISE THE RULE OFF THE BOARD

CORD GOES THROUGH PULLEYS AT EITHER ENDS

Parallel rule.

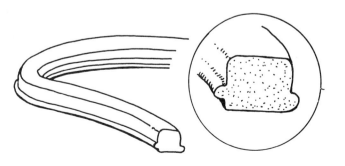

Flexible curve.

Drafting tape is a thin flexible crepe tape used to hold down drawings. It is similar to masking tape but with less adhesive—the tape peels off cleanly.

Straightedges, made of heavyweight stainless steel, come in various lengths for use as cutting and lining guides.

Aluminum rulers come in various widths and from 6 inches to 144 inches in length with printed divisions (which wear off with use). About one fifth the cost of steel straightedges, they can be used for the same tasks and also for measuring. Aluminum blades are much softer than steel blades, so you must be cautious when cutting. Avoid the narrower one-inch-wide rules for lengths of more than one foot; they bend out of shape.

Centering rules are aluminum rules in lengths of 6 to 48 inches. One edge is standard ruled, the other starts at "0" in the center and is ruled from it equally in both directions. To find a center, place the rule so the same measurement appears on both the left and right of the "0". A convenient length is 24 inches.

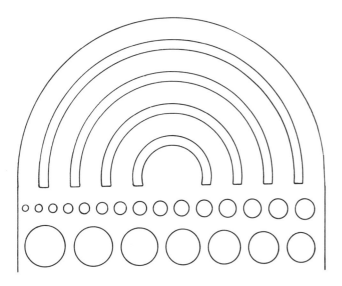

Portion of a circle template.

The *architect's scale* is a device, usually triangular but sometimes flat (for portability), for enlarging or reducing dimensions to fit within the size of a working drawing. Scales come in either hardwood, which is expensive, or plastic, which is perfectly adequate. Look for a scale that is clearly printed; preserve it by not using it as a straightedge for drawing and cutting. The *engineer's scale* looks similar but is divided decimally rather than fractionally.

The architect's scale is generally open-divided, meaning that only the main measuring units are indicated. An extra unit extending beyond the zero is divided fractionally.

On the triangular scale, one edge, marked "16," is fully divided into inches graduated by sixteenths. The other five edges are commonly in 3/32″ and 3/16″, 1/8″ and 1/4″, 3/8″ and 3/4″, 1/2″ and 1″, and 1 1/2″ and 3″. Two scales share each face; they read from opposite directions, and each of the two scales is either twice larger or twice smaller than its fellow. This sharing can be confusing; be careful to stick with the selected scale. A binder clip attached to the apex opposite the selected scale will help.

To use the scale, work from the closest integer back to the zero to make up your whole numbers, then add the necessary fractions beyond the zero to complete the measurement. The number series on the scale is normally used to represent feet. For example, on the 1/4″ scale (stated as 1/4″ = 1′) the 1 represents 1 foot, the 2 represents 2 feet, and so on. But the scales may also stand for other units of measurement. For example if 1/4″ = 1″, then 1 on the scale will represent 1 inch, 2 represents 2 inches, and so on.

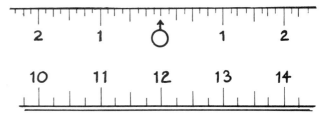

Centering rule.

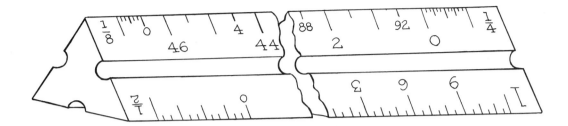

A portion of the architect's scale. Note that two scales share each face; they read from opposite directions, each being twice either larger or smaller than the other. For example, the 1/8 scale reads from left to right and is half that of the 1/4 scale, which reads from right to left. Note too, that this is an open-divided scale: the extra unit beyond the zero is divided fractionally. The two bottom scales, 1/2 and 1, show only the fractional unit.

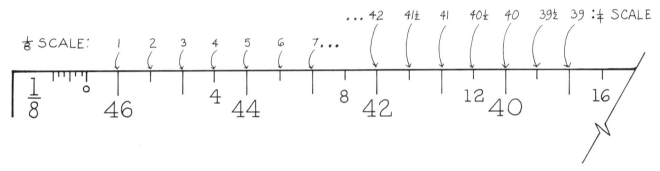

A close-up of the 1/8 scale. For simplification, the 1/8 scale is numerated by 4's, e.g., 0, 4, 8, 12, 16, etc. The large numbers (46, 44, 42, 40) are the numerations of the 1/4 scale by 2's.

Note, for example, that 44 on the 1/4 scale is 5 on the 1/8 scale. Portions of both scales are fully enumerated above the drawing to make this clearer.

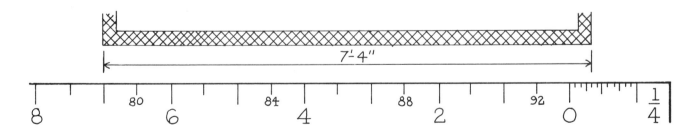

Reading the scale. Work from the closest integer back to the zero to make up your whole numbers, then add the necessary fractions beyond the zero to complete the measurement.

The scales 1/8″ = 1′ and 1/4″ = 1′ are commonly used for plans and elevations, but smaller scales like 3/16″ = 1′ or even 3/32″ = 1′ could be used for larger areas. Details are drawn 1/2″ = 1′, 3/4″ = 1′, 1″ = 1′, or even 1 1/2″ = 1′ or 3″ = 1′ if required. You should work with the commonly used scales for easier communication with other people. Also, by limiting yourself to a few scales, you will become familiar with them and be more able to visualize their enlargement.

Compasses are available in many sizes, materials, and designs for drawing circles and measuring. Although compass sets offer the advantages of a case and a cheaper unit price, you'll probably be better off picking up instruments as you need them. Satin-finish metal is less slippery than polished metal and doesn't show tarnish and fingerprints as readily.

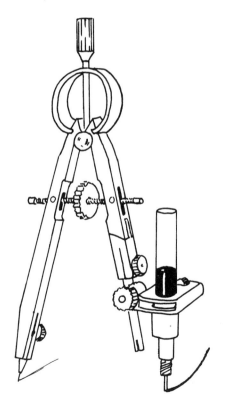

Bow compass with a universal adapter holding a technical pen.

The bow compass is the familiar compass of the drafting set. Choose one that can accept both leads and technical pens. (Since technical pens are not standardized, you need either a universal adapter or holders for each brand of pen you own, or you must use only one brand of pen and the holder for it.) It is difficult to draw small circles with a bow compass. As the circle widens, the legs get progressively less perpendicular. The angled-leg feature of the better compasses alleviates this.

The beam compass consists of two independent legs, one with a point and one with a lead. The legs travel along a beam, and can be tightened in place. The points remain perpendicular; beams may be added on to extend the radius.

Trammel points are, in effect, the two legs of the beam compass which can be attached to a ruler or piece of lathe. Thus, the circumference of the circle need only be limited by the length of the beam employed. The inexpensive models attach to a wooden ruler by means of a slot and screw cap. The more expensive trammel points carried by some drafting equipment houses attach with clamps and so can fit a wider variety of beams.

The blackboard compass is the familiar large, cheap, wooden compass from the classroom. Adapted with a pencil stub, it is useful for drawing circles quickly.

Dividers are two equal length metal legs hinged at the top and pointed at both ends. They are used to transfer dimensions and to divide, enlarge or reduce drawings. *Proportional dividers* are shaped like an X with the center of the cross secured with a movable set screw in a channel. By moving the screw, the ratio of one end is altered to the other from 1:1 to 1:10. They are used for enlarging and reducing, and converting feet and meters, yards and meters, etc.

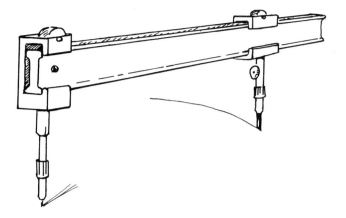

Beam compass.

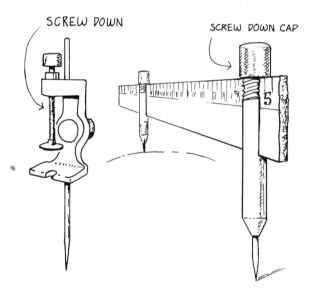

SCREW DOWN

SCREW DOWN CAP

5

Adjustable trammel points (left) and yardstick trammel points (right).

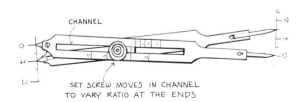

CHANNEL

SET SCREW MOVES IN CHANNEL
TO VARY RATIO AT THE ENDS.

Proportional dividers.

Leads and Pencils

Standard lead holders are metal or plastic tubes that hold lead in their central barrel. Press the button to open the clutch and free the lead to lengthen, sharpen, or retract it; release the button to close the clutch and regrip the lead. Clean and constant in weight and balance, the lead holder can accommodate the full range of leads.

Extra-fine lead holders are similar to the above but accept the much finer .03 or .05 mm polymer leads. The lead needs no sharpening and gives a consistent-width line excellent for drafting, but the leads clog and break easily and are much more expensive than standard leads.

Leads are thin graphite and clay sticks to be used in a lead holder, in a hardness range from 6B (very soft) through 9H (extremely hard). A starting selection is:

4H—for precise drawings and faint lines. It holds its point and lasts forever, but, since it cuts into the paper, it is hard to erase.

2H—a balance between the qualities of 4H and the general-purpose leads.

H, F, and HB—general-purpose leads. H, of course, is harder and HB softer, with F midrange. They combine the accuracy and cleanness of the H range with the ease of flow and erasability of the Bs.

B, 2B, and beyond—dense and easy flowing for sketching, lettering, and shading. They erase well but smudge easily and wear rapidly.

The apparent hardness of leads is affected by the softness, texture, and humidity of the paper used.

There are also soluble and waterproof colored leads, and leads for use on films.

CHUCK   RELEASE BUTTON

Standard lead holder.

Colored pencils are available with different characteristics of softness, lead width, solubility, and color range. "Prismacolor" pencils are intense, light resistant, and waterproof, and come in 60 excellent colors.

A *lead pointer* is a small, closed, weighted, sharpening device containing a circular band of abrasive. Place the lead holder with the lead extended in the hole of the pointer and twirl. The longer the lead that is extended, the sharper the point. This device is convenient, relatively clean, and another item to clutter up the desk. Pocket pointers are available. Leads may also be sharpened with a sandpaper block of tear sheets or on scrap abrasive. These are cheap, portable, and dirty.

The *electric sharpener* is the electric can-opener of the drafting world. It's for serious sharpeners.

Lead pencils are available in a hardness range of 6B through 9H. They must be sharpened with a knife, sandpaper, or pencil sharpener. You may redeem the stubs with a stub holder.

Also available are specialty pencils of various types:

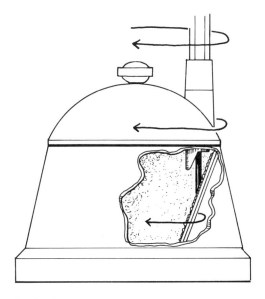

Lead pointer.

A *Stabilo pencil* is a wooden pencil with eight different colors of waterproof, nongreasy leads used for soft and slick surfaces like paint, metal, glass, acetate, and photos. It erases easily or may be wiped off with turps or paint thinner (test the surface first).

A *marking pencil* (China Marker) is a paper-wrapped pencil with a pull string around a thick wax core in several different colors. It is similar to the Stabilo but is harder to point and, being softer, may be better for tender surfaces like fresh paint (test the surface first).

A *charcoal pencil* is paper-wrapped or wood-clad. They come in white and several hardnesses of charcoal and can be sharpened and erased (test first) like a pencil.

Charcoal is a form of carbon in natural-stick (vine), compressed-stick, pencil, and powder, in a number of grades, for sketching, shading, and pouncing. It is dirty and may stain.

Pens, Inks, Dyes, and Opaque Whites

Technical or Hollow Point Pens: The point is a hollow tube containing a wire, which controls the ink flow. They come in eight to a dozen line widths depending on the manufacturer. A starting selection is sizes 00, 1, and 2.5; size 1 is good for general purpose use. They give a line of uniform thickness, can take waterproof ink, and are used for drawing, inking and lettering. Start them with a light tap or shake; heavy shaking will only increase the clogging. Store them full with the point up. Keeping them in a closed jar raised above a little water will hinder clogging. Clean with cool water with a touch of bleach *or* ammonia added, or, in an ultrasonic machine. Never use alcohol or hot water. Stainless-steel points are adequate for paper; jewel or carbide points are necessary for films.

Fountain Pens: You may want a fountain pen for sketching and drawing. The "Pelikan 120" is a fine, inexpensive, old-fashioned piston pen that is available in three regular and three italic iridium-pointed, gold-dipped nibs. Cheaper pens have poorly finished stiffer points of base metal that snag in the

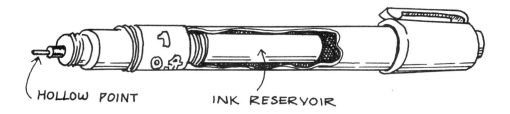

HOLLOW POINT   INK RESERVOIR

Technical pen.

CASTELLTG. Pen No.	RAPIDOGRAPH Pen No.	MARS Pen No.	RAPIDOMETRIC (Metric Size)
	6 X 0		
	5 X 0	5 X 0	.13
	4 X 0	4 X 0	.18
3 X 0	3 X 0	3 X 0	.25
2 X 0	2 X 0	2 X 0	
0	0	0	.35
1	1	1	
2	2	2	.50
2.5	2.5	2.5	.70
3	3	3	
		3.5	1.00
4	4	4	
5		5	1.40
6	5	6	2.00
7	6		

Actual technical-pen line-width comparisons. All of the above lines were drawn under the identical conditions with the stated pen and Higgins Black Magic ink on the same polyester drafting film. The line width indicated in millimeters is that stated by the manufacturer to be the correct line width for that pen size. Because U.S. size designations do not identify actual line width, the only true comparison between brands can be made by comparing metric line widths. (Courtesy Adcom) paper. The "120" will not take waterproof inks; use fountain-pen inks like "Pelikan 4001." Self-filling pens, because they are flushed periodically as you fill them, cause fewer problems than cartridge pens. If you won't be using your pen for more than a few weeks, clean it with cold water before storing. To keep ink from collecting in the cap, always hold the pen upright and place the cap on it.

Pelikan Graphos: An interchangeable nib pen that uses waterproof ink loaded into the barrel with a dropper. It features three feeds and sixty points for lettering, drafting, and calligraphy. Either buy the pen and add points as needed, or start off with one of the three assortments in a case. Unfortunately, the pen is not made to be carried around; the cap will not fit over the nib.

Markers (Marking Pens): The ubiquitous disposable dye marker comes in a variety of point widths, styles, and materials, and in many colors, both waterproof and nonwaterproof. Use them for sketching, coloring, drafting, and drawing. They dry quickly, especially if not capped, and the dyes tend to migrate, i.e., they travel through overpaints or substrata.

Waterproof Black Inks (India Ink): An opaque, waterproof mixture of finely ground carbon with a waterproofing agent like shellac. It deteriorates in storage—buy from a dealer with a rapid turnover and purchase no more than you can use in six months to a year. There are many different inks available with varying densities and flow qualities. Select an ink for its use: whether for technical pens, wash, brush drawings on paper, film, etc. Pelikan is a good general-purpose ink, usable in technical pens

for widths .35mm (0) and up. Below .35mm (0), use a thinner ink like Artone "Fine Line" or Steig "FW."

Fountain Pen Inks: None is completely waterproof; the permanent inks will wash out, leaving a stain. Pelikan's colors are pure and intense.

Dyes: Aqueous, unbindered solutions of pure dyes are brilliant, transparent, not light safe, and very tricky to work with. Dyes are used for finished artwork, and for designs for textiles and printing, because they closely resemble the effects of textile and printing inks. Remove dyes with bleach. "Dr. Martin's" and "Luma" are two good brands.

Opaque white (Touch-Up White) is used to cover mistakes. As with waterproof ink, there are many formulations on the market, with different opacities, flow, and water-resistance characteristics. Steig's "Pro White" is a good all-purpose white. Their "Luma Designer's White" is bleed-proof but a little harder to handle.

Erasers

Start with the softest eraser to disturb your work least. For paper and general purpose, vinyl erasers like Faber-Castell's "Magic-Rub" or Staedtler's "Mars-Plastic" have replaced everything except the kneaded eraser, which is shapeable to fit small areas. For waterproof ink, try fluid-impregnated erasers like Pelikan's "PT 20" or Faber-Castell's "TGK 7092," a knife to scrape off the ink, or an electric eraser.

Dry Cleaning Pads and Cleaning Powders (Cleaning Pounce): Eraser compounds are sold either in a small, porous, cloth bag or in a canister.

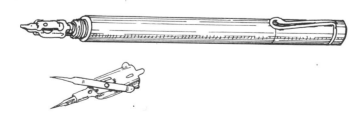

Pelikan Graphos, with a closeup of the interchangeable drawing nib.

They are used to keep surfaces clean while drawing, to prepare tracings for inking, and for a final tidy-up.

Eraser Shields: A stainless steel template that shields the drawing while an eraser is worked through its holes.

Drafting Brush: A long, soft-haired brush for whisking off drawing surfaces. Removes dirt without smudging.

Push Pins and Adhesives

Push Pins: Metal- or plastic-headed tacks with sharp, strong points, they come in 3/8", 1/2", and 5/8" lengths. Use the 5/8" pins for hanging murals, for securing the ends of snap and level lines, and for any other operation that requires extra holding power.

Rubber Cement: A solution of rubber in a highly volatile thinner that is easily removable, usually without staining. Since it dries rapidly, keep the cement either in a small, four-ounce dispenser jar or buy an airtight brush and jar combination and fill it from a separate bulk container. Use rubber-cement thinner to dilute the cement as it thickens. Fully hardened lumps will be difficult to dissolve; add them to your rubber cement ball for cleaning up excess cement. Rubber cement is not a permanent adhesive. Under the best of circumstances it will not last more than a few years; at worst, as with heat or a poor pasteup job, it won't last more than a few weeks. You can either buy a rubber-cement thinner dispenser or convert a lighter fluid or oil can to such use. The dispenser lets the thinner be squirted accurately in small amounts where needed to dissolve bonds. Use thinner with caution, as it contains benzol, which is both toxic and highly flammable.

For temporary bonds, apply the cement to one surface and join immediately. For more permanent bonds, coat both surfaces and, when they are thoroughly dry, join them as you would contact cement by either (1) lightly touching them together then pressing, or (2) tipping them together at the top, interleafing a clean sheet of paper between the coated surfaces and pressing the coated surfaces together as you carefully withdraw the clean sheet. The surfaces will bond as they touch; repositioning is extremely difficult.

You can also try one-coat cement. It is stickier than regular cement and may not clean up as well.

Dry Mount: A heat-sensitive adhesive sheet placed between surfaces to be joined and bonded under heat and pressure in a special press. The process is fast, clean, and easy. The major drawback is the cost of the presses.

Wax Coaters: Adhesive wax dispensed in either a small handheld strip waxer or a machine with rollers. For nonpermanent use, like pasteups, adhered work can be easily repositioned. It is clean and quick.

Spray Adhesives: Aerosol sprays for permanent mounting of photos and artwork, e.g., 3M's "Photomount" #6092; and repositioning artwork, e.g., 3M's "Spuramount" #6065.

Mounting Adhesive: A dry adhesive sheet that is repositionable until rolled down with a brayer, e.g., 3M's #567. Permanent, clean, won't bubble or peel, it is clear enough for mounting transparencies.

Tapes: Consider either a double-coated tape such as 3M's "Scotch #400" or a transfer tape such as 3M's "Scotch #463", which consists of the adhesive coating only. The latter provides fast, neat adhesion.

Surfaces

Papers are made in a multitude of colors, textures, compositions, weights, and absorbencies by a few large manufacturers who sell them to converters, who, in turn, package them in rolls, sheets, and pads under their brand names.

Common terms for paper finishes are:

Cold-Press (C.P.): Paper that has been run through hot rollers to give it a smooth, polished surrougher in texture than:

Hot-Press (H.P.): Paper that has been run through hot rollers to give it smooth, polished surface suitable for tight renderings.

Smooth, Plate, High: A smooth surface for fine

linework.

Medium: A slightly textured surface for all techniques.

Rough: A rough surface for bolder work in pencil, wash, charcoal, or paint.

Kid, Vellum: Denotes a medium, matte finish. The term, originally meaning a fine animal-skin writing surface, has been transferred to papers that resemble the old vellums.

Commonly used papers and boards include:

Drawing Paper: For drawing, available in a wide range of finishes, colors, textures, weights, and fiber contents.

Tracing Papers and Films: Available in rolls or sheets in a wide range of strengths, transparencies, widths, permanence, erasability, finishes, and costs. Select a paper for the particular purpose in mind, balancing utility and cost. You can, for example, use the cheaper papers for in-house roughs and the more expensive papers and vellums for presentations. Films are used where strength and transparency are most important.

Bristol: An all-purpose, double-faced, quality drawing paper used for finished drawings. Bristol comes in from one to five plys, indicating the number of sheets (plys) that are laminated together. One ply is like a stiff bond, while five ply is almost one millimeter thick. For presentations, you can mount bristol to a heavier board for support.

Color-Aid, Color-Vu: Oil-based ink silk-screened on a white-paper ground, in a wide variety of colors. The variety, evenness, and intensity of the colors make it useful for designs, backgrounds, and presentations. Unfortunately, the colors may vary noticeably from batch to batch, the colors change as they age, and the surface soils extremely easily.

Illustration Board: A stiff backing board surfaced with bristol in assorted textures and shades of white for finished drawing and painting. Thickness may be designated as: *lightweight* (about 1 mm) and *heavy weight* (about 2 mm); or *single thickness* (1/16") and *double thickness* (3/32"). It may be *single mount* (bristol on one side) or *double mount* (bristol on both sides). Double mount may be used on both sides and is good for model making, since it is of a uniform color and, being double surfaced, is warp resistant.

Mat Board: Similar to illustration board but with a wide selection of colored and textured papers laminated to its surface instead of the bristol.

Showcard Board, Poster Board: Smooth surfaced, moderately priced boards in a variety of colors for sign work, printing, screening, and brushing. They come single and double thick, one or two sided, and indoor or waterproof (for outdoor use).

Foamboard: A polystyrene foam core faced with either kraft or white coated paper in 1/8", 3/16", and 1/4" thicknesses and 30." by 40", to 48" by 96" sheets. Used for displays, models, mounts, and backing. It cuts easily with a knife and, for its thickness, is quite warp resistant.

A *paper cutter* is either a hinged knife and table, which can cut both board and paper, or a rotary blade on a horizontal arm, which is really only good for paper. The better machines, like the Dahle, feature precision cutting—the paper doesn't move as the blade encounters and cleaves it—self-sharpening, automatic clamping, and greater safety. Proper cutters are a great convenience, but quality cutters are expensive. Unless you cut a lot of paper and boards, you can get by with a mat or X-Acto knife and a straightedge.

To get started you will need, at the minimum: a drafting surface; a parallel rule or T-square; a 14-inch 30-60 degree triangle and a 12-inch 45-degree triangle; drafting tape; an architect's scale; a compass; a set of circle templates; a lead holder and assorted leads; a lead pointer or sandpaper; a pen, either a technical pen with a #1 point, or a Graphos set, and free-flowing waterproof ink to go in them; a fine-line marker; opaque white; a fine pointed brush; a vinyl eraser; rubber cement in a container with a brush; and a roll of tracing paper. You can add other equipment and materials as you find the need for them.

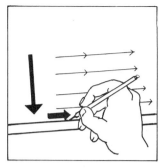

Draw horizontal lines from left to right working from top to bottom.

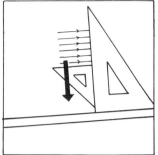

Draw a series of short horizontals by positioning a triangle on your parallel bar and moving a smaller triangle along the stationary triangle's vertical edge.

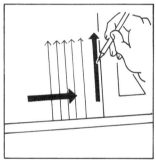

Draw verticals from bottom to top, moving from left to right.

Draw inclined lines with triangles.

Pull, don't push, your pencil or pen along, inclining it out from the straightedge at a slight angle. Rotate pencils as you move them to keep them evenly pointed (no need to rotate extra-fine leads).

Prevent ink from running under your guide instruments by using bevel-edged equipment or raising their edges.

Techniques

Position your paper on the drawing board (to the left if you're using a T-square to minimize aberration) and fasten the top edges with drafting tape on an angle. Pull the sheet taut and fasten its bottom corners. The parallel bar, as it moves, may roll up the bottom tape. To prevent this, you can either fold a piece of tape over on itself and place it under the sheet, adhering the sheet to the board, or raise the rule on strips of mat board.

Draw horizontals from left to right using the parallel bar or T-square as a straightedge. You can draw a series of short horizontals by positioning a triangle on your parallel bar and moving a smaller triangle along the vertical edge of the stationary triangle. Draw verticals from bottom to top using a triangle held firmly against the parallel bar or T-square. Draw inclined lines with triangles, those other than the 30–60–90 and 45–45–90 of your triangles, by working the two together or by using an adjustable triangle.

Pull, don't push, your pencil or pen along, inclining it out from the straightedge at a slight angle. Rotate pencils as you move them to keep them evenly pointed or use extra-fine leads. When using ink, work away from your completed areas so as not to drag across wet lines.

Keep your work clean by keeping your hands and tools clean. Dry cleaning pads or cleaning pounce dusted on the surface of important drawings will keep them clean as you work. Occasionally, wipe your tools and board off with mild detergent and water. You can also use alcohol or rubber cement thinner, but test an inconspicuous spot first.

Erase with the gentlest eraser to start; shift to the more abrasive ones as necessary. Erase away from yourself in a circular motion so as not to grind the eraser particles into your work, holding the paper down firmly to prevent wrinkling. An eraser shield will protect adjacent areas.

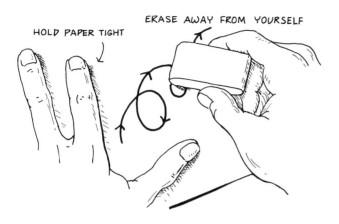

HOLD PAPER TIGHT

ERASE AWAY FROM YOURSELF

Erase away from yourself in a circular motion, holding the paper down firmly.

Draft systematically following a regular order:

1. Lay out the drawing either with light lines or through a succession of overlays.

2. Draw all circles and segments of circles.

3. Draw irregular, curved lines.

4. Draw straight lines, horizontals first, verticals next, then angles. Draw in the heavy lines; follow with the light ones.

5. Complete the drawing with dimensions and lettering.

Circles are easiest to draw with a template (note the four centering ticks at the circle's edges). If you can't find the right size on your template, use a compass. Set the compass either against a scale (taking care not to damage the scale) or on a line drawn for that purpose. Set the point of the compass on the center of the circle and rotate the compass clockwise, holding it at a raking angle. To avoid puncturing your paper, you can place a scrap piece of board at the circle's center. To avoid misalignment in corners with radii, draw the circle segment first, then connect the straight line to it.

Draft systematically, following a regular order.

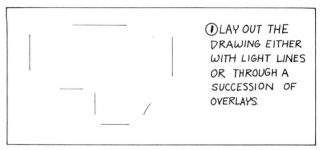

① LAY OUT THE DRAWING EITHER WITH LIGHT LINES OR THROUGH A SUCCESSION OF OVERLAYS.

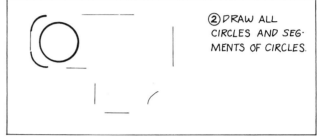

② DRAW ALL CIRCLES AND SEGMENTS OF CIRCLES.

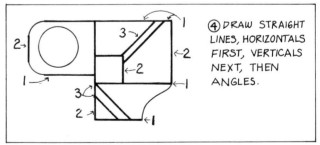

③ DRAW IRREGULAR, CURVED LINES.

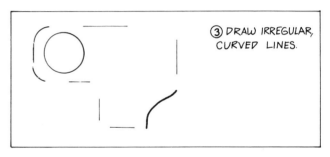

④ DRAW STRAIGHT LINES, HORIZONTALS FIRST, VERTICALS NEXT, THEN ANGLES.

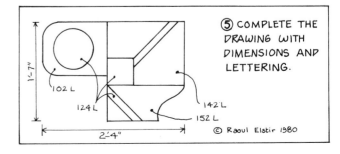

⑤ COMPLETE THE DRAWING WITH DIMENSIONS AND LETTERING.

© Raoul Elstir 1980

124

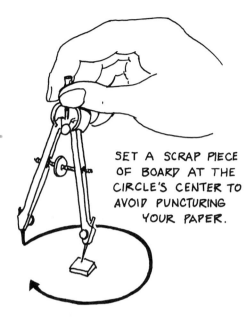

SET A SCRAP PIECE OF BOARD AT THE CIRCLE'S CENTER TO AVOID PUNCTURING YOUR PAPER.

Rotate the compass clockwise, holding it at a raking angle.

Lettering

It will be easiest to design and distribute the lettering for your drawing if you put it in last. It should be firm, decisive, and confident. Usually, 1/8 inch is adequate for dimensioning and 1/4 inch for titles. Thicken up letters over 3/16 inch high, lest they look too light.

Single stroke gothic, the most commonly used style, is easy to draw, but lower case, serif, or anything you're comfortable with that's appropriate to the subject is fine. As you practice, you'll work out your own "handwriting." You may letter either freehand or use a small triangle to guide the vertical strokes.

Draw your horizontal guidelines in lightly. As an aid, you can use a lettering guide (parallelograph) such as the Ames lettering guide, which is a small plastic device with a series of spaced holes in a movable wheel. Adjust the wheel to change the line spacing, place your pencil in the holes and slide the guide across the paper, drawing your lines as you go.

ABCDEFGHIJKLMNOPQRSTUVWXYZ 1234567890
PLAN SECTION DETAIL PLANFILE

abcdefghijklmnopqrstuvwxyz
estimate contract agreement

ABCDEFGHIJKLMNOPQRSTUVWXYZ
WOOD CONCRETE STEEL MARBLE

ABCDEFGHIJKLMNOPQRSTUVWXYZ 1234567890
RENDERING PERSPECTIVE SCHEMATIC WATERCOLOR

ABCDEFGHIJKLMNOPQRSTUVWXYZ 1234567890
STRUCTURAL DESIGN ENGINEERING PLANNING

Lettering examples. (Courtesy Jim Knox)

Make the spaces between the lines equal to or a little less than the heights of the letters. Space between the letters by eye. Vertical letters like E, H, or I want more room between them than open letters like A, L, or V. Make the space between the words equal to the width of the letter O.

There are many lettering stencils, templates, systems, and transfer letters on the market. To use the transfer letters, draw light guide lines, line up the letter, burnish it to transfer it from the sheet, move the sheet, and continue for the remaining letters. When you're finished, lay one of the wax sheets which separate the letter sheets over your copy and burnish the whole to make it more permanent. Then, erase your guide lines.

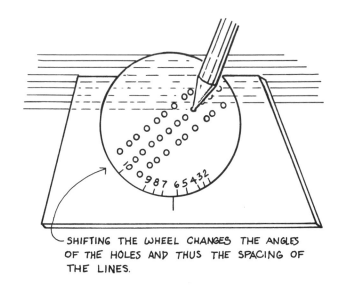

SHIFTING THE WHEEL CHANGES THE ANGLES OF THE HOLES AND THUS THE SPACING OF THE LINES.

The Ames Lettering Guide.

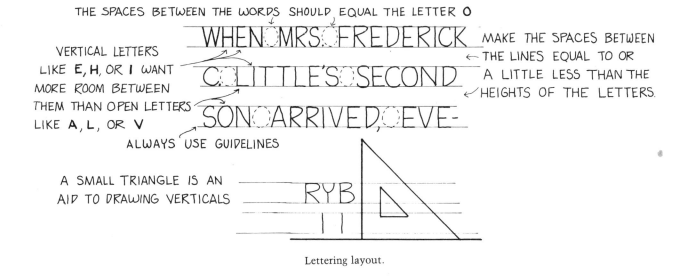

THE SPACES BETWEEN THE WORDS SHOULD EQUAL THE LETTER O

WHEN MRS FREDERICK
C LITTLE'S SECOND
SON ARRIVED, EVE-

VERTICAL LETTERS LIKE E, H, OR I WANT MORE ROOM BETWEEN THEM THAN OPEN LETTERS LIKE A, L, OR V

MAKE THE SPACES BETWEEN THE LINES EQUAL TO OR A LITTLE LESS THAN THE HEIGHTS OF THE LETTERS.

ALWAYS USE GUIDELINES

A SMALL TRIANGLE IS AN AID TO DRAWING VERTICALS

RYB

Lettering layout.

19. Presenting Designs to a Client

Format

You will often need to submit preliminary designs to a client. There are no hard rules for the format, which derives from the natures of the artist, the client, and the job. Presentations should be clean, neat, confident, and professional. Trim edges, sanding them if necessary, erase smudges, avoid glue lumps and loose, flapping pieces.

Establish a scale and stick with it. Hopping about will only confuse everyone. Try to standardize your boards; it will make them easier to handle and store. Supplement your artwork with texture and color information and actual sample materials.

Make photocopies, photographs, or traced copies of everything you send out, for your records in case of loss and for phone or mail reference. Keep your rough designs and calculations until the job is completed. Often you'll want to resurrect an abandoned idea or trace a thought back to its origins.

Presentations are valuable to show prospects how you work, for job souvenirs, and to give to clients. You can assure their retention by stating it in your contract.

Lest they be separated or mislaid, label each item or each nondetachable group of items with such information as your name, logo, date, copyright, address, job title, and scale. Be consistent here also. You may hand letter your presentations, using an architectural or other legible style, or you may use transfer type, a rubber stamp, or a lettered, typed, or printed gummed label.

Approvals

Unless you enjoy excellent rapport with a client, have your designs approved in writing. It will protect you should questions arise about who gave you the authority to proceed, or if your contact should pass from the scene. You may have your work initialled on either the front or back, or you may write out a brief notation like, "Approved _____ Date _____" on the back or on a separate cover sheet. Some approvals are conditional on changes by the artist; determine if your alterations need also be approved.

Three Phases of Presentations

Presentation may follow three phases: (1) *rough*, (2) *comprehensive*, and (3) *final design*.

1. The *rough* is the exploratory phase, where you can consider and present many rough solutions to a design problem. It will save time and money if the client is willing to accept informal sketches on tracing paper, but have this understood in advance.

2. *Comprehensives* are a refinement of your rough designs, with indications of color, details, texture, and materials. They may be mounted or not, depending on the formality of the client.

3. The *final design* is the culmination of the preceeding design phases and should accurately prefigure the final art. Scale figures, adjacent surfaces, material swatches, and renderings of stage settings and colors and textures will enhance verisimilitude.

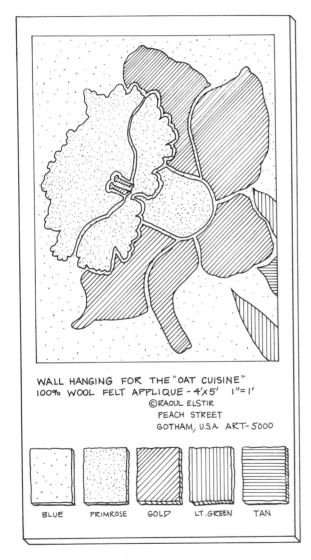

A presentation final design.

Finished designs may be either *flat* or *dimensional* (models).

For a flat finished design, select media and materials compatible with the effect you wish to convey. For example, you may use cut and pasted colored paper to represent the uniform, bright colors of applique fabrics; painted fabrics or colored drawings to represent woven textiles; paintings accompanied by detail studies for murals; and colored paper or washes for hard-edged paintings. Vellum will save you time by letting you trace, rather than transfer, your designs. Mount your designs on mat board or foamboard, and mat or frame them if they are paintings. Protect them with Mylar or acetate folded over and taped with transparent tape to the back (looks slick and changes can be marked on it with a grease pencil), flap them, or frame them under glass.

Dimensionality often cannot be conveyed adequately through drawings—you may have to provide models (they take much more time, so budget accordingly). Choose materials that correspond to the final art. Foamboard has a dimension of its own, resists warping, and can be cut and painted easily. Mat board is similar, but thinner and more likely to warp. The better grades of mat board are the same color throughout. Both can be covered with paper, paint, tapes, films, sculptmetal, or modelling paste. The actual intended materials can also be used: wood, plywood, metal, plaster, glass, stone, and plastic. Some artists, e.g., monumental sculptors, have models made for them by the subcontractor who'll be doing the final art, or by professional model-makers.

Consider how your model will be transported and stored; make it sturdy enough to survive handling. Disassembly features may help also.

See Hohauser's excellent *Architectural and Interior Models* (Bibliography) for more information.

Two Ploys

In the section on pricing, I mentioned several ploys used by clients to lower artists' fees. There are two other ploys involving presentations.

The first is the "knock-off" or "bump-off," particularly notorious in the garment or textile industries. It works this way: When you present your designs to a prospect, he excuses himself ostensibly to show them to someone in another room—his boss or a head designer. While he's out, however, he quickly traces or photocopies your work, and then returns it with some remark about its unsuitability. You won't know it's happened unless you see a slightly changed version in a dress store several months later.

You can protect yourself in several ways. If you suspect a prospect, don't let your designs out of your sight. If asked to leave your work on speculation, you may (1) say that the designs are already committed to another showing and offer to return with them at a better time, (2) propose that you accompany your designs for their presentation to the other party, or (3) leave them on receipt of a signed form that contains such wording as:

These original designs are submitted to you in confidence for the sole purpose of soliciting your orders, in consideration of which you agree not to copy or cause them to be copied or modified directly or indirectly. All artwork developed from these designs is to be returned to us, unless the designs are purchased by you. . . .

and include instuctions for their return.

In the second ploy, the client negotiates a contract with the design and final art phases separate, and with the artist deferring, as is the usual case, his profit to the final art phase. When the designs are finished to the client's satisfaction, the client withdraws from the contract, pays the artist what amounts to less than his anticipated fee, and hands the designs over to a cut-rate fabricator for their execution, thus realizing an overall savings.

You can forestall this (and to an extent the previous) gambit by copyrighting your work and including a clause to that effect in your contract. Should it be played on you, you have the normal alternatives in an infringement situation: You may ask for compensation or threaten a lawsuit. Also, you can loudly disclaim the design's execution to all who will listen.

There are no easy answers for being had. Choosing reputable clients and avoiding speculation are easier said than done. Of course, copyright your designs, but a shnorrer can make small changes in them and claim your designs are his own, leaving you with the option of proving your original authorship in court.

20. Transferring Designs and Making Patterns

Designs are transferred for three main reasons: (1) To evolve a design through a series of studies without having to redraw the previous study each time. Example: Working out a design through tracing paper overlays. (2) To move a design from one surface or medium to another. Example: Transferring a completed tracing paper design onto bristol or fabric. (3) To change the scale of a design while moving it. Example: Transferring a mural design from the small study to the wall.

Choose a particular transfer method on the basis of: cost, ease, the number of copies required, the need for scale change, the surface involved, equipment availability, and accuracy.

There are three principal categories of transfer methods: *manual*, *projection*, and *photomechanical*.

Manual Transfer

There are five principal manual transfer methods: *tracing*, *transfer paper*, *rub-off*, *fabric transfer pencil*, and *graphing off*.

Tracing

The process: Place a sheet of tracing paper over the design and trace the design on the tracing paper. Alternatives to tracing paper are: tracing film; opaque paper made transparent either permanently with varnish or shellac, or temporarily with a nonstaining, nonbuckling solvent, like rubber-cement thinner; or, by working on a window or light table.

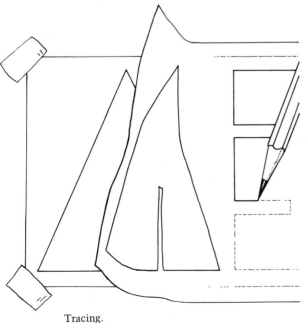

Tracing.

Comments: Tracing is quick and simple. It is the principal method for developing designs, because the previous design can be easily modified as it is traced. Tracing produces only one copy at a time, and each additional copy takes the same amount of time. To eliminate tedious duplication, photomechanical reproduction methods may be combined with tracing for working up complex designs.

Transfer Paper

The process: Place a sheet of transfer paper between the design and the other surface (*other surface* in this chapter designates *that surface to which you are transferring your design*). Go over the design with a stylus, pencil, or colored pencil (which will mark what you've gone over), thus transferring the design to the other surface. You may use either a commercial transfer paper such as "*Saral*," a wax-free, erasable paper available in five colors; *graphite paper*, an erasable, graphite-coated paper; or typewriter *carbon paper*, a waxy, permanent paper that is cheap but difficult to erase. You can also make your own transfer paper by rubbing a soft pencil, charcoal, or pastel on a piece of tracing paper. To make the paper darker, repeat the operation several times, spreading the pencil, charcoal, or pastel with rubber-cement thinner applied with a brush or cotton ball between each rubbing.

Comments: Transfer is good for a wide range of surfaces. It produces only one copy at a time, and each additional copy takes the same amount of time. It is principally used for transferring designs from one surface to another, e.g., tracing paper to drawing paper, board, or canvas. Where the results are critical, test this and any other process on scrap material.

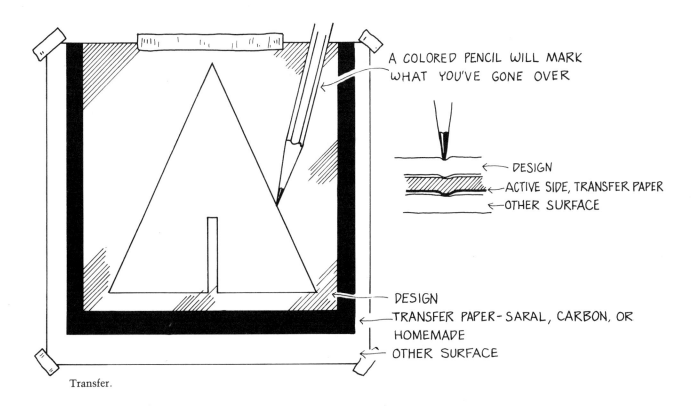

A COLORED PENCIL WILL MARK WHAT YOU'VE GONE OVER

DESIGN
ACTIVE SIDE, TRANSFER PAPER
OTHER SURFACE

DESIGN
TRANSFER PAPER - SARAL, CARBON, OR HOMEMADE
OTHER SURFACE

Transfer.

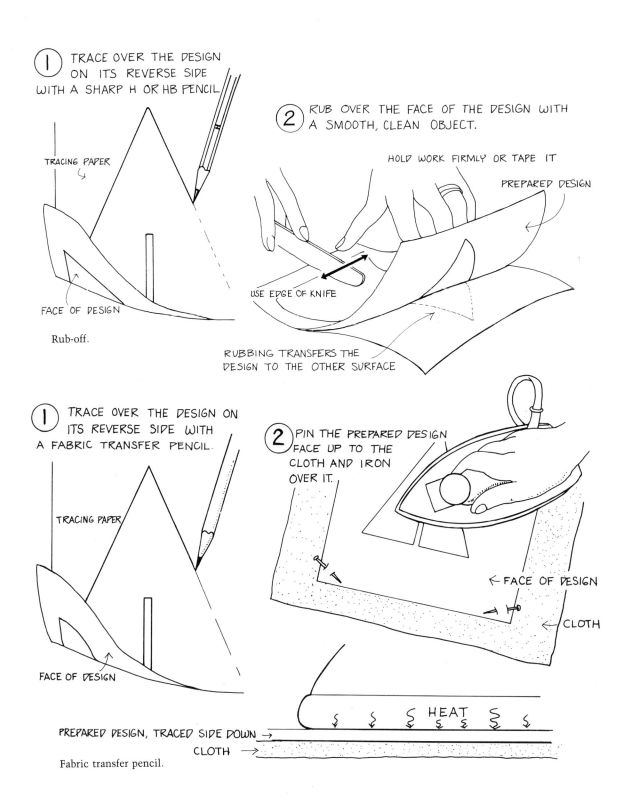

① TRACE OVER THE DESIGN ON ITS REVERSE SIDE WITH A SHARP H OR HB PENCIL

TRACING PAPER

FACE OF DESIGN

Rub-off.

② RUB OVER THE FACE OF THE DESIGN WITH A SMOOTH, CLEAN OBJECT.

HOLD WORK FIRMLY OR TAPE IT

PREPARED DESIGN

USE EDGE OF KNIFE

RUBBING TRANSFERS THE DESIGN TO THE OTHER SURFACE

① TRACE OVER THE DESIGN ON ITS REVERSE SIDE WITH A FABRIC TRANSFER PENCIL.

TRACING PAPER

FACE OF DESIGN

② PIN THE PREPARED DESIGN FACE UP TO THE CLOTH AND IRON OVER IT.

FACE OF DESIGN

CLOTH

HEAT

PREPARED DESIGN, TRACED SIDE DOWN →
CLOTH →

Fabric transfer pencil.

Rub-Off

The process: Trace over the design on its reverse side with a sharp H or HB pencil and secure it face up to the other surface. Rub the face of the design with a smooth, clean object that will not dry burnish—a spoon or the edge of a table knife, for example. The rubbing transfers the design to the other surface. The design should be on tracing paper, so that it will be both easy to trace from the back and to position on the other surface.

Comments: Preparing the design takes no longer than any tracing process. A good original can yield five or more copies with equal rapidity. Use rub-offs when you wish to make very accurate multiple copies, as for a textile design repeat.

Fabric Transfer Pencil

The process: You can adapt the rub-off technique for fabrics by substituting for the H or HB pencil a *fabric transfer pencil* available in needlework and yard-goods shops. Trace over your design on its reverse side with the fabric transfer pencil, attach the traced design rightside-up to a piece of cloth, and iron over it, transferring the design to the cloth. Keep the pencil sharp, as the heat will spread the waxy line, which is difficult to remove.

Comments: Unlike a pencil rub-off, fabric transfer pencil yields only one good copy. Use it when you want to transfer intricate designs, such as lettering, to fabric, and for embroidery and crewel. Use pouncing for larger scale designs, for appliqué, and when you need to clean the transferred pattern off the fabric easily.

Graphing Off

The process: Draw a regular grid over the design, starting at one corner, if it is an overall design, or working out from the center, if the design is centered. Select a grid scale in keeping with the scale of the design—a dense grid for complex designs; an open grid for simple designs. The grid will be easier to see if you use contrasting colors. With dense grids, you can use different colors for the different units of measurement, e.g., red for feet, blue for half feet, and green for quarter feet, to avoid confusion. Mark the scale along the grid's edges.

Transfer the grid to the other surface by one of the following techniques:

1. *For small canvases and boards with parallel edges,* use a T-square and triangle.

2. *For paper, canvases, and boards that will fit on a drafting table,* use a T-square or parallel rule to mark off the grid.

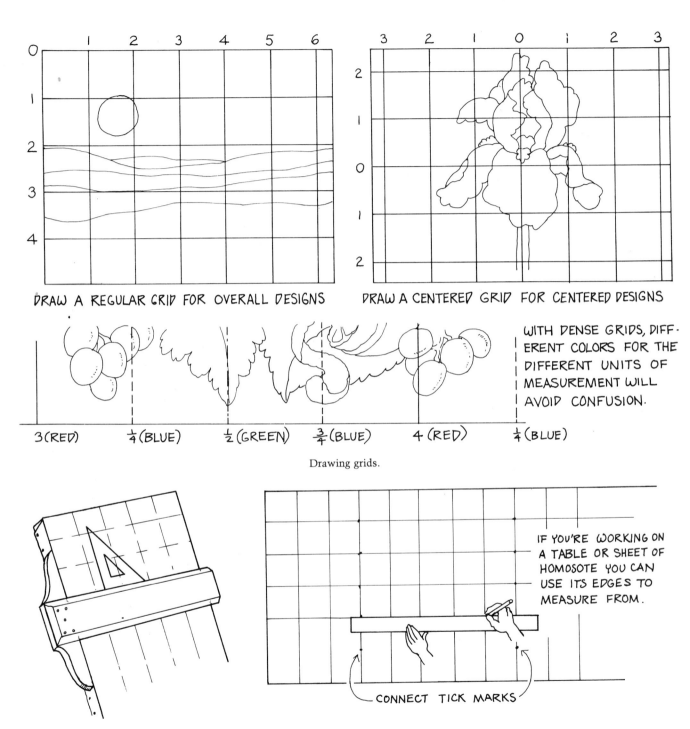

DRAW A REGULAR GRID FOR OVERALL DESIGNS

DRAW A CENTERED GRID FOR CENTERED DESIGNS

WITH DENSE GRIDS, DIFFERENT COLORS FOR THE DIFFERENT UNITS OF MEASUREMENT WILL AVOID CONFUSION.

3 (RED)   ¼ (BLUE)   ½ (GREEN)   ¾ (BLUE)   4 (RED)   ¼ (BLUE)

Drawing grids.

IF YOU'RE WORKING ON A TABLE OR SHEET OF HOMOSOTE YOU CAN USE ITS EDGES TO MEASURE FROM.

CONNECT TICK MARKS

For small canvases and boards with parallel edges, use a T-Square and triangle. For larger boards, canvas, and paper, mark the grid along all four edges and connect the points with a straightedge.

3. *For larger boards, canvas, and paper,* mark the grid along all four edges and connect the points with a straightedge.

Longer lines may be made with a snapline. To do this, purchase a chalk reel in a hardware store and replace the thick line with about a thirty-pound-test braided fishing line, which will leave a thinner mark. Fill the well of the reel with powdered charcoal or chalk. The snapline must be held at one end either by an assistant or a loop secured to a nail or push pin, or by hooking the metal end that comes with the reel over an edge. Pull the line taut; pinch it with your fingers at its center; draw it away from the surface; and, when it's stretched, release it like a bowstring. The line thus formed will be reasonably, but not precisely, accurate.

In cases where only two sides of the surface are parallel (as occurs with lengths cut from a roll of paper) use one of the edges of the paper as a straight edge, align a T-square or a large triangle with it, and draw a perpendicular to complete the third side of the parallelogram. Step off the divisions of the grid along the two edges of the paper from the third side (which you've just drawn), and connect the divisions with a straightedge. Make all your measurements out continuously from the third side. If you measure a long grid with a short ruler and begin each new set of measurements from the end of the previous set, you'll find that by the time you reach the end of the grid, you'll have introduced a considerable error.

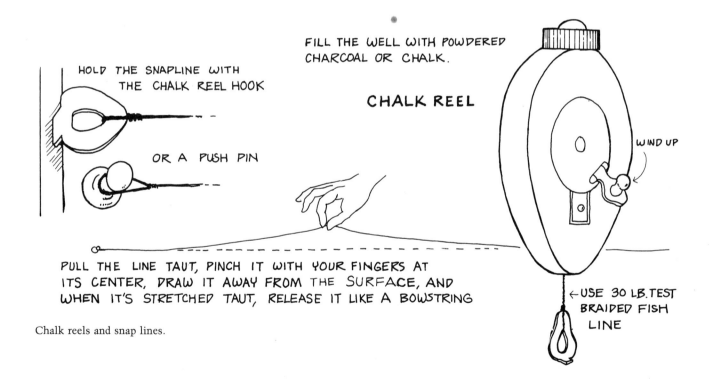

FILL THE WELL WITH POWDERED CHARCOAL OR CHALK.

CHALK REEL

HOLD THE SNAPLINE WITH THE CHALK REEL HOOK

OR A PUSH PIN

WIND UP

PULL THE LINE TAUT, PINCH IT WITH YOUR FINGERS AT ITS CENTER, DRAW IT AWAY FROM THE SURFACE, AND WHEN IT'S STRETCHED TAUT, RELEASE IT LIKE A BOWSTRING

←USE 30 LB.TEST BRAIDED FISH LINE

Chalk reels and snap lines.

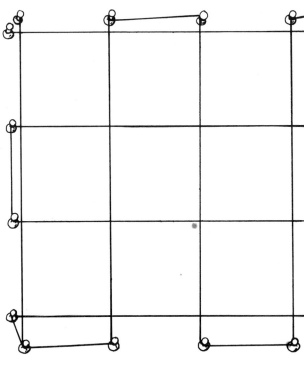

Making a string grid.

4. *For murals and surfaces that you don't want to mark on with a drawn grid*, make a grid of string. Mark your coordinates around the perimeter of the other surface, stick 5/8-inch push pins (which are less likely to pull with the strain than the ordinary shorter pins) into each coordinate point and interconnect the points with a weaving of string. A thin, braided, fishing line or kite string in a contrasting color works well.

If you can't pin into the wall, you can build a separate frame next to it to receive either the pins or headed nails.

Establish reference points for coordinates on a wall by: (1) measuring up from the floor, (2) measuring in from the edge of the goods, (3) using a *line level* (a length of string with a small bubble level tied into its center) to align points on the wall, (4) using a *mason's level* (a level four feet or more long), or (5) using a *water level*. To use a water level, fill a length of 3/8-inch clear, flexible

Establish reference points for coordinates on a wall.

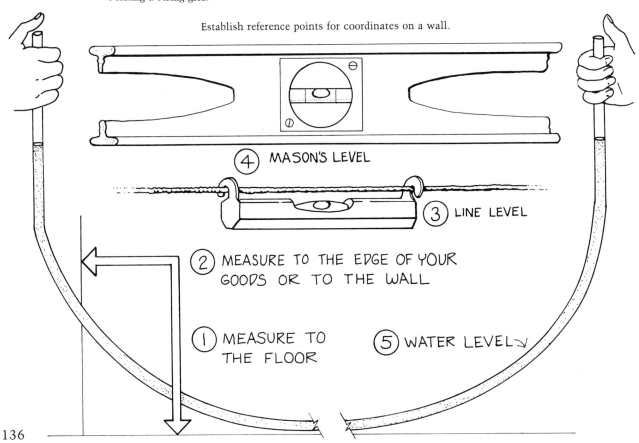

④ MASON'S LEVEL

③ LINE LEVEL

② MEASURE TO THE EDGE OF YOUR GOODS OR TO THE WALL

① MEASURE TO THE FLOOR

⑤ WATER LEVEL

polyethylene tubing with water either at a tap, by siphoning, or by sucking on it like a straw. Make sure there are no air bubbles. Hold your thumb over one end of the tube and align the water level in your end of the tube with a point on the vertical axis of a grid you've established with a mason's level. Have an assistant align the water level in the other end of the tube with a point approximately corresponding to your own on the other vertical axis, also drawn with the mason's level. As long as you keep your end capped, the water will not move in the tube, so your assistant needn't cover his end. After a discrete warning, lift your thumb. The water will seek its own level. When the water settles, the two levels will exactly correspond, and you can mark their heights on the vertical axes.

Once the grid is established, transferring the design is easy. Either start at a corner and work across, or connect the main junction points. Take care, especially with large and elaborate designs, not to lose your way. Refer back to the original periodically to check for accuracy.

Some designs are so simple that you won't need a grid. For example, if you're transferring a carrot from a design to a wall, rather than going to all the trouble of making a graph, simply triangulate the carrot's bottom by measuring in from the design's bottom and two edges, locate the carrot's top in the same way, locate its sides in one or two places, and, finally, connect your reference points.

Comments: Graphing off is one of the three principal methods for transferring designs for mural work. The other two are either pounced or transfer-paper cartoons; or slide, opaque, or overhead projection. Cartoons can be laborious. Projection requires specialized equipment, and may be impractical because of the size or nature of the design, or the size or light level of the room.

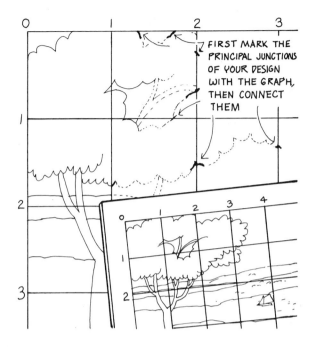

Work across, connecting principal junction points.

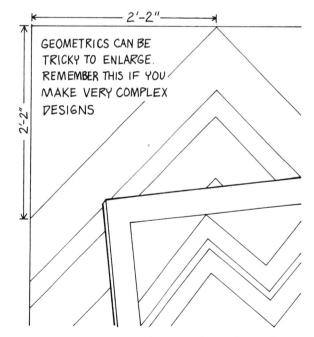

For simple designs, measure from the edges to locate the main reference points.

Projection Transfer

There are four principal types of projection equipment: *slide projectors*, *opaque projectors*, *visualizers*, and *overhead projectors.*

Slide Projectors

The process: Ordinary slide projectors are excellent for transferring designs. Their bright, sharp images can easily be enlarged or reduced by moving the projector or the other surface. Slides are very flexible: you can make complete, traditional underpaintings; you can combine elements from several slides; and you can change the scales of the slides' components. Their principal disadvantages are the time, trouble, and expense of taking slides and having them developed (especially if you only need one or two shots in a hurry), and the necessity of working in a darkened room when you copy them.

Since it is hard to see accurately in the projector's glare, it can help to roughly locate your design first with an easily visible material like charcoal or tape. Project the slide and line it up with your marks. Sketch in the outline and turn on the lights to check the placement. When satisfied, complete the tracing. You can either do a simple outline, or a full rendering in charcoal or paint.

If the other surface will transmit light (e.g., a stretched, primed canvas) you can use rear projection. Reverse the slide, focus the image on the back of the canvas, and trace it from its face. Some definition may be lost, but you will eliminate the impediment of working in your own shadow.

Comments: Projection—whether slide, opaque, or overhead—is useful for accurately transferring designs or photographs (slide and opaque projectors only) while changing their scale. Of the three methods, slide projectors give the sharpest image and greatest enlargement.

Opaque Projectors

The process: Bright lights within the opaque projector reflect off the art placed in the machine and throw the art's image out through a large lens. Any object, regardless of its opacity, within the size range of the machine, can be projected in full color.

Opaque projection is easy and fast, since the art can be used as is, but, because it works by reflected rather than transmitted light, it has many disadvantages. The image quality is much dimmer and fuzzier than that of a slide projector, and while a slide projector can throw a usable image on the side of a building, the opaque projector can throw an image that is only good for a dozen or so square feet. Also, the art is difficult to adjust inside the machine and likely to toast if the ventilation system is inadequate.

Opaque projectors range in cost from the ten-dollar models advertised in comic books to those costing over five hundred dollars. More money will get you a larger, brighter image and a larger copy acceptance. We have a Seerite that cost under a hundred dollars and works acceptably. Whichever machine you're considering, try it out before you buy it.

Comments: Opaque projection is particularly useful for transferring opaque artwork within a limited range of magnification. Its principal advantage is that any art, within the size and enlargement range of the machine, may be used without further modification.

Visualizers

The process: Visualizers comprise various precision optical devices. The type known as the viewer (often generically called the "Lacey Luci," after a former manufacturer) is an internalized opaque projector. The art is placed on a copyboard and bright lights reflect its image up through the viewer onto the back of a frosted glass screen, measuring about 14 by 16 inches, in front of which the operator sits and copies the image onto tracing paper. Visualizers enlarge and reduce accurately about three or five fold without distortion, and the rear projection feature eliminates the user's hand shadow. Visualizers, however, need a curtain or a dark room, are bulky, and cost at least five hundred dollars.

Comments: Visualizers are particularly useful whenever accuracy and precise scale change are required. Examples are: converting diverse artwork into the same scale, e.g., coordinating illustrations for a publication; or, converting a photograph into line art. They find their greatest application in the graphic arts.

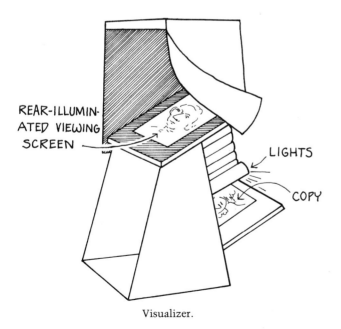

REAR-ILLUMIN-ATED VIEWING SCREEN

LIGHTS

COPY

Visualizer.

Overhead Projectors

The process: In the overhead projector, light shines up through the art placed on the projection stage into the adjustable projection head, where a mirror reflects it out at an angle. The head's adjustability lets you modify the angle of reflectance to obtain a perfectly rectilinear image. Overhead projectors will take about a 9- to 10-inch square piece of art and clearly enlarge it many times in a fully illuminated room, but, as with any optical device that functions by light transmission, the art must be absolutely transparent. Mylar and acetate films work; tracing paper is too opaque.

The machine is versatile: you can draw on film with Stabilo pencils, film inks, and transparent colored markers; apply transfer letters and symbols to the film; or use a transparency-making copier. Overhead projectors are popular with schools; your local audiovisual person may be able to give you a demonstration. Also, for free information on making transparencies write: 3M Company, Visual Products Division, 3M Center, St. Paul, MN 55101.

Comments: The principal advantage of overhead projection over other projection methods is that it can operate in a normally illuminated room. Its principal disadvantage is that art used with overhead projectors must be fully transparent. Its other advantage over slide projection is that it bypasses the photographic interlude. The advantage of overhead projectors over opaque projectors and visualizers is their greater enlargement capability.

Photomechanical Transfer

There are many photomechanical transfer methods. Four of the most common are *black line*, *blue line*, *Xerox*, and *photostat*. All require expensive equipment, which confine their purchase or lease to large offices, but many duplicating and printing services are available to do the work for you. Except for the Xerox, their main use is in architecture and the graphic arts.

Black line, blue line, and Xerox make fast and cheap copies. Some machines have modest enlargement and reduction capability. All are monochromatic except for the recently introduced color Xerox.

Photostats make negative paper photographs of line art, which they can either enlarge or reduce. Positives must be photographed from the negative print. The process is reasonably quick and produces sharp copies ideal for graphic arts.

TRANSFER METHODS

Manual Transfer Method	Enlargement	No. of Copies	Advantages	Disadvantages	Used For
Tracing	None	1	Quick and simple. Designs may be modified in the process	Laborious. Not suited for final designs on opaque materials	General copying. Evolving designs
Transfer Paper	None	1	Useful for wide range of surfaces. Saral, graphite, and homemade papers erasable	Laborious	Transferring designs from one surface to another, e.g., tracing paper to board
Rub-Off	None	5 or more	Accurate. Subsequent copies quick	Laborious	Accurate multiple copies, e.g., textile design repeats
Fabric Transfer Pencil	None	1	It and pouncing only transfer methods for fabrics	Laborious Not readily erasable	Fabrics, particularly intricate designs like lettering, crewel, and embroidery
Graphing Off	Unlimited	1	Cheap. Flexible. No special equipment needed	Laborious. Dirties other surface. Designs must be completely drawn	Murals and other large scale enlargements

PROJECTION METHODS

	Art Accepted	Enlargement/ Reduction Scale	Room Illumination	Image Quality	Advantages	Disadvantages	Used For
Slide Projectors	Slides	Great, image breaks up with distance	Darkened	Excellent	Clear image, great enlargement and reduction. Equipment widely available and familiar	Needs photographic interlude and darkened room. Except for rear projection, artist must work in his own shadow	General transfer work, tones. Any work that requires great scale change
Opaque Projectors	Any art that will fit projector, regardless of opacity	Limited, 10–15 x enlargement. Possibly some reduction	Fully dark	Poor to moderate	Art requires no preparation	Image quality usually poor. Needs fully darkened room. Image deteriorates rapidly with enlargement. Artist must work in his own shadow	General transfer work from opaque material
Visualizers	Any art that will fit projector regardless of quality	Enlarges/ reduces about 3–5 x	Fully dark, or curtained viewing booth	Excellent	Art requires no preparation. Sharp, distortion-free image. No hand shadow	Limited scale change. Needs dark environment. Machine expensive and bulky	Graphic design and other fields that need exact copywork
Overhead Projectors	Fully transparent line art	At least 25x, image breaks up with distance	Normal	Good to excellent	Uses unprepared transparent art. Works in regular room illumination. Image adjustable to eliminate distortion	Art must be fully transparent. Accepts no tones. Artist must work in his own shadow	Transparent line art copywork. General transfer work that requires considerable enlargement

Patterns

Patterns are used to repeat a design rapidly, easily, and cleanly. You might, for example, make a pattern if you wanted to reproduce a design for a number of identical artworks, or duplicate a motif within an artwork.

Patterns are also used to keep a substrate clean. For example, if you are transferring a design to a delicate wall covering (such as a wallpaper in the case of a mural) or fabric (in the case of a wall hanging), you would make a pattern because it is accurate and readily erasable. Were you to sketch or develop the design directly on the wall or fabric, you would not be able to keep it clean.

While rub-off will produce more than one copy, *pouncing* is the best general-purpose pattern-making method. Once you've made your pattern, pouncing is very fast—you can pounce a thirty-foot mural in less than ten minutes, start to finish—and the pattern will last until the paper wears out.

Making a Pounce Pattern

A *pounce pattern* is a perforated pattern through which a fine powder (*pounce*) is dusted (*pounced*) to transfer a design.

1. Transfer your design to a piece of paper. Any paper that's neither too soft nor too thick can work, but you'll get good results from a 20 pound white bond paper such as is sold for poster use. For true edges, use paper the same width as the design; therefore, keep a selection of commonly used widths in stock. For widths greater than the maximum available, join pieces together on the back with tape. For in-between widths, use the next larger size, keeping one edge as the straight edge and measuring the other edge in from the side. You may trim off the overage, but it's not necessary.

2. Pin the paper with your design on it to a length of felt tacked to a wall or laid on a table. Trace over the design with a *pounce wheel*, or, for very tight work, a stylus, *pin vise* (a stylus held in a handle or vise), or a tool made from a large needle set in a hole drilled into a length of dowel.

The pounce wheel (also called a tracing or perforating wheel) is a small, spiked wheel that rolls freely on an arbor fixed to a short handle. The Grifhold Company makes one of aluminum in four different wheel options, each of which comes with a collar that loosens to swing curves. Buy a selection; they only cost a few dollars each. Model #9, which has 21 ¼-inch-long teeth, is good for fine work and tight curves, but the numerous teeth produce closely spaced holes that weaken the paper so it tears easily, and the teeth's shortness makes running along a straight edge difficult. Model #12, which has 15 7/16-inch-long teeth, is faster and easier to operate, but is too large for close work.

An *electric pouncer*, which burns holes with intermittent sparks, is available for production work. Don't use the blunt-toothed dressmaking wheels; they only press the paper and do not puncture it.

Use straightedges and flexible curves as guides for critical lines. Don't worry about mistakes; you can seal them with tape from the rear (so the pounce bag won't rub them loose).

3. Flip over the pattern and rub the back gently with fine sandpaper to enlarge the holes in order to make a clearer pouncing.

4. Secure the pattern to the other surface. Pour several tablespoons of pounce into a small, porous bag or the toe of a child's cotton sock. Use powdered charcoal for light surfaces and powdered chalk or corn starch for dark surfaces. For fabrics, use only corn starch, since it cleans off relatively easily. Add a tiny pinch of pigment or powdered paint to the corn starch if more contrast is needed. Daub the pounce bag on the pattern with a light tap-and-wipe motion. The tapping forces a little of the powder through the mesh of the bag, and the wiping distributes it over the pattern. Lift up the pattern carefully to check that you've pounced everything. The pouncing will have replicated in powder the exact perforations of the pattern.

5. Roll up the pattern, label it on its edge, and put it away for its next use.

1. TRANSFER YOUR DESIGN TO A SHEET OF PAPER.

2. PIN THE PAPER TO A LENGTH OF FELT AND TRACE OVER IT WITH A POUNCE WHEEL.

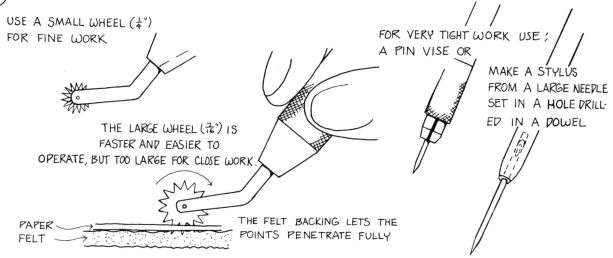

USE A SMALL WHEEL ($\frac{1}{4}$") FOR FINE WORK

THE LARGE WHEEL ($\frac{7}{16}$") IS FASTER AND EASIER TO OPERATE, BUT TOO LARGE FOR CLOSE WORK.

PAPER
FELT

THE FELT BACKING LETS THE POINTS PENETRATE FULLY

FOR VERY TIGHT WORK USE: A PIN VISE OR

MAKE A STYLUS FROM A LARGE NEEDLE SET IN A HOLE DRILLED IN A DOWEL

3. FLIP OVER THE PATTERN AND RUB THE BACK GENTLY WITH FINE SANDPAPER TO OPEN THE HOLES MORE TO MAKE A CLEARER POUNCING.

4. SECURE THE PATTERN TO THE OTHER SURFACE, DAUB IT WITH A LIGHT TAP AND WIPE MOTION OF THE POUNCE BAG.

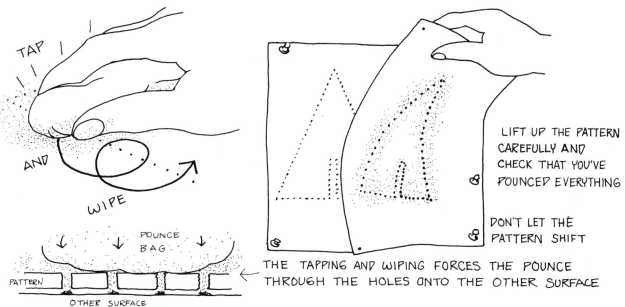

TAP

AND

WIPE

POUNCE BAG

PATTERN

OTHER SURFACE

LIFT UP THE PATTERN CAREFULLY AND CHECK THAT YOU'VE POUNCED EVERYTHING

DON'T LET THE PATTERN SHIFT

THE TAPPING AND WIPING FORCES THE POUNCE THROUGH THE HOLES ONTO THE OTHER SURFACE

5. ROLL UP THE PATTERN, LABEL IT ON ITS END, AND PUT IT AWAY.

Making a pounce pattern.

21. The Studio

Most of us work in oversized closets while dreaming of vast, airy studios the size of barns. If you've ever worked in a barn, or a large studio, for that matter, you will know that the spiritual benefits of spaciousness are balanced by the practical concerns of keeping the place clean, orderly, and in repair; and the costs of heating, cooling, taxes, and the mortgage or rent. Furthermore, the higher your expenses, the more money you'll have to earn in order to cover them. Actually, you only need enough space to accommodate your largest average (not your largest conceivable) work plus enough room to view your work from an adequate distance—that, and room for your equipment, your office, and some storage.

If you're building from scratch or considering extensive renovations, you can profit from the services of an architect. He can help you with the layout, materials, and lighting. An imaginative architect can transform unlikely prospects into exciting, workable spaces. As with other professionals, remember that you may be able to exchange services.

Many artists have successfully combined their workplace with a sales gallery. Avery Faulkner, the architect, observes:

Americans love to see how things are made, like power plants and factories, and not simply the product. The public doesn't need pedestals and the gallery atmosphere. Many clients want to see the art in the space in which it was created and get an idea of how they can display it in their own settings. Consider the studio as not just a workshop, but as a magnet.

If you choose to follow Faulkner's advice, you can open your studio to the public and set regular hours, or be available by appointment, or have periodic open houses. You'll need to promote yourself (see Chapter 8), especially if you're not in a tourist area or a regular shopping street. Also, be sure to check into liability insurance, zoning, parking, and access.

Surfaces

White is the preferred color for studio surfaces because it maximally reflects light without tinting it. Semigloss and gloss paints are easier to maintain than flats, but they can cause annoying reflections. Homosote, a paintable, soft, gray cellulose product, is an excellent panelling choice, especially for mural walls. It takes push pins readily and holds them without tearing. If the wall becomes unsightly, a little sanding, spackle, and paint will quickly freshen it up.

Concrete is cheap, smooth, and sturdy for the floors, but hard on the feet. You can cover concrete with carpet, vinyl, or wood, or lay resilient mats on the areas where you stand. If you don't cover concrete, seal it with a clear sealer or paint it with rubberized paint, heavy-duty floor paint, or catalyzed epoxy to eliminate dusting and facilitate cleaning.

Light

Lighting can so dramatically affect the perception of art, especially if the art is in color, that, if you're doing commissions in your studio, you should either attempt to replicate the character of the illumination that will ultimately be provided for your work or at least periodically view the work under similar lighting conditions to check its color balance and emphasis. You can imagine the problems of museums that must show works together that were executed under a diversity of lighting conditions, or, worse, cannot reproduce artificially in their windowless galleries the natural light under which so many works were done. Gordon Anson, the lighting expert of the National Gallery of Art in Washington, D.C., spectacularly demonstrated this to me when he fully opened the automatic skylight louvers for the room in the new East Wing in which the Matisse cutouts are displayed. Suddenly, brilliant daylight flooded the room, and for the first time I could see that Matisse had masterfully set all his colors vibrating within the same plane. But, as the timer switch inexorably took hold, and the incandescent light returned, the yellows, reds, and oranges sprung forward in a pulsating glow, while the blues and violets resumed their places in the background.

The amount of light you'll need for various tasks depends on a number of factors, which include: (1) figure/ground contrast—it requires much less light to see black lines on white paper than black lines on brown paper; (2) size of the task—it requires much less light to read headline type than eight-point type; (3) familiarity of the material—it requires much less light to read words in sentences where there are contextual clues than series of unrelated numbers; and (4) your age—the older you get, the more light you need. One study showed that the average person over 50 may need more than ten times the light to see as well as a 20 year old.

Glare, which is annoying brightness, causes both discomfort and fatigue as your eyes constantly adjust to sharply varying light levels. The change in the eye's pupil size is not instantaneous, and the time-lag for adjustment increases as you grow older. Two types of glare are: *direct glare*, which comes from looking directly at an unshielded light source; and *reflected glare*, which is the reflection of a light source into the eye. The reflections may be hard *specular reflections*, as off a shiny object like a mirror, or more diffused *veiling reflections*, as from a less obviously reflective object like the matte pages of a book.

Color temperature is a measure on the Kelvin scale (which is similar to the Centigrade or Celsius scale, but starts at absolute zero) of the degree of whiteness of a light source. It is based on the phenomenon of the changing light emission and color of a body as it is heated—an iron bar or tungsten light filament going from dull red, through yellow-orange, to white and blue-white, ever increasing in brilliance as it grows hotter. *Correlated color temperature* is the term used for light sources other than incandescent metal and the sun or sky. Thus, fluorescents and other gaseous discharge light sources are given a Kelvin rating equivalent to that of a comparable incandescent metal source. The distinction may not be made, however, in common usage. Some typical color temperature readings are: sunlight at dawn, 1800 K; general-lighting tungsten lamps, 2600–3000 K; warm white fluorescents, 3000 K; tungsten floodlamps, 3100–3400 K; cool-white fluorescents, 4200 K; noon sunlight, 4870 K; north skylight, 7500 K; and clear northwest blue sky, 25,000 K. Note the wide color temperature variations for natural light. We'll return to this shortly when we discuss artificial lighting.

Measuring Light Intensity

If you are satisfied with the present lighting level of your studio, fine, but if you are designing a studio or are planning to consult with a lighting engineer, you may need to know something about recommended light levels.

The basic measurement for the intensity of light is the foot-candle (fc), equal to one lumen per square foot, or about the amount of light produced by a plumber's candle at a distance of one foot. Working outdoors, where a typical reading in an open field on a clear day at noon in summer might be 7,000 to 10,000 fc, our eyes readily adjust to the sunlight, although glare may be troublesome, and the light will be suitable for most any task. Indoors, we must assure adequate light, and recommended light levels have been established for guidance. Some figures are: for art galleries, 10–15 fc for works on paper, and 20–30 fc for general lighting; school art rooms, 70 fc; rough drafting, 150 fc; detailed drafting, 200 fc. While there are no specific recommendations for artists' studios, you can see that general illumination of 150 to 200 fc should be adequate, or you could have an ambient level of 70 to 100 fc (as with an art room) and use supplemental task lighting for detailed work.

You will require a foot-candle meter to measure foot-candles. Unfortunately, there are no conversion tables for a photographic light meter—the results would be too inaccurate. General Electric's #214 light meter sells for under $50, if you wish to buy a meter, or you may be able to borrow or rent one from a lighting engineer or lighting store.

Natural Light

Daylight varies greatly according to the time of year, the time of day, and the cloud cover. An overcast sky is two-and-a-half to three times brighter overhead than at the horizon; a clear sky is normally brighter at the horizon, that is, of course, away from the sun's immediate vicinity. The amount of daylight that enters a room depends on these factors, plus the cleanness of the air, the cleanness, size, angle, and transparency of the fenestration, and the light reflected off the ground. Ground light can contribute more than half the daylight in a room, as when the earth is covered with water, snow, white concrete, or similar highly reflective materials. And, since it comes from a lower angle, ground light can reach farther into a room than light from the sky.

Most artists, given the choice, prefer working under natural light. It is free, vibrant, and intense, but easy on the eyes and most probably more healthful since we, as a species, evolved under it. Direct sunlight coming from the east, south, and west can cause some problems. It is constantly moving; it is direct, creating sharp light and shadow contrasts and glare; it can vary markedly in intensity as clouds obscure the sun's face; and its color shifts appreciably from dawn through dusk. Diffusors, such as translucent panels or curtains, will ameliorate these difficulties somewhat.

North light, traditionally associated with artists, is sunlight reflected off the sky. It is diffuse, indirect, directionally constant, and bluish in color. North windows, however, release heat in winter, with none of the compensating heat gain of windows that face the sun. To conserve energy, you can devise insulating curtains, shutters, or panels to cover windows when they're not in use.

Fenestration

Side windows (windows set in the lower wall) provide ventilation, a view, and daylight. But the light from them may not penetrate very far into the room, and the windows can be a source of glare.

Clerestory windows (windows high in the wall) can be added to let daylight fully illuminate a room. There are formulas for calculating the optimal relationship between the size and configuration of side wall windows, and the clerestory's size, setback from the window wall, angle, and height above the floor to provide the desired interior light levels (see Callender, *Time-Saver Standards*).

Skylights: Skylights have many advantages: they don't take up wall space, their light can fully penetrate a room, they provide up to twice the il-

THE AMOUNT OF DAYLIGHT WHICH ENTERS A ROOM DEPENDS ON:

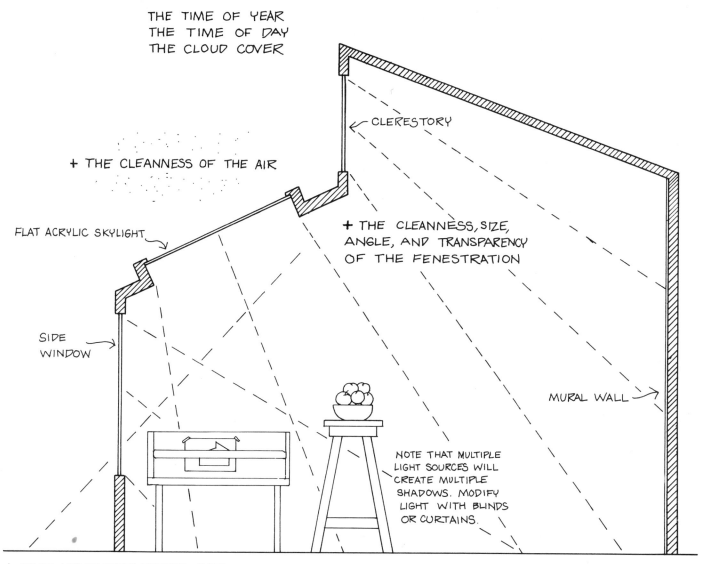

THE TIME OF YEAR
THE TIME OF DAY
THE CLOUD COVER

+ THE CLEANNESS OF THE AIR

CLERESTORY

FLAT ACRYLIC SKYLIGHT

+ THE CLEANNESS, SIZE, ANGLE, AND TRANSPARENCY OF THE FENESTRATION

SIDE WINDOW

MURAL WALL

NOTE THAT MULTIPLE LIGHT SOURCES WILL CREATE MULTIPLE SHADOWS. MODIFY LIGHT WITH BLINDS OR CURTAINS.

+ THE LIGHT REFLECTED OFF THE GROUND

Daylighting.

lumination of comparable vertical windows, they don't create glare, and, if set in a roof that slopes 30 to 60 degrees, their light issues at an angle that produces the clearest modeling for realistic painting. But, skylights can be a chronic source of leaks; they often cost more than other fenestration; and, because hot air rises, they lose more heat than comparable vertical windows. Large circular or squarish skylights are, from an illumination standpoint, preferable to small or elongated ones, because the former reduce fatiguing dark/light contrast.

Skylights function like a local light source, e.g., a light bulb, and not like the sky itself. Their light attenuates as distance increases. That is to say, when you climb a ladder to a skylight or light bulb, the light becomes stronger; when you climb a ladder outside, you can detect no change in light strength.

Architects have tables for determining the fenestration size, shape, construction, angle, cleanness, orientation, and height above the floor necessary to produce a desired light level. One computation posits the sky as a uniform light source of known brightness. Thus, if you design for light admission adequate for the late afternoon of an overcast day in December, you can predict that in 42 degree north latitude (the vicinity of Providence, RI), for example, the sky will be brighter 85 percent of the time, twice brighter 50 percent of the time, and thrice brighter 5 percent of the time. The remaining 15 percent (when the sky will be duller than the constant) may require supplementary artificial illumination.

A CLEAR SKYLIGHT WITHIN THE 30°-60° RANGE...

60°

30°

PRODUCES THE CLEAREST MODELLING FOR REALISTIC PAINTING.

TRANSLUCENT SKYLIGHTS DIFFUSE THE LIGHT...

PRODUCING DIFFUSE MODELLING.

Skylights and modelling.

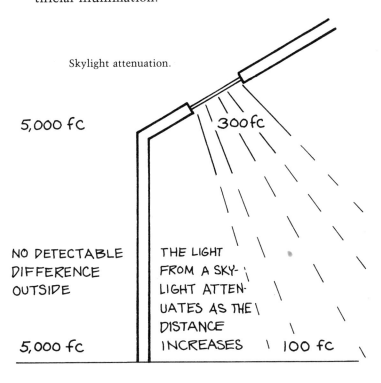

Skylight attenuation.

5,000 fc

300 fc

NO DETECTABLE DIFFERENCE OUTSIDE

THE LIGHT FROM A SKYLIGHT ATTENUATES AS THE DISTANCE INCREASES

5,000 fc

100 fc

If you don't want to get that technical, look for a skylight in a studio or other room comparable to your own studio in size and reflectance, and then duplicate the skylight, modifying its configuration as you see fit. Or, measure the light admitted through a north side window and calculate that a similar-size north skylight will let in twice the light if the day is clear, and two-and-a-half times the light if the day is cloudy. Thus, for example, if you get a reading of 100 fc six feet from your window on a sunny day, you may assume that a similar-size skylight will deliver 200 fc on that same day.

Skylight Types

Plastic domes: Lightweight, clear, easy to install and trouble free, plastic-dome skylights come in a wide variety of styles and shapes and are the most popular skylight for domestic use. They are more expensive than homemade varieties, and like any acrylic, they scratch easily. They consist of an extruded metal frame and one or more curved acrylic sheets (the additional sheets eliminate condensation and add insulation) set on a curb built into the roof.

Metal skylights: Metal skylights are custom made in a wide number of patterns by sheet-metal shops, roofers, and skylight specialists. Their framing is of galvanized steel or aluminum, and the "lights" (panels or panes) are of either ¼-inch wired glass (which is heavy and sometimes subject to cracking), other types of safety glass, or plastic.

Flat acrylic skylights: A flat acrylic skylight (one or two sheets of acrylic set in a curb in a sloping roof) is the least expensive skylight and reasonably easy to build. We have a 4- by 8-foot unit similar to the one illustrated, built several years ago for less than $300, that has served perfectly. Note that the design avoids piercing the acrylic with fasteners; in fact, fasteners are not recommended. You can add additional interior bracing, or use your roof joists, to support large sheets, as the plastic isn't very stiff.

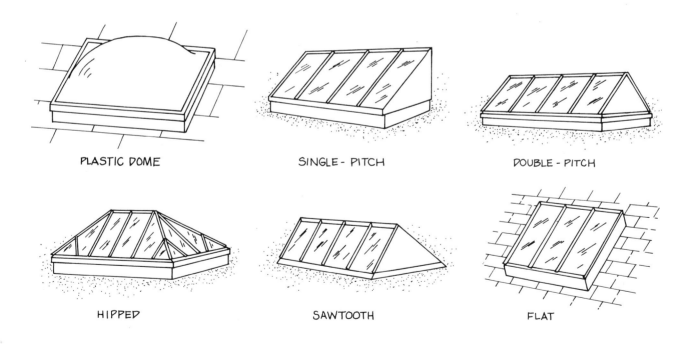

PLASTIC DOME   SINGLE - PITCH   DOUBLE - PITCH

HIPPED   SAWTOOTH   FLAT

Skylight types.

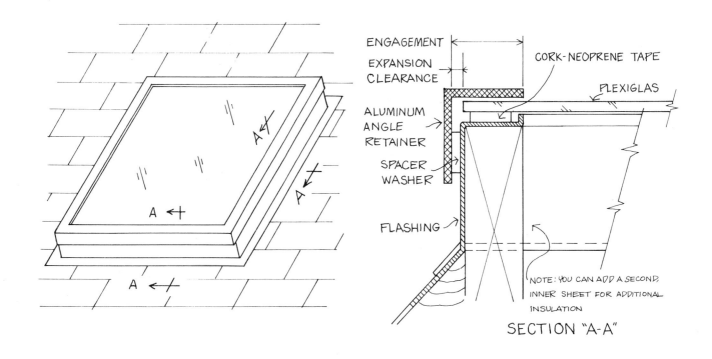

SLOPING FLAT SHEET APPLICATION

ASPECT RATIO = 1				ASPECT RATIO = 2				ASPECT RATIO = 3				ENGAGEMENT	EXPANSION CLEARANCE	
LIGHT SIZE	LIVE LOAD p.s.f.		DEFLECT. *	LIGHT SIZE	LIVE LOAD p.s.f.		DEFLECT. *	LIGHT SIZE	LIVE LOAD p.s.f.		DEFLECT. *		PLEXIGLAS SPAN	CLEARANCE **
	40	30	20			40	30	20		40	30	20			

(Table - "1" (INCHES) PLEXIGLAS THICKNESS)

ASPECT RATIO = 1 LIGHT SIZE	40	30	20	DEFLECT.*	ASPECT RATIO = 2 LIGHT SIZE	40	30	20	DEFLECT.*	ASPECT RATIO = 3 LIGHT SIZE	40	30	20	DEFLECT.*	ENGAGEMENT	PLEXIGLAS SPAN	CLEARANCE **
48 x 48	.187	.187	.187	$1/2$	24 x 48	.187	.187	.187	$3/16$	16 x 48	.187	.187	.187	$1/16$	1	24	$1/16$
60 x 60	.187	.187	.187	$3/4$	30 x 60	.187	.187	.187	$3/8$	20 x 60	.187	.187	.187	$1/8$	1	36	$1/8$
72 x 72	.250	.250	.187	1	36 x 72	.250	.250	.187	$5/8$	24 x 72	.250	.187	.187	$1/4$	1	48	$1/8$
84 x 84	.375	.375	.250	$1\,1/4$	42 x 84	.312	.250	.250	$3/4$	28 x 84	.250	.250	.187	$3/8$	1	60	$3/16$
96 x 96	.500	.500	.375	$1\,1/2$	48 x 96	.312	.312	.250	1	32 x 96	.312	.250	.250	$1/2$	1	72	$3/16$
108 x108	.625	.625	.500	$1\,5/8$	54 x108	.375	.312	.250	$1\,1/4$	36 x108	.375	.312	.250	$5/8$	$1\,1/8$	84	$3/16$
120 x120	.750	.750	.625	$1\,7/8$	60 x120	.375	.375	.312	$1\,3/8$	40 x120	.375	.312	.250	$7/8$	$1\,1/8$	96	$1/4$
																108	$1/4$
																120	$5/16$

* MAXIMUM LONG TERM DEFLECTION DUE TO WEIGHT OF PLEXIGLAS MATERIAL ONLY.
** CUT PLEXIGLAS SHORTER THAN ACTUAL SKYLIGHT FRAME DIMENSION BY THE AMOUNT INDICATED.

TABLE -"1" PLEXIGLAS SHEET THICKNESS SELECTION IS BASED ON TOTAL DEFLECTION UNDER UNIFORM LIVE LOAD LIMITED TO 5% OF THE SHORT SIDE, OR 3", WHICHEVER IS SMALLER.

A plan for a flat acrylic skylight (recommended for use between 6° and 75° roof pitch). (Adapted from Rohm and Haas drawing #1006, sheet application data courtesy Rohm and Haas)

150

Avoid the cheaper corrugated or flat reinforced fiberglass panels (Filon is one brand name), which color and impede the light. They also diffuse it, which may, or may not, be an advantage.

Artificial Light

Until you've seen a simultaneous demonstration, you can scarcely appreciate the vast differences between artificial light sources. General Electric at Nela Park in Cleveland, OH, Sylvania in their Danvers, MA, lighting center, and Lightolier in their Manhattan showroom display adjacent, diversely illuminated white painted alcoves that contain identical, multicolored samples. Viewed side by side, the color differences of the samples under the various lights are remarkable, but even more so are the walls of the booths seen obliquely so that they line up like fanned cards. The whites—dingy blue-gray under the cool-white fluorescent, cotton-candy pink under the warm-white fluorescent, sunny warm under the tungsten halogen, or jaundiced under the incandescent—are eloquent. See one of the exhibits if you can (call in advance for an appointment).

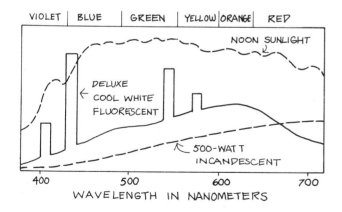

The relative spectra noon sunlight, deluxe cool-white fluorescent, and 500-watt incandescent (adapted from General Electric, *Light and Color*).

Incandescent

Incandescent lamps are easy to install, and the fixtures and bulbs cost less initially than fluorescents. They provide a point source of light readily adaptable to most architectural treatments, and a wide range of bulb types and wattages that will fit one standardized socket. Their color temperature is decidedly yellow, normally averaging about 3000 K, but we have come to consider incandescent light as standard for artificial illumination, probably because it was introduced first and through decades of use has become familiar.

For economy, you may wish to use incandescents primarily for supplemental and accent lighting (where their greater flexibility will be most advantageous) and use the more efficient, diffuse fluorescents for ambient lighting. If you mix the two, keep them at distinctly different levels to avoid a clash in color temperatures. Quartz-halogen (tungsten-halogen) lamps, although initially more expensive than conventional incandescents, provide a cleaner, purer white light that remains uniform over the 4,000 or so hours of their normal life. These qualities have led to their acceptance for general museum illumination. A good all-around lamp is the 250-W PAR-38 quartz-halogen flood or spot. PAR stands for "parabolic aluminized reflector," and the 38 indicates the size, which is expressed in one-eighths of an inch at the lamp's maximum diameter; i.e., 38 one-eighth-inch units or 4¾ inches.

Fluorescent

Fluorescent tubes are more efficient than incandescents: they yield three to four times more light per watt, last seven to ten times longer, and produce far less heat. However, they are less flexible, adapt less readily to architecture, sometimes hum and flicker, and the *luminaires* (the complete lighting unit: tube, socket, and fixture) are initially more expensive.

Fixtures are important for assuring efficient, glare-free illumination. *Parabolic reflector luminaires* deliver the maximum amount of light in the nonglare zone, which occurs 30 to 60 degrees from the vertical. The direct rays of the 1- to 30-degree zone cause veiling reflections, and the oblique rays of the 60- to 90-degree zone cause direct glare. For comparison, strip or industrial luminaires are about 200 times brighter than the surrounding ceiling; parabolic luminaires are only one-and-a-half to two times brighter. Unfortunately, quality fixtures are quite expensive, and unless you are contemplating public display space, strip or industrial reflector fixtures will suffice. If glare is a problem, shift your work around and wear a hat or eyeshade.

There are two considerations in tube selection: the *color temperature*—how warm or cool the light is—and the *color rendition*—the selective enhancement of colors caused by the tube's particular pattern of spectral energy distribution. Two tubes may look the same, i.e., have the same color temperature, but produce entirely different color renditions.

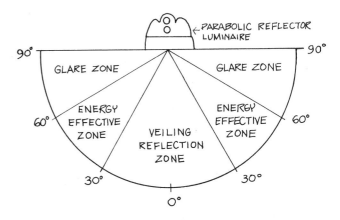

Parabolic reflector luminaire with the glare, energy effective, and veiling reflection zones marked (adapted from Lightolier, *Recessed Fluorescent Lighting*)

COLOR EFFECTS OF ARTIFICIAL LIGHT SOURCES

	Correlated Color Temperature	Apparent Tint Given White Surface	Blue	Green	Red
Daylight Fluorescent	6500°K	Light Blue	Cools, enhances	Brightens, imparts blue hue	Greys, dulls, imparts violet hue
Design White Fluorescent	5200	Slight Blue	Enhances, appears crisp	Brightens, cools	Enhances, crisp color
Cool White Fluorescent	4300	Slight Blue	Slightly greys or darkens	Greys, except blue-greens	Greys and darkens
Deluxe Cool White Fluorescent	4100	None	Lighter, clearer, cooler	Clear, light	Clear, rich, vibrant
White Fluorescent	3500	Slight Yellow	Greys darker shades, clears lighter shades	Bright, clear, slightly yellow hue	Dulls darker shades, yellows lighter shades
Warm White Fluorescent	3050	Light Yellow	Clear, rich	Light shades bright and clear	Light shades clear, bright
1000 Watt Incandescent Tungsten Halogen	3000	Light Yellow	Yellowish hue, dulls, darkens	Dark shades warmed, darkens, yellow hue	Slight yellowing of bright reds. Enhances
Deluxe Warm White Fluorescent	2950	Slight Yellow	Warms, deepens	Deepens, enriches, warms	Bright, rich
100 Watt Incandescent	2870	Light Orange	Dulls, darkens	Darkens, brownish hue	Enhances

(Courtesy GTE Sylvania)

No consensus exists on the choice of an ideal fluorescent for artists' use, in part because there can be no definitive color temperature for natural light, and because color preference is so personal—one artist might fancy a color rendition disdained by another. You may be happy with Deluxe Cool White, which, according to GE, gives the best overall color rendition of the standard tubes; but if you're particular, investigate those tubes especially designed for critical situations like museums, art studios, and photo labs. These include GE's Chroma 75 and Duro-Test's Color Classer, both of which match the 7500 K of north skylights; the Verilux tube used by the New York Met and other museums, which measures 6200 K, (close to the International Commission on Illumination [C.I.E.] 6500 K standard for perfect daylight—a June day at noon with a slight overcast); GE's Chroma 50 and Westinghouse's 5000 K Ultralume, both of which match midsummer noon daylight; and Sylvania's Natural White at 3684 K. All claim to deliver optimum color balance, but any of these should be a significant improvement over standard tubes, such as daylight, cool white, natural white, white, warm white, or deluxe warm white, which tint white and falsify colors.

Fluorescent light, as does sunlight, produces ultraviolent emissions that can fade or deteriorate susceptible materials like some paints and textiles. If you have projects that will expose vulnerable materials to fluorescents for an extended period, say in excess of six months (or even less in some cases), you should consider either installing UV screening filters on your luminaires, or using a non-UV-emitting tube, such as the Verilux VLX/M.

All luminaires decrease in efficiency with time because of the accumulation of dirt, which can cut light by as much as 20 or 30 percent, and the gradual deterioration of the tubes or bulbs. To maintain maximum output, keep your luminaires clean, and don't wait until they burn out to change them. You can tell when to change a light by either following the schedule supplied by the manufacturer or by measuring the light's output when you first install the tubes or bulbs and then replacing them when it drops 20 percent.

Task Lighting

We can distinguish at least five task-lighting situations: (1) ambient or overall lighting, (2) desk work, e.g., drawing, drafting, and jewelry making, (3) table-height work, e.g., preparing materials, painting, weaving, potting, (4) diagonal and vertical work, e.g., easel painting, sculpture, vertical weaving, and (5) mural walls. Ambient lighting in the range of 100 to 200 fc or more supplied by combinations and artificial light should suffice for situations 1, 2, 3, and 4. Where the ambient level is insufficient for a particular task, you can supplement the lighting with auxiliary artificial lights or skylighting.

Lighting a mural wall can be the greatest challenge because of the need for uniform illumination, with neither hot spots nor shadow pockets. The optimum angle of the light source should be 30 degrees from the vertical: a lesser angle will rake the surface and emphasize its irregularities; a greater angle can cause reflections and cast your shadow. For daylighting, you can use a strip of either skylights or clerestory windows. For artificial light, consider two-tube fluorescent industrial reflector fixtures hung in a continuous strip along the length of the wall and aimed roughly at its midpoint. The continuous strip will avoid the dead spots of intermittent fixtures, and the double tubes will minimize the top-to-bottom fall-off that may occur at lower light levels. You may want to angle the luminaires to the wall slightly and build a baffle in front of them to bounce more light onto the wall and reduce glare in the room. Incandescents, because they are point sources, will not be as satisfactory—it will be hard to blend them smoothly even with well-designed wall-washer units, and the many lights will create multiple shadows.

Contact a GE regional office (of which there are forty or so around the country), your local utility, or your lighting fixture supplier for assistance in determining your specific light needs.

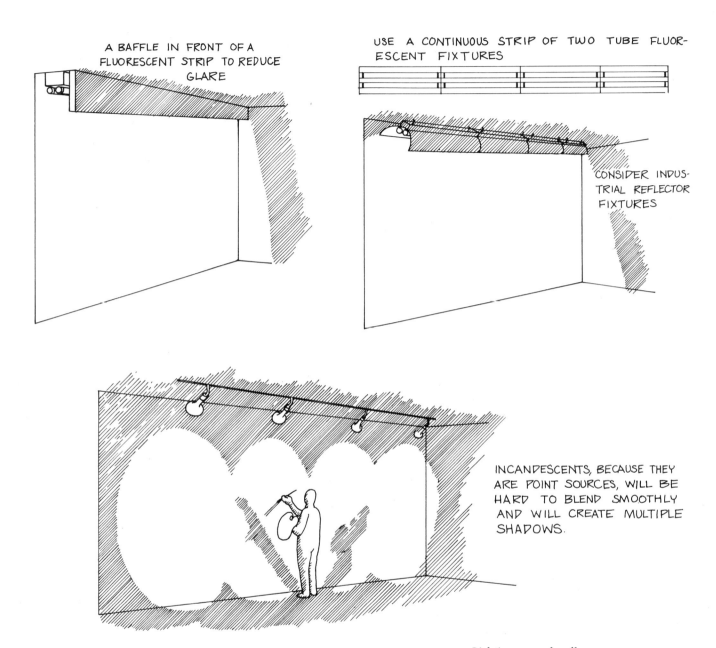

A BAFFLE IN FRONT OF A FLUORESCENT STRIP TO REDUCE GLARE

USE A CONTINUOUS STRIP OF TWO TUBE FLUORESCENT FIXTURES

CONSIDER INDUSTRIAL REFLECTOR FIXTURES

INCANDESCENTS, BECAUSE THEY ARE POINT SOURCES, WILL BE HARD TO BLEND SMOOTHLY AND WILL CREATE MULTIPLE SHADOWS.

Lighting a mural wall.

Studio Equipment

Easels: If you do large or heavy work, buy a sturdy, adjustable studio easel with a screw-wind raising mechanism. The large easels grow quite tall when fully raised, so if your ceilings are low, check the final height to make sure you have clearance. If you do exceptionally wide work (in excess of say six feet) you may need two easels to support it, and a second easel is useful for holding a mirror for self-portraits or for painting two pictures simultaneously. A rigid, lightweight wood or aluminum portable easel is useful if you work outdoors. Always test an easel, whenever possible, before you buy it.

Taborets: You can make a very serviceable taboret out of an old kitchen base cabinet. Enlarge the top with a piece of plywood if you wish, and add a set of wheels so you can roll it where needed. Use the drawers for storing paint, mediums, and brushes, and the top for cans of brushes, jars of mediums and cleaner, and palettes. You can hang oversize palettes and tools from the taboret's sides as well.

Scaffolding: For low work, use a strong, flat seated chair, a stepping stool, or make yourself a step platform. For higher work, use an *extension plank* (matchsticks) made of extensible interlocked pieces of wood or a rigid *scaffold plank.* Ordinary

A taboret adapted from an old kitchen base cabinet.

boards are too limber unless they are supported at frequent intervals or braced at their edges. Set the plank on a matched pair of heavy-duty wooden ladders. A pail shelf on the ladder may be handy, but it can get in the way of the plank. An *extension trestle ladder*, a step-type ladder with an extendable central ladder, will let you increase your scaffold height without commensurately increasing that of the step ladders.

Other Requirements

A deep laundry tub or janitorial sink with a water-resistant shelf on the side for storing wet equipment will be desirable. If you work with materials like plaster that can clog your pipes, ask a plumber about special traps and settling basins. If the studio shares a house septic system and you're using noxious solvents that can kill its essential microorganisms, you may require a separate system for the studio.

Plan for enough electric service for your present and anticipated power needs. Separate circuits for lighting and heavy-duty power equipment will help to keep your lights on when the equipment breakers trip. Locate outlets close to task areas to avoid extension cords as much as possible. You can install strip outlets where you'll be using a lot of equipment. Mount them along the ceiling to keep the wiring off the floor, and, if you wish, hang a cord reel to retrieve and store the wire when it's not in use.

An exhaust fan set high on the wall or over the activity location is essential if you work with harmful fumes. If you're using air-conditioning, remember that a closed system will not remove fumes, only recirculate them; you'll need to bring in fresh air and cool it.

North-lit studios with expanses of windows and skylights are energy inefficient in cold climates in the winter time. You may want to consider south, east, or west facing windows, which can be blocked off when the studio is not in use, for passive solar collectors, or active solar collectors on the ground or roof.

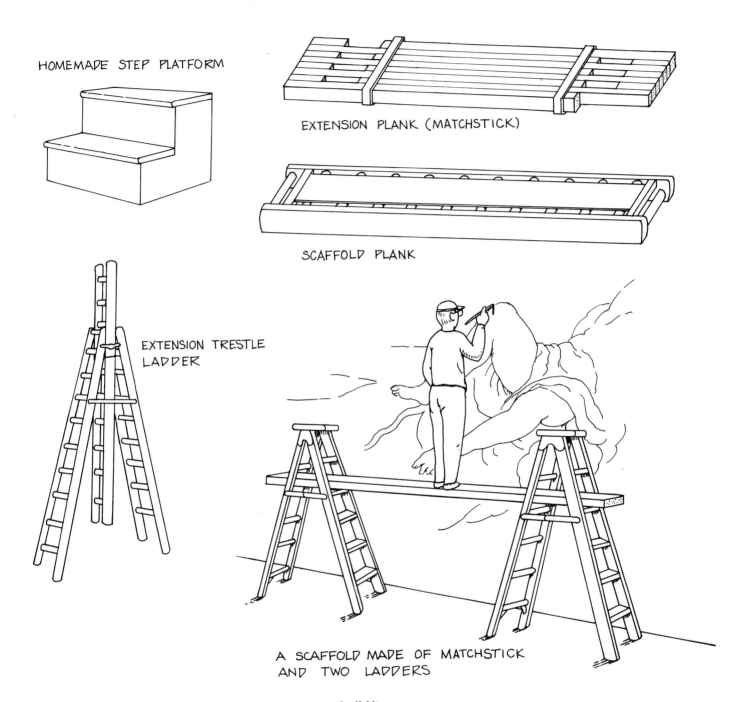

HOMEMADE STEP PLATFORM

EXTENSION PLANK (MATCHSTICK)

SCAFFOLD PLANK

EXTENSION TRESTLE LADDER

A SCAFFOLD MADE OF MATCHSTICK AND TWO LADDERS

Scaffolding.

Workshop

A workshop is always handy, but it's essential if you're going to make your own frames, boxes, bases, and stretchers, and perform routine maintenance. You may wish to locate it in your studio (for craftspeople and sculptors, the workshop and studio may be one and the same), but if you're a painter, you may object to sawdust and debris collecting on your wet paint.

Some workshop considerations are:

Convenience: It should be close to the studio to minimize transferring tools and materials.

Access: It should be accessible for delivery trucks, heavy equipment, and bulky supplies like sheets of plywood, crates, and lengths of lumber.

Utilities: It should have necessary water, electricity, phone, and heat. A separate electric box with a disconnect switch is a good idea. Four 15- to 20-ampere circuits should be sufficient, and heavy-duty equipment will need 240-volt service. Space electrical outlets every six feet if possible, and add strip circuits or a multioutlet strip at the workbench for hand power tools. Make sure that whatever you do conforms to the local codes. Reflecting light fixtures and light-colored, reflective surfaces will reduce the foot-candles needed.

Ventilation: You should have adequate ventilation to remove fumes and dust.

Size: In general, 10 by 12 feet is a minimum for a separate shop, but much depends on the room's proportions, your equipment, the traffic pattern, and the functions performed there.

Layout

Make cutouts of your equipment and do a layout on paper to at least ½" = 1' scale. Think through typical jobs and place the equipment in their best relationships: for example, lumber will come from the storage rack, go through the power saw, and on to the workbench or sawhorses. Assign storage close to the task area—hand tools near the workbench, saw blades by the saw. Allow sufficient space around each power tool, e.g., a saw or planer will need a lot of room at either end to feed and remove lumber; a drill press requires but a few feet on three sides. Mounting equipment on lockable wheels allows it to be stored against the walls and rolled to a cleared space in the room or outside for use.

An outside workplace is a blessing, especially when it comes to messy chores like sanding, sawing, and priming. A level concrete pad works best; minimize the threshold between it and the shop or you'll have trouble maneuvering your equipment over it.

The Workbench

The workbench is your center of activity. You can build or buy them new; often you can find good used benches. (I have a run of butcher-block-topped kitchen cabinets that work quite nicely.) The height of the workbench will depend on how tall you are and will be a compromise between the height for those activities like nailing and planing (which should be about waist high for leverage, comfort, and safety) and close work like soldering and gluing (which would be more conveniently done higher up). A height of 32 to 34 inches is average, but try out some tables, kitchen counters, or benches in schools or shops to gauge the best size for you. Surface the top with hardwood or yellow pine, linoleum, masonite, or plywood. A flush base will be a great help in keeping things clean, but allow an open place for a chair or stool. Large work is always a problem for benches set against a wall. One alternative is to position the bench in the middle of the floor either permanently or on lockable wheels. Another alternative is to supplement the bench with sawhorses.

Accessories

You'll want to mount a sturdy *mechanic's vise* somewhere along your bench. A corner is handy if you have clearance around it. Select a vise with at least a 3½" opening and with both regular and pipe jaws, which you can cover with wood or masonite to protect your work. Bolt-on vises are more rigid, but clamp-on or vacuum bases will allow you to remove the vise for storage. A *woodworking vise* that mounts on the edge of the bench is convenient for holding wood for sawing, planing, and carving.

Sawhorses are invaluable as supports for painting, sawing, sanding, and assembly. You can build them from scratch, use readymade metal brackets to assemble them, or buy metal sawhorses or a multipurpose device like Black and Decker's ''Workmate,'' a combination vise and sawhorse. For delicate work like framing, cover the top with carpet rolled over the edges and attached from underneath. Heights can be 24 inches for sawing, 29 inches for painting, sanding, and assembly, and 36 inches for measuring-table bases. Try to have most of your sawhorses the same height so you can use them together for large jobs that need a number of horses. Storage can be a problem. Keep the cross supports up high so the horses can be stacked, or use fold-up models or those that can be disassembled.

A *backstand* is convenient for supporting long work for the saw and planer. Have it adjustable to accommodate machinery of different heights.

Hand Tools

Unless you have careless or sticky-fingered employees, buy good tools the first time around. Look for quality materials, superior finishes, and close tolerances for long life and satisfactory performance. More money usually buys a better product, but sometimes it only buys silly gimmickry. Get recommendations from a case-hardened tool nut or a reputable dealer. The following is a quick list of some basic tools:

Hammers: A solid 13- or 16-ounce rim-tempered claw hammer with a metal, wood, or fiberglass shaft is good for all-around use. As needed, add specialty hammers like tack hammers for driving light nails and brads. A 1- or 1¼-pound rubber mallet is just the thing for banging together stretchers and hammering down paint can lids.

Nail sets: Purchase them either as a set or as needed for driving finishing nails below wood surfaces, e.g., setting picture-frame nails.

Saws: Hand sawing requires considerable skill. There are two basic types of hand saws—*rip saws*, for cutting with the grain, and *cross-cut saws*, for cutting against the grain. *Back saws*, which have a rectangular profile, are used for cabinetry work, like cutting picture-frame moldings. *Hack saws*, which consist of an adjustable metal frame, are used for straight metal cutting.

Screwdrivers: Buy a set of *standard* (slotted) and *Phillips head* screwdrivers or acquire them as needed. Match the screwdriver to the screw size to avoid damaging the screw or the work. *Cabinet-tip* screwdrivers have a straight shaft, without the flare at the blade, to fit into tight holes. *Spiral-ratchet screwdrivers*, which are used for quantity work, have forward, reverse, and rigid settings, and a chuck for changing bits.

Pliers: Lineman's pliers, which have side cutters for wire cutting, or adjustable *slip-joint pliers* are good for general purposes. Use *long-nose pliers* for fine work and wire bending; *lockjaw pliers* (plier wrenches) for locking parts in a firmer grip or holding work to protect your hands when grinding or hammering; and adjustable *channel pliers* (pump pliers) for holding large objects and squeezing brads into picture frame backs.

Adjustable wrench: A 6- to 9-inch adjustable wrench is handy for tightening nuts and bolts. Sets of *Allen wrenches*, *open-end wrenches*, and *box wrenches* will complete your ensemble.

Measuring devices: Buy a 12-foot or longer steel tape, 3/4 inch wide, stiff enough not to buckle when you measure vertically. A metric scale on one side will prepare you for the future and make computations like division easier for the present. Use a 50- or 100-foot tape for measuring large sites and for murals. You may also want to carry a small tape in your car or briefcase for impromptu measurements. A *folding wood rule* with a 6-inch metal extension is useful for making exact measurements across open spaces like doors or frame openings; the *combination square* is useful for testing squareness, marking 45-degree angles, and measuring, and as a marking gauge; and the *rafter square*, for testing

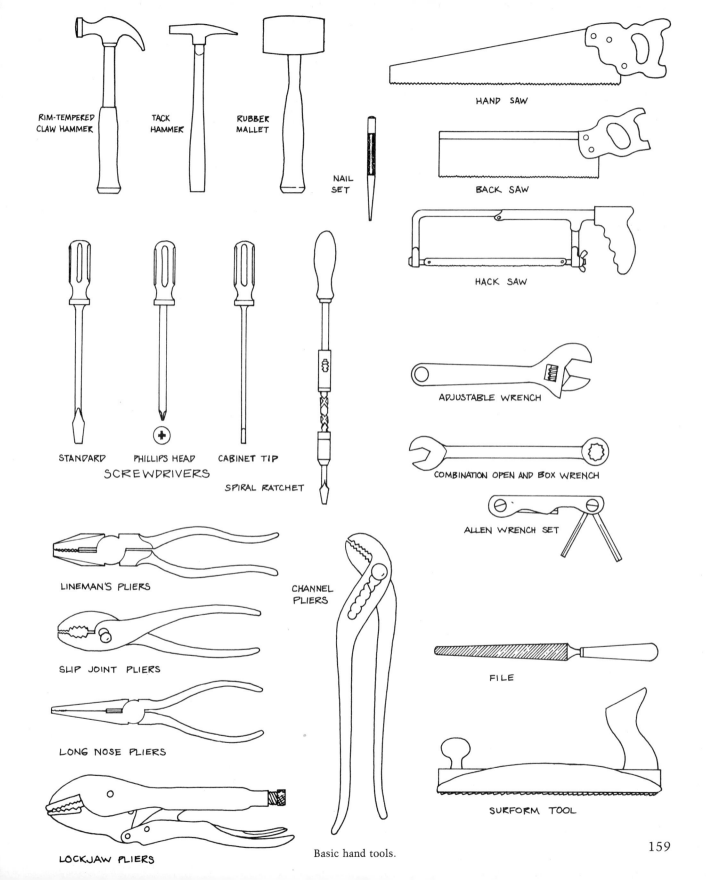

RIM-TEMPERED
CLAW HAMMER

TACK
HAMMER

RUBBER
MALLET

NAIL
SET

HAND SAW

BACK SAW

HACK SAW

STANDARD

PHILLIPS HEAD

CABINET TIP

SCREWDRIVERS

SPIRAL RATCHET

ADJUSTABLE WRENCH

COMBINATION OPEN AND BOX WRENCH

ALLEN WRENCH SET

LINEMAN'S PLIERS

SLIP JOINT PLIERS

LONG NOSE PLIERS

LOCKJAW PLIERS

CHANNEL
PLIERS

FILE

SURFORM TOOL

Basic hand tools.

159

frames, canvases, and panels for squareness. Use the short *torpedo level* for routine work, the *line level* hung on a string for long spans, and the long *mason's level* for mural work.

Files: Used for removing material, files come in a variety of lengths, cross sections, tooth patterns, and roughness. Often sold without a handle, you can either buy a handle, or fashion one from a dowel or a corn cob. The *Surform tool*, a nonclogging plane/file combination, is good for the fast removal of wood and other soft materials.

Clamps: Essential for holding parts together for assembly, you can start with a selection of metal *C-clamps* or *adjustable bar clamps*, and add wooden *hand screws*, *pipe clamps*, *spring clamps*, and *miter clamps* as needed.

Sandpaper: Sandpaper comes in a wide assortment of grades, abrasives, and backings; select the right combination for the job. You'll get your best price at a volume paint or hardware store that sells the paper in bulk, rather than in prepackaged units. Use sandpaper with a rubber sanding block.

Safety equipment: Don't be a hero. Protect your

More basic hand tools.

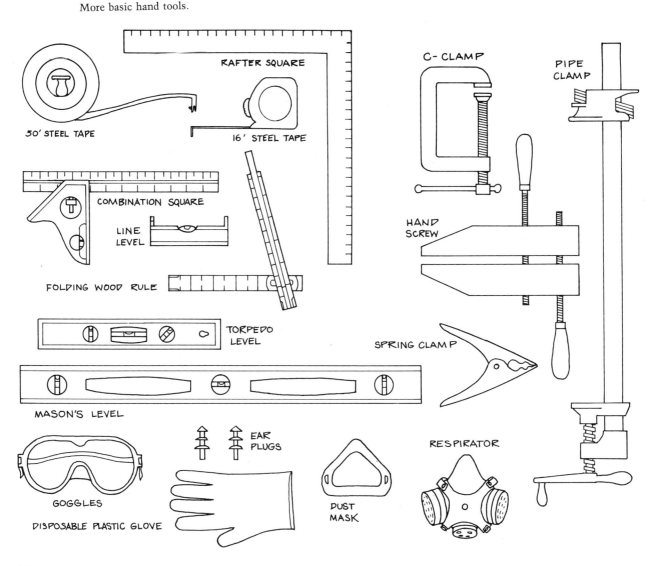

RAFTER SQUARE

50' STEEL TAPE

16' STEEL TAPE

COMBINATION SQUARE

LINE LEVEL

FOLDING WOOD RULE

TORPEDO LEVEL

MASON'S LEVEL

GOGGLES

DISPOSABLE PLASTIC GLOVE

EAR PLUGS

DUST MASK

C-CLAMP

PIPE CLAMP

HAND SCREW

SPRING CLAMP

RESPIRATOR

eyes with *goggles* or a *safety shield* when using power equipment, hammering brittle materials, or grinding; protect your ears with *ear plugs* or *ear muffs* when using noisy power tools; your hands with *rubber gloves* or *disposable plastic gloves* when working with irritating substances; and your respiratory tract with a *dust mask* when sanding in close quarters or a *respirator* when using noxious solvents or creating metal fumes. (A respirator is no substitute for a mask with a separate air supply for especially hazardous substances or rooms with inadequate ventilation.)

Power Equipment

Power tools have dropped in price over the years, so that now many are competitive with their hand-tool equivalents. Some electric drills, for example, cost no more than good-quality hand drills. Power tools allow the amateur to accomplish quickly and easily tasks like sawing, routing, and planing that were once the exclusive preserve of experienced professionals.

Buy tools as you need them, considering your current requirements along with features that you may want in the future. Before making a purchase, you may want to perform a job a few times to see if a power tool really would help, and you may try to borrow or rent one for a trial (remember, however, that rental tools are often in scabrous condition).

As a general rule, you get what you pay for. More money buys longer life, a larger motor, better bearings, more features, and finer finishes. You won't require a high-quality tool's performance for infrequent or quick jobs, and sometimes you may want to make an inexpensive stopgap purchase when you know that an improved version soon to come on the market will supercede it. Multipurpose tools can save money and space, but this saving may be offset by the time it takes to switch the accessories around, the break in the work rhythm caused by the switching, and the fact that no multipurpose tool does individual tasks as well as equipment designed specifically for that one purpose.

When I first started buying power tools, I would doggedly quiz acquaintances and conscientiously scrutinize *Consumer Reports*. Now, however, I have consolidated my purchases to a single manufacturer for four main reasons: I can buy from one or a few stores rather than search the town; I can get all my equipment serviced in one location for a predictable price; the tools are dependable and compatible and the controls and directions similar; and if I move up the line, I have a good idea of what I'll be getting. You, of course, can buy from whomever you choose. I happen to buy from Black and Decker (B & D), which is not only located in my area (so I can call headquarters if I have a question) but is also the world's largest portable-tool manufacturer with over one hundred service centers in the United States. B & D produces four lines of tools: ''Great Buy'' (green case), which are excellent values perfectly adequate for intermittent use; ''Value-Plus'' (orange case), better quality with step-up features; ''Best'' (gold case), the top of the home-use line; and ''Trade'' (gray case), industrial quality for continuous use. Look for B & D's frequent sales or stop in one of their service centers for bargains in reconditioned tools that have been returned under warranty.

Drills: If you're going to buy only one power tool, it should be the versatile electric drill, adaptable to grind, polish, sand, screw, and mix paint. A 3/8'' variable-speed, reversing drill will provide sufficient power and features for most jobs. If you'll be drilling into rock, cement, or masonry, consider a combination drill/hammer drill. The percussive action of the hammer/drill option removes masonry-type materials far more efficiently than carbide bits used with an electric drill. Use twist drills for drilling wood and metal, carbide drills for masonry and concrete, plastic drills for plastics, screwdrills for pilot screw holes in wood, and spade bits to bore large, fast holes in wood. Finishing nails make cheap, nonbreakable bits for small holes. A polishing and sanding kit and paint mixer are two useful accessories. A vertical stand for converting the drill for use as a drill press is not worth buying. They don't work well.

Jig saws: If you only want one power saw, make it a jig saw. They're pretty safe, and while primarily used for cutting curves, they also will cut straight lines, but by no means as well as a circular saw. Two-speed or variable-speed options let you choose the best speed for the job. Trade machines can cut faster and handle thicker sections of wood. Quality blades saw more quickly and last longer, provided you don't force or twist them. Dozens of blade styles are available; match the blade to the job.

Finishing sanders: Finishing sanders greatly expedite finish sanding. Newer models, which use a half sheet of sandpaper, cover 50 percent more area than the old one-third sheet machines. B & D's trade sander combines high speed (10,000 orbits per minute) with one-half-sheet capacity for extra-fast removal. Dust-collector bags are a help, as are hose attachments to vacuum cleaners, but the latter can be awkward because they drag across the work.

Belt sanders: For really fast straight-line wood removal, belt sanders are best. They churn up a lot of dust, so a dust-collector bag is a must.

Disc sanders and polishers: Use disc sanders and polishers for fast sanding and polishing. The two machines are similar, but the polisher operates at 2400 rpm, and the sander at 4000 rpm. To be efficient, combination machines must offer both speeds with no loss in torque.

Circular saws: Circular saws are invaluable for cutting large sheets of material. Straight cuts are not difficult with practice and a sharp blade. Again, match the blade to the job. The new smaller, 5½-inch models are still large enough to handle lumber and plywood. The standard 7¼-inch models are heavier and cut faster.

Routers: Use the router for cutting decorative edges and trim, and dadoes. For most purposes, one-half horsepower is satisfactory. The bits are quite expensive, because they must be made of high-grade steel, or carbide-tipped, since resharpening would destroy their profile.

Radial-arm saws: The radial-arm saw is an excellent multipurpose machine for cross cutting, ripping, and mitering. With attachments, it can drill, sand, and polish as well. But don't expect miracles of it: some attachments may be ineffectual, and, with age and use, the radial-arm saw itself will become progressively less accurate for precision work like cutting picture-frame molding.

Power miter boxes: Power miter boxes are designed for one purpose: to cut accurate miters. As such, they do a far better job of mitering picture-frame molding than the more versatile table and radial-arm saws.

Vacuum cleaners: You'll want a shop vacuum to pick up sawdust and other mess. The wet-and-dry machines can suction both liquids and solids, but the dry-only machines have bigger hoses that will pull in larger debris. You can often couple them to dust-producing machinery like saws to suck in the dust as it's generated. Smaller canister machines take up less space.

Storage for Shop and Studio

Efficient storage is always a challenge. Plan for it from the very first to save time, loss, and duplicate purchases. Used kitchen cabinets (which you can often locate through advertisements, acquaintances, or builders) work well. They're neat, functional, relatively inexpensive, and keep out the dust. Look for cabinets with lots of drawers, preferably hung on roller tracks. Place them as you would in a kitchen, with the top cabinets at a convenient height above the bottom ones to allow room to work under them, and, if you wish, to hang things from them. Store items near where you'll be using them, and keep the heavier objects in the bottom cabinets for ease and safety. For small tools like screwdrivers, files, and chisels, you can mount racks, spring clips, or magnetic strips to the inside of the doors, taking care to allow sufficient clearance for closing. Put the most frequently used items in the front of the drawers, and if you wish to separate them, build dividers or use the dividers designed for holding kitchen utensils or silverware. You can fasten screw-top glass jars to the undersides of the top cabinets by attaching the lids with two screws.

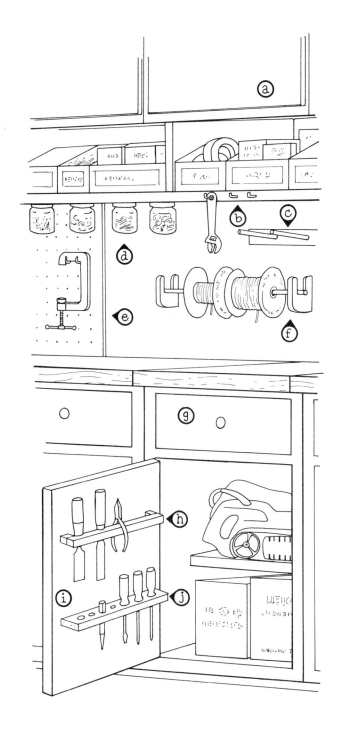

Open shelving is another possibility. Use 3/4-inch plywood or chipboard, or shelving-grade lumber, and nail and cleat or dado the sides, or use adjustable standards and brackets. You may combine the shelving with built-in arrangements for desks, files, and other equipment.

Store hand tools in drawers or hang them from walls and cabinet doors with spring clips, racks, nails, hooks, dowels, or pegboard. When you've laid your tools out on the pegboard to your satisfaction, you can draw outlines around them to cue their replacement. Wall storage is convenient and visible, but has disadvantages: tools are more likely to fall and break, or injure people; they are a danger and temptation to children; and they are more apt to rust. Tools hung over a permanent barrier like a

Shop storage. (a). Top cabinets, (b) A support shelf hung from the top cabinets. Cardboard small-parts bins rest on the shelf, and tools are hung on it with L-hooks or nails, (c) Angled dowels set in a board to hold tools, (d) Screw-top glass jars attached to the underside of the shelf with two screws through their lids, (e) Peg board—outline your tools to aid in replacement, (f) Wire spools held on a removable rod supported by brackets, (g) Base cabinets, (h) Tool rack made of 3/4″ × 3/4″ molding, (i) Be sure to allow clearance for closing the door, (j) Tool rack made of holes drilled through the board.

A picture rack.

workbench will overcome the first two objections.

Store hardware and small parts in glass jars; in plastic, metal, or heavy-cardboard storage bins; in small parts cabinets; or in odd containers like cigar boxes, bread pans, and margarine cups.

Store lumber in racks hung from the ceiling or wall, or on shelves. A retaining lip will help keep the lumber in place. Some people have a scrap bin for the bits and pieces that accumulate. Either stack plywood and masonite sheets against the wall (where they may warp) or build a rack from lumber or of heavy-weight, slotted, steel rack components.

Store rolled blueprints, plans, and patterns in tubes held in bins or in compartmented bins. Store flat plans, drawings, paper, and boards in flat (also called map or plan) files or build plywood racks. Store canvases in vertical racks or hang them from slide-out panels.

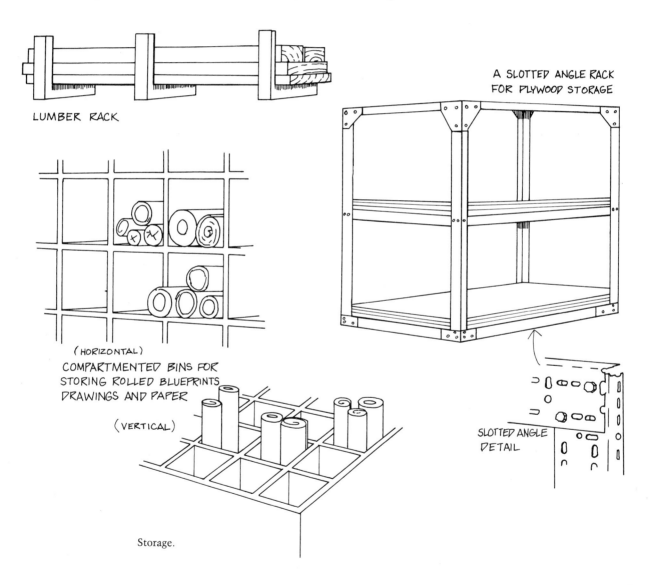

LUMBER RACK

A SLOTTED ANGLE RACK
FOR PLYWOOD STORAGE

(HORIZONTAL)
COMPARTMENTED BINS FOR
STORING ROLLED BLUEPRINTS
DRAWINGS AND PAPER

(VERTICAL)

SLOTTED ANGLE
DETAIL

Storage.

22. *Photography*

Photography is an art form at least the equal of any other technical complexity. I must, therefore, assume a basic knowledge on your part and confine this discussion to taking photographs for your portfolio and as a record of the work that leaves your studio. The last section, ''Further Study,'' lists suggestions for increasing your general knowledge.

Hiring professional photographers is quite expensive and out of the question for routine copywork. A day's professional shooting time can easily cost as much as a good camera, so photography is one area where it really can pay to do it yourself. Clients are unreliable as a source of photographs—because the expense is so great, most jobs are not photographed. Even if your job is photographed, you cannot control, unless you can participate in the cameraman's expenses, how your work will be handled or if you will have access to the prints. Therefore, unless you have a dependable photographer friend or can afford, and have access to, a professional's services, you must acquire the skill and equipment to take respectable photographs yourself.

Cameras

By far the most commonly used camera is the single-lens reflex (SLR). The 35mm size is lightweight, easy to operate, relatively inexpensive, and readily available. Its slides fit the standard projectors. The SLR viewing system allows the subject to be seen through the lens, thus eliminating the parallax problem of the optical viewfinder (parallax is the discrepancy in the position of the object as seen through the lens and through the viewfinder).

The disadvantages of the 35mm camera are:

1. Its length-to-width ratio does not match that of standard 8- by 10-inch photographic paper. The enlarged ratio is closer to 7- by 10-inch, so 8- by 10-inch prints made from it must be cropped in some way. You can compensate for this problem by composing your subject in the viewfinder of your camera to exclude the ends that will be cropped off with enlargement, or you can cut down standard paper to match your full image.

2. Its enlargements generally have lower contrast and resolution, and coarser grain than enlargements from bigger-format negatives. You can compensate for these problems by using higher resolution, more contrasty films like Kodachrome 25.

3. Except for special lenses, it has no correction mechanism for parallel-line convergence

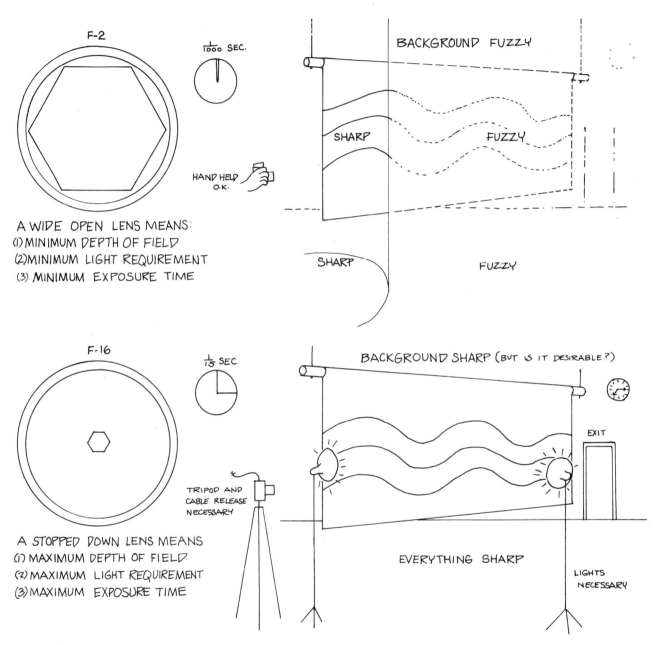

F-2

$\frac{1}{1000}$ SEC.

HAND HELD O.K.

BACKGROUND FUZZY

SHARP   FUZZY

SHARP   FUZZY

A WIDE OPEN LENS MEANS:
(1) MINIMUM DEPTH OF FIELD
(2) MINIMUM LIGHT REQUIREMENT
(3) MINIMUM EXPOSURE TIME

F-16

$\frac{1}{15}$ SEC.

TRIPOD AND CABLE RELEASE NECESSARY

BACKGROUND SHARP (BUT IS IT DESIRABLE?)

EXIT

A STOPPED DOWN LENS MEANS
(1) MAXIMUM DEPTH OF FIELD
(2) MAXIMUM LIGHT REQUIREMENT
(3) MAXIMUM EXPOSURE TIME

EVERYTHING SHARP

LIGHTS NECESSARY

Cameras have two interrelated adjustments: the exposure time (expressed in fractions of a second) and the lens opening (f-stop).

(the convergence of straight lines, such as those of tall buildings, which is caused by tipping the camera upward to include a full scene). You can correct convergence in three ways. First, you can minimize tipping by (a) using a wide-angle lens to include more of the scene (but this will introduce distortions of its own), (b) moving the camera back, to take in more of the scene, (c) moving the camera to a higher position, and (d) using a telephoto lens with (b) and (c). Second, you can use an adjustable PC (perspective-control) lens. These, however, are expensive. Third, you can tilt the photo paper easel during enlargement, but this will alter the length and width ratios of the subject.

You may also want a Polaroid camera for quick photographs to test lighting set ups; to photograph work in progress to send to clients; to document work that leaves your studio; or for a record of job sites that you visit.

There is an abundance of other cameras that offer different film sizes, formats, focusing systems, and features. Of special interest for architectural photography is the *view camera.* Its adjustable film plane will correct parallel-line convergence, and its large negative size produces sharply detailed prints. The view camera's expense and unwieldiness, however, confine it largely to the professional photographer.

Look for a camera that is well built and easy to operate. If you intend to use it for enlargements, it should have superior optics. Balance the initial cost against its overall quality, features, and ease of repair, and the availability of parts and accessories.

Cameras have two interrelated adjustments: the *exposure time* (expressed in fractions of a second) and the *lens opening* (f-stop). Each increase in exposure time doubles the length of time light is admitted to the film. Conversely, each increase in the f-stop doubles the amount of light admitted to the film. Thus, the total irradiation is equivalent at f-2 at 1/1000 second, f-2.8 at 1/500 second, f-4 at 1/250 second, all the way through f-16 at 1/15 second. The exposure remains constant, but the *depth of field* (the range along the lens axis in which the image is in focus) will change, because the image sharpens as the lens aperture is reduced. For example, at f-2 with the lens wide open, only a small central portion of the image will be in focus, whereas with the lens stopped down to f-16, the whole image from side to side and from front to back should be sharp. However, you'll require much more light for your exposure at f-16 than at f-2.

Lenses

Select lenses equal in quality to your original equipment, lest you get inferior results; and similar in operation, lest you become confused as you interchange them. Many lenses perform best in their midrange or within one f-stop of either end. The difference may not be noticeable in slides, but it can be critical in enlargements. Take a test series for each lens with your camera on a tripod, blow up the negatives, and examine the results, particularly for fall-off at the edges.

Lenses are rated by their *speed.* A "fast" lens will admit a lot of light at its widest f-stop, say f-1.4, whereas a slower lens, say f-4, will admit 1/16 as much light. Fast lenses are useful for available-light photography. Their greater expense is not warranted for object photography, where you will want the depth of field produced at the other end of the scale, say at f-16 or f-22.

Lenses are divided into three groups according to their *focal length* (the distance from the film plane to the optical center of the lens focused on infinity).

Normal Lenses. Lenses of 40mm to 55mm are called "normal" because they best reflect the eye's perception. They are used for general photography and copywork.

Wide-Angle Lenses. Lenses of less than 40mm focal length take in more of a scene without moving the camera. The shorter the focal length, the greater the distortion, but the more of the scene included. Indispensable for shooting on location, especially in interiors where it is often difficult to get back far enough from the subject, a 35mm to 24mm lens is a sound choice for the first additional lens.

Telephoto Lenses. Lenses of more than 55mm focal length work like telescopes, bringing distant objects closer. The longer the focal length, the greater the magnification but the narrower and flatter the field. Telephotos are used primarily for inaccessible subjects, but the shorter ranges are also advantageous for avoiding the perspective distortion that can occur when photographing objects with normal lenses. A short telephoto of about 105mm, which produces about 2x magnification is a good choice for a third lens.

Film

Because there is a bewildering array of films in diverse combinations of speed, resolution, and color balance, you should concentrate on and become thoroughly familiar with a limited selection—say one black-and-white and two color films—one outdoor and one incandescent.

Most of your work will probably be in color. There are two types of color film: *slide* (also called positive image or reversal) film, and *negative* film.

The advantages of slide film are: it can be

a

b

Three photos of Dubuffet's *La Chiffoniere* taken from the identical position with (a) a wide-angle lens (24mm), (b) a normal lens (55mm), and (c) a telephoto lens (100mm).

168

viewed directly without printing; it can be projected; it has greater resolution, color saturation, and contrast (which may be just as much a disadvantage); and it can be printed on high-resolution material like CIBA. Its principal disadvantage is its narrow exposure latitude.

The advantages of negative film are: it yields more accurate skin tones and pastels; it has greater exposure latitude; and it has softer contrast and resolution (which may be just as much a disadvantage). Its principal disadvantages are that it cannot

be projected, and it must be printed to be evaluated.

For enlargements, especially those of more than 4 by 5 inches, a slower *speed* film (or lower ASA rating) will give greater sharpness. The ASA rating is a numerical expression of the amount of light needed to expose a film properly. Slow films, ASA 25 through 40, have fine grain and excellent sharpness. They are "contrasty," which means they favor subjects that have gradual variations between light and dark. As the film's speed increases, so does the grain and, therefore, the resultant lack of sharpness, whereas the contrastiness decreases.

Color balances of films differ. Kodachrome, for example, enhances the reds, Ektachrome, the blues, and Fujichrome, the greens.

Color films are designed either for *natural (outdoor, daylight)* light or for *artificial (indoor, tungsten)* light. Artificial-light films are further divided into use with either 3200 K "tungsten" bulbs (Type-B film) or with 3400 K "photolamp" bulbs (Type-A film). In practice, many photographers find the 200 K difference unimportant and use the films and bulbs interchangeably.

Black-and-white films are easier and cheaper to use than color films. They can be valuable for black-and-white reproduction, and for dimensional art to emphasize its depth and texture.

For starters for 35mm use try:

Panatomic X, a very fine grain, ASA 32 black-and-white film available in 20- and 36-exposure rolls.

Kodachrome 25, a very fine-grain, ASA 25 color-reversal (color slide) film for daylight use. Available in 20- and 36-exposure rolls. It's contrasty in bright sunlight—it works best in hazy sunlight or open shade. A skylight filter will reduce bluishness when shooting in the shade, distant scenes, the mountains, and sunlit snow scenes. For a 3200 K tungsten bulb, use a Kodak No. 80B filter and drop the ASA to 8. For a 3400 K photolamp, use a Kodak No. 80A filter and drop the ASA to 8. (If you're using a camera with a built-in meter, simply take the reading with the filter in place.)

Kodachrome 40 (Type A), a very fine-grain, ASA 40 color-reversal (color slide) film for use with 3400 K photolamps. Available in 36-exposure rolls only. A Color Compensating (CC) filter is necessary for exposures longer than 1/25 second. For a 3200 K tungsten bulb, use Kodak No. 82A filter and drop the ASA to 32. For daylight, use a Kodak No. 85 filter and drop the ASA to 25. (If you're using a camera with a built-in meter, simply take the reading with the filter in place.)

Equipment

Don't entrust a good camera to a cheap tripod. There's nothing more frustrating than to watch a tripod slowly collapse after you've spent fifteen minutes meticulously composing the perfect shot.

Choose a sturdy, well-made, easy-to-carry tripod with an elevating head that tilts and pans, one that's stable even when extended. To check a tripod for vibration, mount your camera on it, balance a lightweight object on the camera, and snap the shutter with a cable release. If the object falls, reject the tripod.

You will need lights for most interior shots and for copy work. The least expensive are folding metal light stands and clip-on reflectors. Look for porcelain sockets, 12-inch reflectors of decent size and weight, and the same quality hardware, extensionality, and locking features that you seek in a tripod. The reflector and bulb in combination with the strung-out electric cord tend to make lightweight stands top-heavy, so test them in the store,

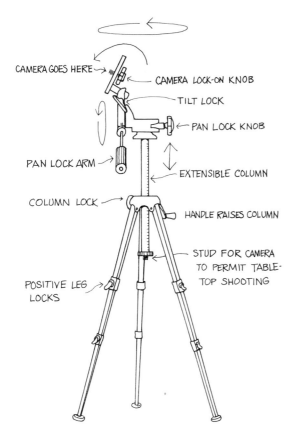

Tripods.

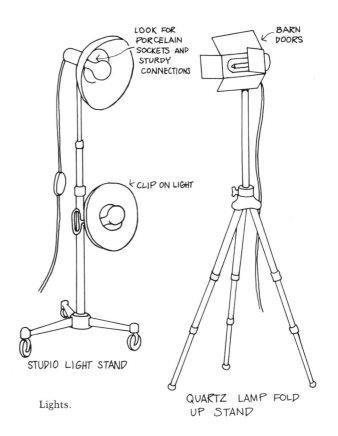

Lights.

fully extended and plugged in, before you buy them.

Use 500-watt, 3200 K or 3400 K bulbs matched to your color film. For black and white, use either. The bulbs have a life of two to eight hours (switching them off and on will decrease it) and they change color temperature as they age.

Quartz lamps (also called *quartz-halogen*, and *tungsten-halogen*), which are more expensive than regular photo bulbs, offer a constant color temperature, long life, and light weight. You can buy a convenient twin-lamp set, complete in a carrying case, with collapsible stand, barn doors (adjustable shutters), and extension cords that you can use both in your studio and on location. Additional units will give you more flexibility in lighting a scene.

Add equipment as you need it: a camera bag, filters, separate light meter, cable release, lens shade, extension tubes, ad infinitum. Your dealer will be more than happy to help with their selection.

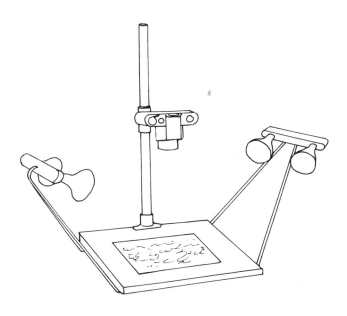

A commercial copyboard.

Copying

Copying is the term used for making accurate photographic reproductions of prints, paintings, drawings, crafts, sculpture, and similar objects. For small work you can use a set-up of lights attached at 45-degree angles to a horizontal copyboard. You can purchase a ready-made assembly or you can buy the components and put it together yourself. Alternatively, you can position the artwork vertically, mounting it on a wall or placing it on an easel, sawhorse, or table top, or in a natural setting outdoors.

You may shoot outdoors in direct or diffused sunlight taking care to select flattering backgrounds and to lighten deep shadows with a reflector that you can make out of crinkled aluminum foil attached to a lightweight board. With artificial light, start out with a pair of lamps set at 45-degree angles from the subject and adjust their height, distance, and angle for the best illumination. Add lamps as you need them. Take meter readings over the subject to ensure that you're lighting it evenly. You can modify the light with barn doors, by attaching tracing-paper diffusors to your lamps, by placing scrim diffusors in front of them, or by bouncing the light off a white umbrella, panel, ceiling, or aluminum reflector.

Bracket (taking exposures one stop on either side of the meter reading) your exposures and experiment with the light arrangements. Make careful records for your future guidance.

When photographing two-dimensional objects, make sure the object and the camera are level to avoid distortion. You can test both with a carpenter's level or purchase a small bubble level that attaches to your camera.

If you're shooting for your portfolio, be especially attentive to selecting complementary lighting and backgrounds. Choose attractive colors, patterns, and accessories and make sure they are clean and unwrinkled.

Location Shooting

Don't rely on available light for location shooting. Come prepared with everything you can think of—lights, extension cords, camera bag, tripod, ladder or footstool, and plenty of film. A grip (assistant) will prove invaluable in carrying equipment, setting up, holding lights, and, in busy places, directing traffic and guarding your things. Always secure permission to photograph on private property. Businesses may not want you shooting during work hours; besides the confusion it causes, there may be safety and insurance problems.

Study the illustrations in superior interior-design and architectural magazines like *Interior Design* and *Architectural Record* to learn how the pros compose and light their shots. Notice their use of props to add color, interest, and scale, and their different camera angles, and carefully determine where they have placed their principal and auxiliary lights. Move your lights around, switch lenses and camera angles, use bounce and fill lights, and, of course, bracket your shots—anything for that superlative exposure. As needed include a standard color card close enough to the camera to be read in order

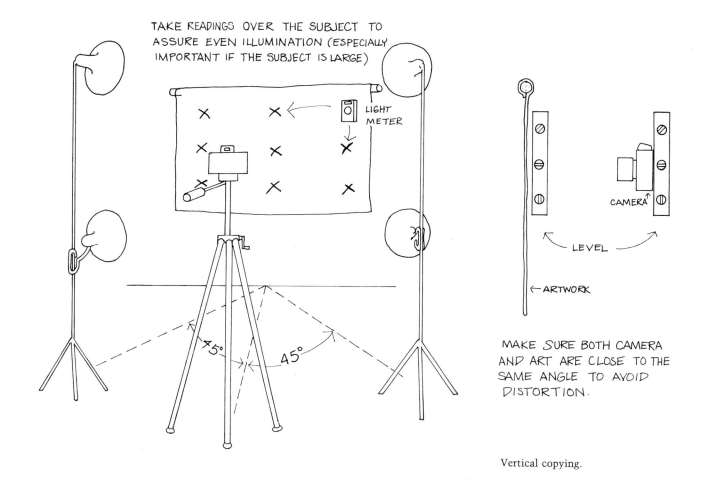

TAKE READINGS OVER THE SUBJECT TO ASSURE EVEN ILLUMINATION (ESPECIALLY IMPORTANT IF THE SUBJECT IS LARGE)

LIGHT METER

45° 45°

LEVEL

← ARTWORK

CAMERA

MAKE SURE BOTH CAMERA AND ART ARE CLOSE TO THE SAME ANGLE TO AVOID DISTORTION.

Vertical copying.

to help key color balancing in the darkroom. Like the pros, expect to use a lot of film. If you get one good shot per roll, you will be doing well.

You must obtain a *model release* from any person who appears recognizably in photographs that you will use for advertising or other commercial purposes—without the release you could be sued. Obtain *model release forms* from photo stores and have them signed, preferably, at the time you take the picture. Parents or guardians must sign for minors. Photos for your portfolio are not considered commercial and do not therefore require releases.

Developing and Printing

Having gone to the trouble of taking good photographs, don't pinch pennies on development. Send your film to Kodak or a reputable local company. Use mailers if a camera store isn't convenient. You can make slide copies in your camera by exposing the same shot several times, or you can select the best developed slide and have duplicates made of it. In-camera duplicates will be equal, of course, to the original slide, but you can't be certain that the shot you're repeating is a good one. Duplicate slides give you more control, but they are more contrasty and therefore less detailed in the highlights and shadows than original slides. The differences may not be all that noticeable when you project the duplicates, but enlargements made from them will be considerably less sharp than those made from originals.

Label slides with the title, size, and medium, and indicate the lower left corner with a red dot. If you're sending slides out, add your name and address, using a rubber stamp or self-adhesive printed labels. Store slides in clear plastic pocket sheets kept in albums, or in drums, trays, or boxes stored in a cool, dry place to reduce deterioration.

Protect important slides and those that will be handled a lot—your presentation set for example—with *double glass slide binders*. These glass-windowed interlocking, rigid mounts that sandwich the slide have several drawbacks however: they are expensive, mounting is tedious, the opportunity for dust accumulation is increased fourfold, and the slide must be unmounted for copying or enlargement.

Kodak will also make enlargements from your slides. Use the cropping guides at your camera store. Otherwise, the cropping that naturally occurs when 35 mm material is printed on 8- by 10-inch paper or its derivatives may not be to your liking.

A preferable, although more expensive, alternative is custom printing, either by a local professional or a talented amateur. Many people have darkrooms these days, and you may find someone who'll print for you at little more than cost. Collaborating with a printer lets you select the best combinations of papers, chemicals, filters, cropping, and exposure and development times to produce the exact effect you're after.

Further Study

Increase your knowledge of photography by working with and observing lab and camera store people and other photographers. Your local museum may have a staff photographer who'll introduce you to copying. Many schools offer photography courses, and the Nikon School travels to dozens of cities each year. For more information and a schedule write: The Nikon School of Photography, 632 Stewart Avenue, Garden City, N.Y., 11530.

23. Paint

Artists often wonder what the best paint is. There is no more a "best" paint than there is a "best" breed of dog. Each paint is a compromise among a long list of possible alternatives. For any paint use, one or several qualities will be most important; you must select the optimum combination available for a particular job and technique. Recognize the ambivalence of some characteristics—quick drying time is desirable for minimizing dust pick-up and repaint time, but undesirable for blending—and the interrelatedness of others—surface hardness is incompatible with great flexibility. And recognize that some characteristics, e.g., adhesion, are clearly desirable, while others, e.g., toxicity, are clearly undesirable.

Paint Characteristics

Paint characteristics may be divided into three phases: preapplication, application, and post-application.

Preapplication Characteristics

Distribution: The availability of fresh stock in the full range of color, container, and finish options.

Packaging: Paints are packaged in a wide range of container sizes—artists' oils in tubes; industrial paints in drums or carloads. Units may be either much too large or too small for your applications.

Shelf Life: The period in which stored paint remains useful. Paints with rapidly evaporating solvents or a lot of drier have shorter shelf lives. Shelf life can often be prolonged by maintaining a low temperature, excluding air from the container, and adding antioxidants, anticoagulants, fungicides, and bactericides.

Economy: The true cost of the paint is a combination of initial cost, shelf life, coverage, and useful life.

Color: The quality, permanence, and range of the colors available. Artists' paints offer the standard in their range of permanent, pure pigments. Most trade-sales paints offer a basic selection broadened by uniform custom tinting, while some of the industrial paints come in only one or two colors. As a rule, the more expensive the pigment, the more likely it will be diluted.

Application Characteristics

Covering power: A function of the pigment, which may be opaque, translucent, or transparent, and its proportion to the vehicle and inert material.

Handling: How well the paint applies. If it levels, blends, drips, spatters, foams, rolls out, sprays, or brushes smoothly. Related to viscosity, weight, and drying time.

Clean up: How easily the paint may be cleaned

from tools and surfaces. Water-based paints have the edge.

Vapor hazard: Odor, flammability, and toxicity, which can be a problem in inadequately ventilated areas, are mainly caused by the vehicle. Water is harmless, of course, while some solvents like xylene and benzene are both highly toxic and flammable.

Drying time: Distinguished as *set up* or *tack time* and *through dry time.* A function of both the pigment and the vehicle.

Adhesion: The ability of the paint to stick to the substrate. Adhesion may be broad based, e.g., to many different substances, or selective, e.g., to one or few substances.

Post-application Characteristics

Durability: A complex equation of the substrate; the paint—its hardness, flexibility and resistance to failures like flaking, checking, and chalking; and the paint's environment—its exposure to weather and stress.

Uniform light reflectance: Depends primarily on the substrate's uniformly absorbing the vehicle. If the penetration is uneven, the paint will appear blotchy.

Burnishing: An undesirable change in reflectance caused by rubbing the paint. Burnishing is usually a fault of the vehicle or the vehicle/pigment combination. Deep-tone flat colors are most likely to burnish, semigloss and gloss paints least likely.

Washability: Semigloss and gloss paints are more washable than flats.

Flexibility: The ability of the paint film to resist cracking when the substrate is flexed, as when a mural is rolled up for shipment.

Solvent Resistance: Resistance to various substances, e.g., acids, oils, foods, water, alcohols.

Fire retardance: The property of rapidly forming an insulating foam (tumescing) when affected by excessive temperatures.

Toxicity: Especially a problem where food and children are present.

Fading: Pigment bleaching caused primarily by sunlight.

Yellowing: Primarily a function of the vehicle; it is most noticeable in light and cool colors.

Categories of Paints

Paint manufacturers categorize paints according to the end use. While you may only use three paints at most: artist's paint, sign paint, and trade-sales paint, it can be helpful to know what else is available should the need arise.

1. *Trade-Sales or Architectural Paints:* The common over-the-counter paint of the paint and hardware stores used for painting buildings, furniture, equipment, etc. Available in a wide variety of colors, finishes, vehicles, and special qualities. Examples are heavy-duty enamel, four-hour enamel, fire-retardant paint, and water-resistant paint.

2. *Chemical Coatings:* Used in factories to coat manufactured items like automobiles, appliances, and equipment. Available in bulk only.

3. *Automotive Refinishing Paints:* Used by automotive refinishers for recoating automobiles.

4. *Industrial Maintenance Paints:* Specially formulated high-corrosion-resistance coatings for maintenance of bridges, machinery, and equipment. Available in bulk only.

5. *Sign Paints:* Artists should become more familiar with sign paints. While they may not meet the high permanence standards of artists' paints, they offer an excellent combination of color intensity, high gloss, durability, application ease, light fastness, package size, drying time, and shelf life. Use them for signs, of course, and for paintings, decorations, supergraphics, doors, walls, and furniture. *Lettering enamels,* designed for lettering on top of painted backgrounds, are more heavily pigmented and therefore more opaque and more expensive than the similar *bulletin enamels,* which are intended primarily for backgrounds. All are light fast when used straight except maroon, which is made from a calcium pigment that doesn't hold up quite as well as the other colors.

Poster colors are dead-flat enamels and have a

slightly different color range than lettering enamels. They are formulated principally for indoor sign use and will not wear well outside. For example, two of Consumer Paint's poster paints, #3006 Magenta and, to a lesser extent, #3007 Purple, are fugitive. Do not use them under direct sunlight either indoors or out, or under ultraviolet-emitting artificial light. Ultraviolet-screening topcoats are available, but as a rule, they are quite glossy.

You can make a semigloss by combining poster paint and sign enamel. Try a test patch before using it, especially if you're placing colors side by side that must have the same sheen. The wearing qualities should be in between those of the two component paints—not as good as sign enamel, but better than poster paint.

Two principal manufacturers of sign paints are: Consumers Paint Factory, Inc., 5300 W. Fifth Avenue, Gary, IN 46406; and T. J. Ronan Paint Corporation, 749 E. 135th Street, Bronx, NY 10454.

6. *Traffic Paints:* For marking road surfaces.

7. *Artists' Paints:* Formulated especially for artists in a variety of vehicles with permanence and purity top considerations.

Vehicles

The following are the principal commercial paint vehicles.

Latices (Latexes): A semisolid, water-dispersion, artificial latex originally derived from synthetic rubber developed during World War II. The initial formula of styrene butadiene has largely been replaced by polyvinyl acetate (PVA), vinyl acrylics, and normal butyl acrylates (NBA) often present as copolymers. Examples are artists' latices (commonly called acrylics) like Liquitex, and latex house paints. They are tough, fast drying, and easy to apply and clean up. Trust the manufacturer to formulate the product properly rather than make your selection based on the vehicle's chemistry.

Polyesters: Used in industrial paints in a catalyzed (two-part: base and hardener) form. Tough and long wearing, they will not air cure, so to seal out air, manufacturers add a substance such as a wax which must be thoroughly removed before repainting.

Epoxies: Extremely tough, catalyzed paints, they have good nonyellowing properties and can be applied as easily as alkyds, but they chalk outdoors. They are becoming available in a more convenient water base. The one-part epoxy oxirane esters sometimes added to trade-sales paints are more for sales appeal than performance; they are no improvement over a good alkyd.

Urethanes: Similar in toughness to epoxies, the catalyzed urethanes contain hazardous toluene diosocyanate. The oil-modified urethane varnishes and paints are tougher than alkyds, but their hardness makes refinishing difficult. The original coat must be thoroughly abraded to ensure adhesion.

Polyvinyl Chlorides: Hazardous, used only for industrial applications.

Acrylics: Solvent-based acrylics such as methyl methacrylate and other derivatives of acrylic acid used primarily for container coatings. They require heat cure.

Alkyds: Thallic anhydride plus a polyfunctional alcohol, alkyds for many years have been the main vehicle for trade-sales "oil" paint. Quite versatile, they're available in quick or regular drying, flat, semigloss, and gloss. Recently they have become available as a vehicle for artists' paints.

Cellulose Lacquers: Industrial finishes, they produce a film through solvent evaporation. Mainly used in coating panels, furniture, and similar manufactured items.

Preparing a Substrate

The final paint film is dependent upon a properly prepared substrate (ground). Artists who are familiar only with the traditional materials like canvas might consider other materials like wallboard, vinyls, metals, and hardboard. The following, a description of the preparation of MDO boards for use with lettering enamels, can be adapted for painting on metal, drywall, and other surfaces as well.

Priming Medium Density Overlay Plywood:

Overlaid plywood, an exterior plywood surfaced with a resin-treated cellulose fiber fused to it under heat and pressure, is available in several product types. Medium density overlay (MDO), with a 28- to 30-percent surface-resin content, has a smooth face that resembles a softer Formica. Sign painters have used it successfully for years in all types of indoor and outdoor signs. To prevent warping, use only double-faced MDO even if the panels are bolted to a wall. Contact your local lumberyard or Simpson Timber Company, 900 Fourth Avenue, Seattle, WA 98164.

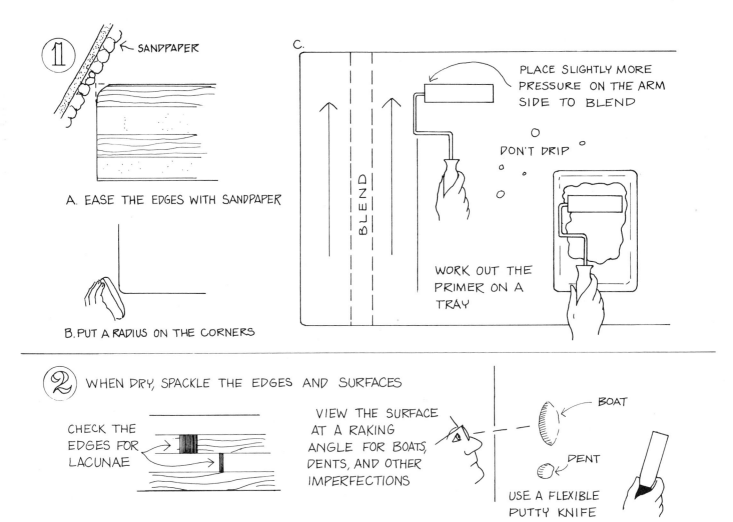

1 — ← SANDPAPER

A. EASE THE EDGES WITH SANDPAPER

B. PUT A RADIUS ON THE CORNERS

C.

BLEND

PLACE SLIGHTLY MORE PRESSURE ON THE ARM SIDE TO BLEND

DON'T DRIP

WORK OUT THE PRIMER ON A TRAY

 2 WHEN DRY, SPACKLE THE EDGES AND SURFACES

CHECK THE EDGES FOR LACUNAE

VIEW THE SURFACE AT A RAKING ANGLE FOR BOATS, DENTS, AND OTHER IMPERFECTIONS

BOAT

DENT

USE A FLEXIBLE PUTTY KNIFE

 3 WHEN DRY, SAND THE SURFACES SLIGHTLY AND DUST THEM OFF

4 REPEAT THE PRIME, SPACKLE, AND SAND CYCLE UNTIL YOU ACHIEVE A VERY SMOOTH, MAT SURFACE.

Priming medium density overlay (MDO) and other flat surfaces.

1. Ease the edges, and put a radius on the corners with sandpaper, a power sander, or a saber saw to forestall splitting. Prime with an even coat of a sign primer like Ronan's Stick-Tite White Metal Primer, a house-paint primer like Hanline's #3651 Latex House Paint Primer, or an artist's gesso. Use a brush or better, a flat-nap roller such as a disposable-sponge roller. First work the primer out on a tray (a Styrofoam meat tray works well) and then apply it with slightly more pressure on the arm side of the roller to blend the strokes together. Work rapidly so the primer will stay wet enough to blend, and don't drip, as drips may show through as brighter or thicker spots. Cover the top and sides evenly. Prime both sides for double-sided or free-hanging pieces, of course. Priming the back may increase warpage resistance for single-sided pieces, but shouldn't be necessary if they are to be mounted to a wall.

2. When dry, spackle the edges and surface imperfections. Indoors, use a ready-mixed commercial spackle. Outdoors, use a waterproof spackle or an auto-body putty like Nitro-Stan.

3. When dry, sand the surfaces lightly with fine sandpaper mounted on a vibrator sander or rubber sandpaper block. Dust off thoroughly with a brush, cloth, or tack rag.

4. Repeat the prime, spackle, sand cycle one or more additional times until you achieve an ivory smooth, mat surface. Don't skimp on your efforts. If the surface is well prepared, most lettering enamels will cover with only one coat.

To prime a group of panels, set the panels on boards supported by sawhorses so you have access to their edges or, if you haven't enough horizontal space, prime the faces while they're lying down, then stack the panels against a wall and prime their edges.

Painting with Lettering Enamels

Lettering enamels handle like any top-quality, heavy-bodied alkyd. Apply them with disposable sponge roller covers (which you can cut into smaller pieces if you wish), lettering quills, and brushes, such as show card, lettering, sign writers', one stroke, and other brushes made of soft hairs like sable, sabeline, and ox hair. Liners and script brushes are nice for flowing, fine lines.

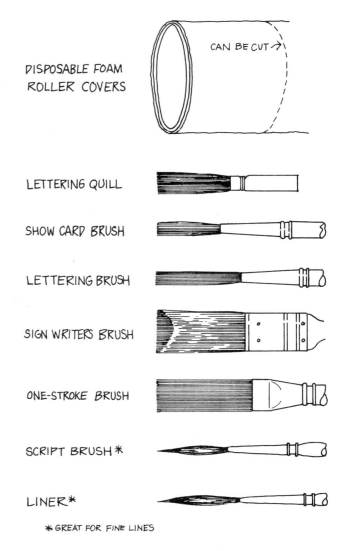

Specialty brushes.

178

Work directly from the can or transfer a little paint to a small container. Disposable paper cups work very well—you can cut and bend out a flap to use as a brush prop and to wipe out excess paint—but only use plain paper cups and not those coated with paraffin. The paint can unobtrusively dissolve some of the paraffin and this will cause streaking, erratic gloss, and uneven drying.

To increase opacity, use two thin coats rather than one thick one. An overly thick layer may wrinkle or skin before its interior can dry properly. A drop or two of kerosene will retard drying time.

Sign enamels tend to skin over rapidly in the can. An anti-skinning agent such as ''Paint-Sav'' added sparingly to the can will prolong shelf life but may seriously retard the drying time of paint films. A safer skinning preventive is to reduce the oxygen in the cans by sealing them tightly, by transferring unused paint to smaller containers, by laying a plastic film like ''Saran Wrap'' on the surface of the paint in the can or by drilling two pour holes in the rim and sealing them with sheet metal screws. Another approach is to buy only as much paint as you can use for a job.

Should a skin form in the can, don't stir it into the liquid paint. Rather, cut away the skin, and strain the remaining paint through a nylon stocking or a throwaway paint strainer.

Clean your brushes in paint thinner or lacquer thinner and either wash them in detergent and warm water or dip them in mineral oil, which will keep them supple. Before using the brushes again, clean out the mineral oil with paint thinner or lacquer thinner.

Hard Edge Painting with Tape

Producing clean, hard edges with masking tape depends on an optimum combination of masking tape, paint, and substrate. Experiment until you find the combination that produces the best results.

Hard edge painting with tape.

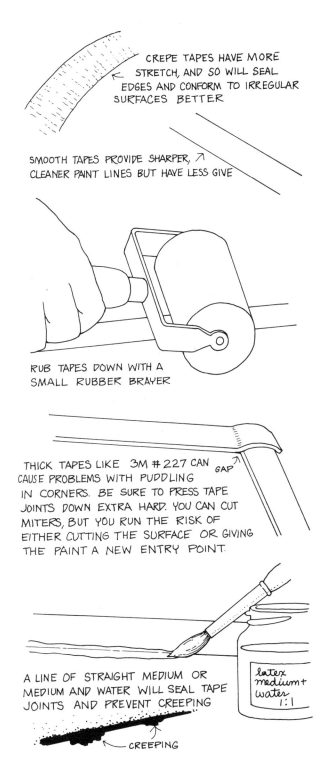

CREPE TAPES HAVE MORE STRETCH, AND SO WILL SEAL EDGES AND CONFORM TO IRREGULAR SURFACES BETTER

SMOOTH TAPES PROVIDE SHARPER, CLEANER PAINT LINES BUT HAVE LESS GIVE

RUB TAPES DOWN WITH A SMALL RUBBER BRAYER

THICK TAPES LIKE 3M #227 CAN CAUSE PROBLEMS WITH PUDDLING IN CORNERS. BE SURE TO PRESS TAPE JOINTS DOWN EXTRA HARD. YOU CAN CUT MITERS, BUT YOU RUN THE RISK OF EITHER CUTTING THE SURFACE OR GIVING THE PAINT A NEW ENTRY POINT. GAP

A LINE OF STRAIGHT MEDIUM OR MEDIUM AND WATER WILL SEAL TAPE JOINTS AND PREVENT CREEPING

latex medium + water 1:1

CREEPING

The tape must adhere to the paint surface enough to seal the seam and not lift prematurely, but not so much as to take the paint with it when the tape is removed. The tape's performance also depends on the *dwell time*, i.e., the amount of time between the application of the paint and the removal of the tape. With flexible-film paints like latices, remove the tape while the paint is still wet; if you wait until the paint dries thoroughly, a jagged edge might result. You can wait to remove the tape until the paint sets up when using hard-film paints like lacquers; they will break cleanly when you remove the tape.

Be sure to use masking tapes, all of which are treated to resist solvents. The cheaper, untreated utility-grade paper tapes used for packaging may dissolve or allow the paint to penetrate. Even so, when using a new tape or paint for the first time, make some tests to confirm the tape's impermeability and to determine the optimum dwell time.

Consider these 3M tapes for masking:

"Scotch" Brand No. 202 Masking Tape: A crepe-backed, solvent resistant, paper tape for general masking applications. Use it for irregular surfaces and to produce curved lines.

"Scotch" Brand No. 218 Fine Line Tape: A top quality, flexible, solvent resistant polyester flat tape for very sharp-curved or straight lines on smooth surfaces.

"Scotch" Brand No. 227 Flatback Masking Tape: A smooth, flat, solvent resistant paper tape for producing clean, straight lines on smooth surfaces.

"Scotch" Brand No. 263 Paint Striping Tape: Similar to No. 227 but with precut slits. Pull out various combinations of the pre-slit portions to produce lines of different widths.

New Products

Recent years have seen the successful entry of alkyd-based paints into the artist's repertory. They are a welcome answer to those who enjoy the fluency, clarity, wet/dry color uniformity, and blending qualities of oils but are bothered by their slow, erratic drying times and film weakness. Alkyds touch dry within eighteen hours, have an even lustre, are virtually non-yellowing, are flexible and should, if anything, be more permanent than oils. Two manufacturers are Winsor & Newton and a small company, P.D.Q., 6059 Larchmont Court, San Jose, CA 95123. I have a large stock of oils and, to use them up, mix them with a non-yellowing alkyd medium compounded for me by Contact Paint and Chemical Corp., 200 South Franklintown Road, Baltimore, MD 21223.

I can suggest two protective top coats for hard use areas. The first is Rohm and Haas's Acryloid B–67 MT, crystal clear acrylic resin soluble in mineral thinner. It is an ingredient of proprietary artists' picture varnishes and is also a paint vehicle. About ½ percent Dow #11 paint additive may be introduced to increase mar resistance.

Another, harder top coat is epoxy polyester varnish, e.g., Fuller O'Brien's Mirror Plate Epoxy Acid and Stain Resistant Clear and Hanline L 6515 Clear Gloss Polyester Epoxy Coating. They are catalyzed (two part), non-yellowing, clear varnishes. If you use an alternate product, make sure it has a UV screener. Properly applied and sufficiently aged, they should permit the cleaning of difficult stains like lipstick and spray paint.

As for the future, Brian J. Heath, President of Winsor & Newton, does not foresee any major changes in the variety of products now available to artists. Rather, he anticipates "a steady stream of refinement in the colors" and that some of the mediums and varnishes "are likely to be superseded by man-made resins which offer . . . advantages to the serious artist in terms of longevity of the finished art work."

24. Picture Frames

Frames are expensive and they take a lot of time to specify, purchase, and fit. But slapdash frames will not only detract from your artwork, they can signal to potential buyers that you don't seem to think enough of your work to present it properly. If you take time to learn about the business and technology of framing, however, you'll be able to use frames more intelligently and pare your costs. I emphasize in this chapter buying, rather than building, frames because I've found that it's more economical, all things considered, and certainly more pleasurable, to spend my time making art, rather than frames.

Choosing Frames

You should match the style, period, materials, and finish of a picture molding to the style and color or your art. A frame tour of a museum will train your eye. Note the frames closely, and pay particular attention to those used with the art that most resembles your own. Consider if the combination is felicitous, and imagine the art without its frame. Better yet, visit the conservator and observe how surprisingly modest even famous paintings can seem when unframed. You may come to see

truth in the observation that almost anything will look good in an important frame.

You'll be limited selecting frames for existing settings. Besides the normal considerations, take into account the period and color of the room, and in particular the color and texture of the wall on which the art will hang.

The frame forms a transition between your art and its background. For example, if you're hanging an orange painting on a wall of a similar color, you'll probably want a contrasting color or metallic frame to separate the art and the wall. If the wall were a contrasting color, a neutral or tertiary color frame would better ease the transition.

Lighting is another key element. If a room is dimly lit, a bold frame will make your piece more prominent. Spotlights in a dark room pick up metal or leaf frames or liners and make them sparkle. By the same token, spots can also glare off glass and gloss-varnished paintings. Wall washes may cast the shadow of a deep frame and obscure your work; use a shallower frame instead.

If theft is a problem, avoid shell frames. They present less attachment surface to the wall and give a thief a better handhold.

Picture Frame Moldings

Lengths is the term used for full pieces of molding. Domestic moldings usually come in *random* lengths, which range between 7 feet and 12 feet; the framer orders the total footage he requires.

SPOT LIGHTS WILL PICK UP METAL OR LEAF FRAMES AND MAKE THEM SPARKLE,

BUT SPOTS CAN ALSO GLARE OFF GLOSS AND GLOSS-VARNISHED PAINTINGS.

Spotlights.

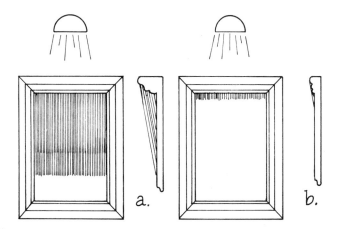

Washes may cast the shadow of a deep frame (a). A shallow frame (b) would be better.

For example, a shipment of 100 feet of random-length molding might be made up of eight lengths of 8 feet, three lengths of 9 1/2 feet, and one length of 7 1/2 feet to equal 100 feet. Imported moldings, which come primarily from Europe and Taiwan, are usually *finger jointed* (a strong, interlocked wood joint recalling fingers pressed together) of smaller pieces combined to form exact 8-foot, 9-foot, or 10-foot lengths. The framer orders the number of lengths he requires, e.g., 10/10-foot lengths to make up 100 feet. When calculating lengths, framers allow as much as 20-percent waste in cutting and as much as a foot loss on either end. There may also be a definite difference in the profile and finish between separate runs of the same molding, so a careful framer will not mix batches.

Chops are mitered pieces of molding supplied to order and ready for assembly into a frame. Chops generally cost twice as much as lengths (but half as much as finished frames). They are easier to ship, and spare the framer the trouble of cutting moldings, the cost of equipment, and the expense of a molding inventory. However, chops are frequently cut carelessly—one bad side will make the entire

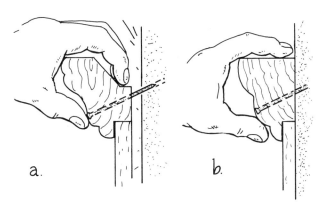

Avoid shell frames (a), they give a thief a better handhold. Flush frames (b) are more frustrating to thieves.

frame unusable—and there's always more resistance met in returning unsatisfactorily cut goods of any kind.

Finished frames generally cost about twice the price of chops and four times the price of lengths. They may be *stock* (ready-made), produced in standard sizes by the manufacturer, or *custom*, made to a customer's specific order. The cheapest frames are power stapled through the sides or backs of their corners, a process that requires a thicker molding than one that is nailed. Staples by themselves are relatively weak, and so the better frames are glued as well. The best frames are glued, cross-nailed from both sides of the corner, and have their nail holes set and filled.

A frame's construction makes a big difference in its cost, strength, and appearance. Be sure you know what you're getting.

Styles and Shapes

Moldings come in a great array of styles, shapes, and *patterns*, i.e., sizes—the same style or shape may be produced in a whole series of widths. The following are some of the more common:

Shell: A molding cut on the bias to save lumber. The frame made from it appears full from the face, but hollow from the side and only a small fraction of it rests on the wall. Shell moldings are cheaper (and they look it) since they use less wood. They are difficult to support while cutting, and large manufacturers, who are their primary users, make special jigs to hold them.

Standard (Colonial): Are highest at the outer edge and flow down to the inner, rabbet (the notch for the artwork) edge.

Reverse: Are highest at the inner, rabbet edge and descend to the outer edge. The design permits a deeper rabbet that can accommodate a thicker canvas.

Reed: Molding grooved in a pattern of parallel ridges.

Cap: A deep profile molding that can be used by itself or with a liner.

Liner: A secondary flat molding, often with an unfinished outer edge, intended primarily as an inner frame in conjuction with a cap, although many work by themselves. Liners may be painted, leafed, or wrapped with materials like linen or velvet. They provide more flexibility in composing frames and can produce a wider frame that is often less expensive than a molding of comparable width.

Scoop: A molding with a concave face.

Strip: A flat strip of molding with neither a rabbet nor a lip. Usually nailed directly to the side of the painting. Always miter a strip; do not butt-joint it.

L or Box: A strip with a lip; used with modern artwork. Box molding has a somewhat thicker top.

High back: A molding cut from 6/4 or 8/4 stock.

O'Keefe: A bull-nosed cap that slants off toward the back.

Metal clad: Thin sheet metal clamped around a milled wood core. It can be cut, glued, and nailed just like a wood molding. Since most metal clads are aluminum, a soft metal that readily scratches and dents, mat and wire-brushed finishes will show less damage than highly polished ones. Stainless steel, a tougher, more expensive metal, holds up much better.

Extrusions: Metal molding, usually aluminum but sometimes stainless steel, extruded from a solid billet. Extruded moldings with wood cores may be joined by normal methods. Hollow extrusions are often sold as chops in packages of two each with ingenious rear-locking assembly hardware.

Compo (Composition): A milled wood base coated with compo, a gesso-like substance, which is then run through metal pattern rollers. Raw compo is always treated with gold leaf, paint, or other finishes. You can easily tell a compo molding by looking at its cross-section—there will be a distinct color and texture difference between the compo and its wood base. Compo is protean; the best and the worst frames are made from it. Look for crispness, depth and fineness in the pattern, and a careful finish.

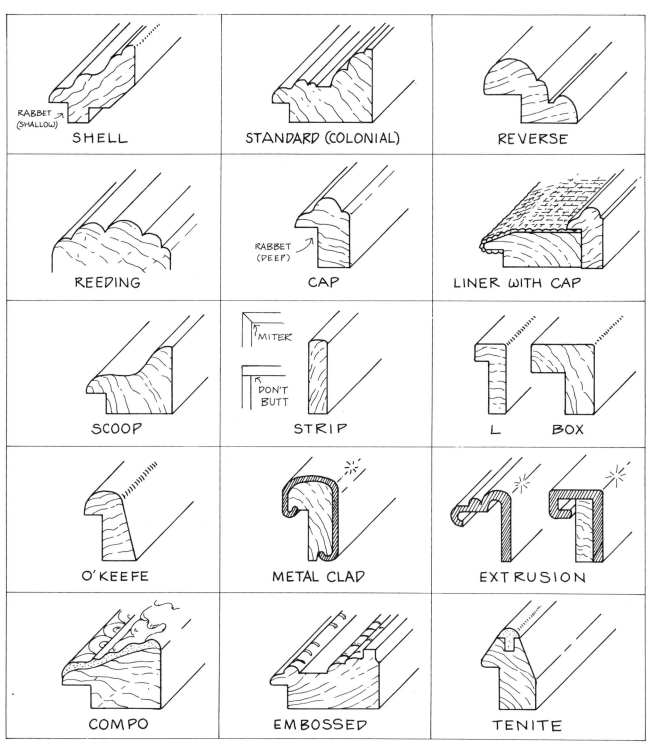

Molding styles.

184

Embossed: Milled wood run through a patterned metal die wheel, which presses a pattern into the wood. Deep patterns require heated dies to burn away the excess wood, often leaving char marks. Not as crisp as quality compo.

Carved: The very finest moldings are hand carved. If price is an insufficient indication, look for tool marks and deep undercutting. Moldings are also production hand carved in cheap-labor countries, but they are an altogether different product, hastily executed and poorly finished. Machine-carved moldings, which can be quite good indeed, are produced on spindle machines.

Finishes

Gold leaf: White or yellow gold leaf is quite expensive, but worth it. A class product, at once brilliant and mellow, it won't tarnish. If in doubt whether real gold leaf has been used on a molding, check the rabbet for scrap bits of gold.

Bronze, aluminum, and other base-metal leaves: Base-metal leaves are less brilliant, more garish, and, of course, cheaper than gold. They will tarnish if unprotected. Check the rabbet for base-metal scraps.

Metal paint: Cheaper still are sprayed bronze and aluminum paint finishes. Only in dim light and under a heavy distress might you mistake paint for leaf. Again, if in doubt, check the rabbet.

Imitation finishes: Compo painted to resemble tortoise shell, bird's-eye maple or other expensive finishes. Well done they're attractive; poorly done, they're tawdry.

Vinyl and other films: Wood core wrapped with vinyl or other films either in solid colors or screened to imitate choice woods and fabrics. The solids may look okay, but the imitations are junk. What's more, they peel off like the bark on a green twig, and when mitered the covering often shrinks back from the cut.

Tenite: An inexpensive, flexible beading of metalized or solid-color plastic used as a decorative insert in wood moldings. It can add sparkle to an inexpensive molding.

Distress, antiquing: Dark paint, rottenstone, and other substances sprayed, painted, spattered, or rubbed over other finishes either to mellow them or to disguise inferior moldings. Artificial finishes may be used to mimic woods like barnboard, driftwood, or wormy chestnut when authentic materials are either rare or of uncertain supply or quality. If rustic textures are too rough; they'll snag clothing and give splinters.

Distressed finishes are wise choices for difficult situations. Already banged up, as it were, they show subsequent damage less and can be repaired more easily.

Paint and varnish: Decorative and protective coatings sprayed, rolled, painted, or wiped on moldings. Stain by itself leaves a rough, absorbent surface. It should be followed by varnish, lacquer, or wax to fill and protect the wood.

Anodize: A permanent chemical color coating for aluminum.

Molding Samples

You'll need molding sample pieces or corners for your own reference and to show to clients. Corners (two short pieces mitered together) give the best indication of the molding's effect, but they generally cost from 50 cents to a dollar and are awkward to carry in quantity. Framers and wholesalers will sell short sample pieces of molding cheaply or even give them to you, if you are a good customer and don't ask for too many. You can cut these pieces to a uniform length if they're not the same size, label the framer's code on the rabbet (if you use more than one source, note the source as well), and glue the pieces with white cement to a two- to three-foot length of felt. You can then roll the felt up for storage, or transport. Moldings follow fashion cycles like clothes, so you'll have to revise your samples occasionally.

Buying Frames

There are many frame wholesalers and manufacturers in the United States—a copy of *Decor* magazine will give you some idea—and they operate in many different ways. They may, singly or in combination, import moldings, manufacture moldings, manufacture custom frames, manufacture stock frames, make chops, and sell to the trade only and/or to everyone. Their ads should tell how they operate. If not, ask.

You can save a lot of money buying frames from a manufacturer—as much as 75 percent of the retail price—but you have to buy in bulk and often in the same style and size. One way to meet the minimum requirement is to pool your purchases with other artists; another is to standardize your painting sizes and buy a group of frames at one time. When you're putting together a show, for instance, you'll find that simple but serviceable frames from a manufacturer will cost you no more than slapping on lath, if you compute your total time and expenses. In addition, the results will be more attractive and more salable. Should you be bidding for a large job that will require a substantial number of similar frames—artwork for hotel rooms, for example—buying from a manufacturer is the only way you can be competitive.

Apart from the need to purchase in quantity, the main drawback to dealing with a manufacturer is service. Unless you buy enough to keep him interested (and for most, that's a lot of frames), you may be put at the end of the line.

If service is the shortcoming of the wholesaler and manufacturer, it is the forte of the retailer. Not only do you get service, but more control, easy adjustments, no minimum-purchase requirements, and a greater selection of moldings (if he deals with a number of wholesalers.) It is advantageous to form a good working relationship with a convenient, careful, and reliable framer who has a good inventory. Introduce yourself, explain what you're up to, and request a professional discount (which should be around 10 to 30 percent, depending on the framer's mark-up and overhead) in exchange for your business. An experienced framer can be a source of valuable advice. He can steer you to bargains on close-out moldings, suggest the best frames for your specific needs, special-order supplies for you, and hustle to meet deadlines. He can even promote your career by touting you to customers and giving your work display space in his shop.

A Visit to a Framer

Anyone who uses frames should visit a framer's workshop to see how they are made. I called on Roger Marino, whose store in Ellicott City, Maryland, is representative of most retail operations around the country. First, we looked at his inventory of over 900 separate moldings, an investment in excess of $60,000. That seemed a lot to me, but Roger says he needs that much to assure an adequate stock and sufficient selection for his customers. He buys at least 100 to 200 feet of molding at a time from a careful selection of wholesalers. Even in these quantities, he finds that his orders are sometimes sidelined until later runs, while the moldings he wants are held for the larger volume customers.

Roger uses two machines to cut molding: *the chopper* (mitering machine, or miter-notching cutoff machine) and the *power miter box*. The chopper is essentially a press with a heavy, very sharp, right-angle blade that cuts a length of molding placed within it into two perfect 45-degree miters.

The power miter box is a circular saw held on an arm that can be swung through 90 degrees. The operator lowers the blade onto molding placed beneath it, rather than moving the molding as with the table saw, or moving the saw on a track as with the radial-arm saw. The power miter box is not as precise, quick, and smooth as the chopper, and it only cuts one miter at a time, but it costs only a fourth of the chopper and, it will cut extrusions. The power miter box is much more accurate than radial-arm or table saws, and since the head is essentially stationary, a vacuum hose can be easily attached to collect sawdust.

For nailing cut moldings, Roger has a miter vise and a bench vise set a few feet apart. He holds the moldings in them either separately, choosing whichever grips the molding best and supporting the ends with wood blocks, or in tandem, with the miter vise holding the pieces to be joined and the bench vise holding the free ends. He cross nails the miters, predrilling them from each side with a cut-off nail held in an electric drill, and glues them with Titebond glue. Then he sets the nails and fills the holes with wax nail-hole filler. Properly nailed and glued, the joints don't need miter clamps and can be handled right away. Any nicks or raw wood that might show at the corners or elsewhere are covered with either marker pens, vinyl wood stain, or a special framer's color blending solution sold in sets by frame suppliers. Canvases are secured in their frames with heavy staples shot from a pneumatic stapler.

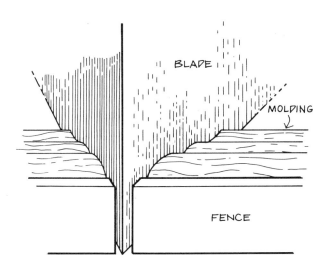

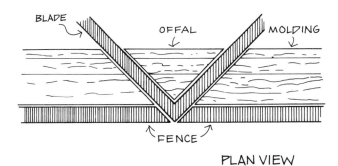

PLAN VIEW

The chopper cuts two perfect miters simultaneously.

Roger uses a $400 "Keeton Mat Cutter" for standard mats and an "Oval Master Mat Cutter," which costs $900, for oval mats. He feels that while hand cutters like the "Dexter Mat Cutter" or an X-Acto knife may give acceptable results in trained hands, they are neither fast nor reliable enough for production work.

Making Your Own Frames

If you want to try making frames yourself, or if there's no decent framer in your area, chops might be your easiest introduction. If possible, buy them from someone nearby whom you can trust to cut the chops carefully, and select a simple molding that'll be easy for you to clamp and nail. You'll need a bench or miter vise to hold the chops and a drill, a hammer, nail sets, glue, a fitting tool or channel pliers for securing pictures in their frames, corner stain, nail-hole filler, screw eyes, and picture wire. As for cutting moldings, if you can't afford a chopper or power miter box, consider a radial-arm saw, which, while no cheaper than a power miter box, is a lot more versatile. Less expensive at about $100 but more precise is the *miter machine*, a miter vise

The miter machine.

with a large backsaw held in a guide at a permanent 45-degree angle. The *miter box*, similar in principle, substitutes a metal bed for the miter vise and is adjustable for any angle between 45 degrees and 90 degrees. Anything less is, in my opinion, a waste of money.

Estimating Large Orders

Occasionally, as when you're mounting a show or specifying a quantity of art, you may need to estimate a large frame order. First separate the job into its components, which may include any of the following: (1) frame, (2) art, (3) glass, plastic, or other protection, (4) mat, (5) backing, (6) assembly, (7) packing, (8) hardware, and (9) installation. Then, consider the items in turn and choose the most suitable options for each. Coordinate the component's sizes, if the final size hasn't been fixed, to minimize waste. I list standard sizes for your guidance.

In other words, if you specify an 18- by 26-inch frame, mat, and glass combination, everything will have to be made to order at a premium. If, however, you could use a 20- by 24-inch frame, which is almost the same area, you can take advantage of cheaper stock components.

1. *Frames:* Consider the frame's width, style, and finish; determine if you'll use a stock or custom size, and if you'll buy from a wholesaler or retailer.

The standard sizes for stock frames are:

5″ × 7″	20″ × 24″
8″ × 10″	22″ × 28″
9″ × 12″	24″ × 28″
11″ × 14″	24″ × 30″
12″ × 16″	24″ × 36″
14″ × 18″	30″ × 40″
16″ × 20″	36″ × 48″
18″ × 24″	

Not all manufacturers offer the full range of sizes, and some may not charge extra for custom sizes in quantity. Don't forget to ask your regular framer if he'd like to bid on a quantity job; he may, in fact, be price competitive, and he'll appreciate your thinking of him.

2. *Art:* Stretched canvas comes in the same sizes as stock frames. Generally there is no appreciable savings in buying the stretchers and canvas separately and assembling them yourself. You will, however, have the option of using a better grade of canvas than comes with stock stretched canvas.

Papers and boards come in a wide variety of sizes. Some common ones are, for illustration and bristol board: 15″ × 20″, 20″ × 30″, 22″ × 30″, 30″ × 40″, and 40″ × 60″; for printing papers: 19″ × 26″, 20″ × 26″, 22″ × 30″, 26″ × 40″, and 29″ × 31″. Papers are generally cheap enough for their size to be subordinated to other components.

3. *Glass, Plastic, and Other Protection:* Glass is harder, cheaper, and easier to keep clean than plastic, but it is heavier and breakable. It is sold in boxes of approximtely 50 square feet of glass each—the area and weight of each box is constant; the number of sheets (lights) varies with the sheet size. Some suppliers will cut a full box to size for a nominal charge. Standard sizes are:

	sheets/box		sheets/box
8″ × 10″	90	18″ × 24″	17
9″ × 12″	67	20″ × 24″	15
10″ × 12″	60	20″ × 26″	14
11″ × 14″	47	22″ × 28″	12
12″ × 16″	38	24″ × 30″	10
13″ × 16″	35	24″ × 36″	8
14″ × 17″	30	(26″ × 32″)*	9
14″ × 18″	29	(30″ × 36″)*	7
16″ × 20″	23	30″ × 40″	6
18″ × 22″	18		

*Not standard frame sizes

Note that glass sizes match that of stock-frame sizes through 24″ × 36″, and also 30″ × 40″.

Plastic is lighter than glass and virtually nonbreakable, but it scratches quite easily and collects static to such an extent that it can pull and hold an unanchored print to it. An antistatic polish will help somewhat. Plastic is manufactured in 4- by 8-foot sheets, which must be cut to order, although some wholesalers do carry stock sizes. Acrylic, the most widely used plastic, is manufactured through either casting or extrusion. Cast acrylic is clearer but more expensive; extruded acrylic is cheaper but may show the extrusion roller marks. One side frosted acrylic, advertised as nonglare, is also available.

Alternatives to glass or plastic include plastic sprays or coatings, Mylar films (available with or without adhesive), and vinyl lamination.

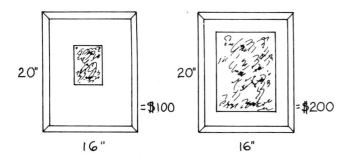

By placing a small piece of art in a large mat, you can reduce the square-foot cost of your product (or vice versa).

4. *Mats:* Mats are not only decorative, but they separate the art from the glass or plastic for better protection. Since mats are cheaper than art, increasing the mat size decreases the total cost per square foot. Alternatives to mats are masked glass, paper mats, and outlines drawn or printed around the art. Common matboard sizes are: 30″ × 40″, 32″ × 40″, 40″ × 48″, and 40″ × 60″.

From *30″ × 40″* you can get, without waste. two 20″ × 30″ pieces, four 15″ × 20″, six 10″ × 20″, and eight 10″ × 15″.

From a *32″ × 40″* you can get, without waste: four 16″ × 20″ pieces and sixteen 8″ × 10″.

From a *40″ × 48″* you can get, without waste: one 32″ × 40″ piece, two 16″ × 20″, four 20″ × 24″, six 16″ × 20″, twelve 10″ × 16″, and sixteen 10″ × 12″.

From a *40″ × 60″* you can get, without waste: two 30″ × 40″ pieces, four 20″ × 30″, six 20″ × 20″, eight 15″ × 20″, and twenty 10″ × 12″.

You can see that it is difficult to coordinate mat-board sizes with stock frames and glass.

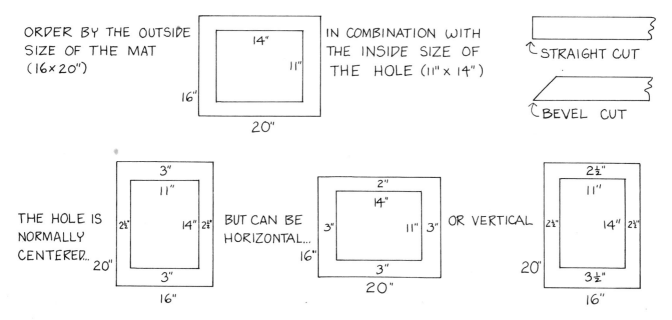

Ordering ready-cut mats.

Ready-cut mats are available in a good range of colors and finishes, and in either a straight or bevel cut depending on the manufacturer. Order them by the outside size of the mat in combination with the inside size of the hole. The hole is normally centered, but some makers may also offer vertical or horizontal placements. For a charge and a minimum order, some manufacturers will make custom dies.

Typical standard sizes are:

Outside	Inside
8″ × 10″	5″ × 7″
9″ × 12″	6″ × 9″
11″ × 14″	8″ × 10″
12″ × 16″	9″ × 12″
14″ × 18″	9″ × 12″
14″ × 18″	11″ × 14″
16″ × 20″	11″ × 14″
16″ × 20″	12″ × 16″
18″ × 24″	12″ × 18″
20″ × 24″	13½″ × 16½″
20″ × 24″	16″ × 20″
22″ × 28″	18″ × 24″
24″ × 30″	18″ × 24″

Note that ready-made mats are available for all stock frame sizes from 9″ × 12″ through 24″ × 30″.

5. *Backing:* Backing may be done with foamboard, mounting board, corrugated fibreboard, solid fibreboard, and, for quality work, neutral ragboard. Select backing on the basis of cost, durability, and rigidity. Foamboard normally comes in 30″ × 40″, 40″ × 60″, and 48″ × 96″ sizes. Backing and mounting board comes in a wide range of sizes including: 30″ × 40″, 31″ × 41″, 32″ × 40″, 33″ × 41″, 34″ × 44″, 35″ × 45″, and 41″ × 61″. Corrugated comes in a wide size range; contact your supplier to determine his inventory.

Assemble frames with channel pliers or a framer's fitting tool.

6. *Assembly:* Assemble frames and art with pneumatic staplers, with brads or finishing nails squeezed in with either channel pliers or a framer's fitting tool; or with points set with a point driver. Damp kraft paper glued to the back edges or tape will give a more finished appearance to the back of the frame.

7. *Packing:* As discussed in the chapter on packing, boxes are customarily made to order to fit their contents, rather than in stock sizes. When you've calculated your order's size and weight, consult a manufacturer for recommendations.

8. *Installation:* If you're doing the installation, you'll have to supply the hardware. Otherwise, ascertain from the client his or the installer's hardware preference. See the chapter on installation for some suggestions.

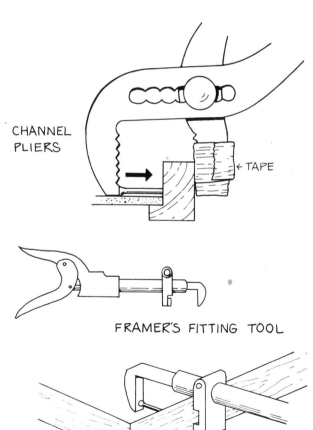

CHANNEL PLIERS

← TAPE

FRAMER'S FITTING TOOL

Alternatives to Frames

Frames aren't always necessary and, in fact, some art forms don't need, or may look better, without them. Some alternatives are:

Boards: Most large suppliers will cut boards to order from the standard 4- by 8-foot sheets of plywood, masonite, or plastic and will often do it better and more economically than you can. Specify that they use a finishing saw blade for smooth edges, and insist on accurate measurements. Remember to take into account the *kerf loss* (i.e., the width of the saw blade, which is about an eighth of an inch for finishing blades) and that the more pieces cut from a sheet, the more the kerf loss and the more mismeasurement will be compounded by a careless worker.

To minimize waste, you should try to use full 4- by 8-foot sheets to best advantage. From a full sheet you can obtain (with allowance for kerf loss) the following pieces: two 48″ × 48″, two 24″ × 96″, three 32″ × 48″, four 24″ × 48″, six 24″ × 32″, eight 24″ × 24″, twelve 16″ × 24″, eighteen 16″ × 16″, twenty-four 12″ × 16″, thirty-two 12″ × 12″, and various combinations thereof. Only one size, by the way, 12″ × 16″, is a stock frame size. Some materials also come in 4′ × 10′ and 5′ × 10′ sizes; these might be more economical for some jobs.

Thin plywood, plastic, metal, and Masonite boards are cheaper, obviously, than thicker sheets, are easier to install, and are easier to prime since they don't require laborious edge treatment. Because they do not project as far from the wall, they are also somewhat less subject to damage. Many clients prefer, however, the greater physical presence of thicker boards.

Boards can be backed on all four edges with a flush, wooden backing frame, which extends the sides and makes the boards appear thicker. Edged boards also have less tendency to warp and are easier to hang with conventional screw eyes and wires. A related method is to fasten two cleats on the back, either along two of the edges, where they can be seen, or hidden, where they will appear to float the board off the wall. Cleated boards, especially those with hidden cleats, are cheap and simple to make, but they're more likely to warp if the boards are at all unstable. Fully edged boards take much more time to make properly, since they require a complete mitered frame and a good fit.

Wraps: Wraps are similar to regular stretched canvases, only the canvas and corners are neatly fastened to the back instead of to the sides of the stretcher, and the painting is continued around the exposed edges. To look most effective, the stretcher thickness should be proportionate to the size of the painting and, be no less than, perhaps, one and one quarter inches. The added costs of heavy-duty or custom-made stretchers, and the extra care in

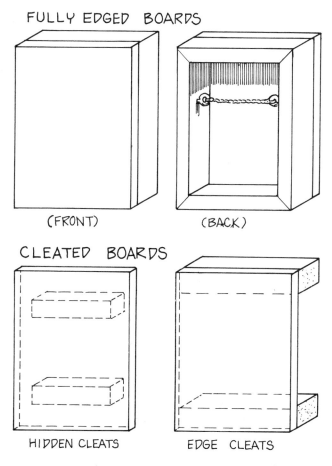

FULLY EDGED BOARDS

(FRONT)   (BACK)

CLEATED BOARDS

HIDDEN CLEATS   EDGE CLEATS

Backed boards.

CONTINUE THE PAINTING AROUND THE EDGES

SHOULD BE AT LEAST 1¼" ($\frac{5}{4}$")

FOLD AND FASTEN THE CANVAS FROM THE REAR

Wraps.

preparation, painting, and subsequent handling often offset any savings from eliminating a frame. Lacking the protection of a frame, wraps are vulnerable, and so they are not especially suitable for commercial installations.

Murals: Murals may be *direct*, i.e., painted right on the wall, or *applied*, i.e., painted on canvas or panels in the studio and subsequently applied to the wall. The savings in direct murals from eliminating the substrate and frame are often cancelled by the added expenses of working on location. Treat the edges of applied murals by either setting the mural into a previously installed molding; attaching a molding after installing the mural; butting the mural flush with similar unmuraled substrates (and feathering the joint if necessary); or setting the mural into an alcove so that it fills the alcove wall to wall.

Murals.

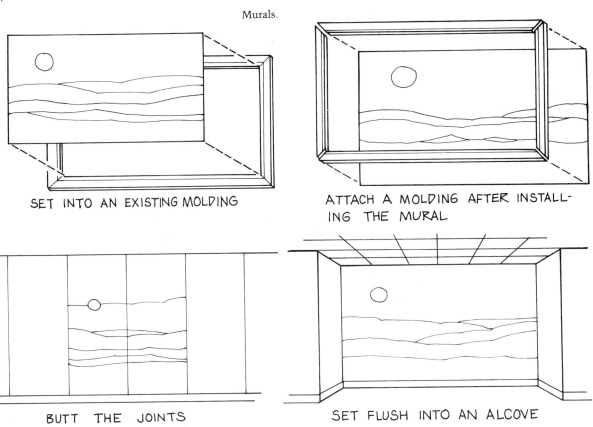

SET INTO AN EXISTING MOLDING

ATTACH A MOLDING AFTER INSTALL-ING THE MURAL

BUTT THE JOINTS

SET FLUSH INTO AN ALCOVE

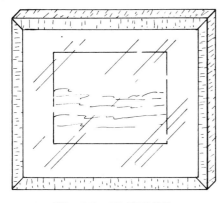

PASSE - PARTOUT

Films: Films such as Mylar or vinyl can be painted or screened, or cut out in appliqué and mounted on walls or boards, either with adhesives or by using self-adhesive films.

Sandwiches: Art can be mounted between clear sheets of plastic or glass and held together with tape (passe-partout), with plastic or metal clips sold for that purpose, or most attractively, with set screws in tapped and threaded holes (plastic only). A more secure alternative to the set screws is to drill through the plastic with a Plexiglas drill, and use two-part Plexiglas fasteners.

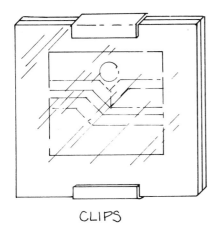

CLIPS

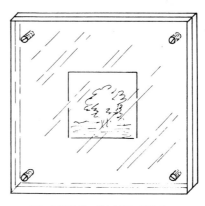

PLASTIC SANDWICH

Passe-partout, clips, plastic sandwich.

25. Installation

You should be familiar with installation methods and materials so that you can design your work for efficient and secure installation. Clients often prefer, and even insist, that suppliers be responsible for installing their own work. The reason is simple. Made-to-order items, be they custom hardware or concrete panels, have a mystifying way of not fitting as specified. In the ensuing go-round, the manufacturer invariably blames the installer (and anyone else he can think of), and the installer blames the manufacturer (and anyone else *he* can think of). The client is left in the middle with heartburn.

Thus, by vesting installation responsibility solely with the manufacturer (you), the client not only pinpoints responsibility but also gains the option of delaying payment until his purchases are properly in place.

Installations pose a number of problems for artists. These include:

1. *Scheduling:* It's often difficult to set an accurate installation date, especially with new buildings. Dates may be postponed time and again, forcing continuous reschedulings. When the word finally does come, it may be with only the shortest notice.

2. *Crews:* While many installations require the help of a number of skilled people, few artists are in a position to keep such people on a regular payroll. Rather, arrangements must be made by the job, and reserving skilled people on a standby basis is difficult.

3. *Distance:* Distance further exacerbates the problems of scheduling and crews.

4. *Skills:* Many of the skills required—managing crews, heavy labor, operating power equipment—are quite foreign to those of making art, and you simply may not possess them.

5. *Insurance:* Installations can demand expensive liability insurance, which may be too high to bill to a single job yet difficult to amortize.

6. *Equipment:* Installations may require elaborate equipment like scaffolds or cranes the arrangement for which will be further complicated by uncertain scheduling.

Installation Policy Options

You should have an installation policy in mind before you seek commissions, and you may want to state it in your brochure.

Some options are:

1. *No installations:* Explain that you are unable to handle installations. It may cost you some clients, but if your work is in demand, this policy is by far the easiest.

Should you not want to do installations but hesitate to appear uncooperative, you can set a price on the service that while not so high as to appear ridiculous, will be high enough to encourage clients to look elsewhere. If your bid is still accepted, the job should, at least, be profitable.

Even if you're not installing your work, especially if it is at all unusual, choose an installation method and communicate it to the installers. Don't make the mistake of assuming that they'll do what's best. Provide clear, detailed instructions and make sure that they get to the persons who'll be doing the actual work. Don't, for instance, write directions on a packing box that may be removed long before your work reaches its final destination. Instead, secure the directions within the inner packing and place a note to that effect on the box.

2. *Installations with the client's crew:* At times a client may want you to work with or supervise his crew. You can charge either a fixed price (which can be included in the contract) or, what's usually less acceptable to a client, your time plus your expenses.

I find the fixed-price arrangement unsatisfactory, because it leaves one too much at the mercy of circumstances. While the client may, with the best of intentions, assure you that events will occur in a predictable fashion at an installation site distant in time and space from his office, often when the time comes the promised crew will not be there because (a) nobody told them, (b) they had more urgent business, or (c) the job site wasn't ready. Should the crew be waiting, they may be (a) hostile, (b) unskilled, or (c) improperly equipped.

To discourage being ill-used, you can (1) stipulate in your bid that you will charge time and expenses if crews and equipment are not present as promised, or (2) that you will be available for a fixed period, after which you'll start your time clock. You may however, have trouble actually collecting the extra money.

3. *Installations by yourself and with your own crew:* There are advantages to installing your work either yourself or with your own crew. You may be able to eliminate much of the packaging; you can control the handling of your work; you may have an additional opportunity to meet the client and to demonstrate your capabilities; and, if you can coordinate the installation with photographing the job, your photo trip will, in effect, be paid for.

On the minus side, installations can be unpleasant and time consuming, and may require expensive equipment and insurance. They can be voyages into alien country; a competent crew will assure you of dependable allies.

Look for resourceful, experienced people. Carpenters and sign men can have such qualities and may be available on short notice. If you need unskilled help to unload and move your work around, firemen, policemen, and students are often free during normal working hours. Another possibility is to schedule installations on weekends or evenings when regularly employed people are at liberty.

You can also subcontract installations, handling it as you would any other subcontractual operation. If you can't be there to supervise, provide clear instructions, and go over the job, on location if possible, to eliminate any misunderstandings.

Fasteners

Base the selection of fastener *types* on (1) the composition of the installation surface and/or subsurface—wood, drywall, concrete, brick, stone, plaster, block, metal, glass, or tile, (2) the weight of the artwork and its size, (3) the nature and amount of stress exerted on the artwork, and (4) the status of the installation—permanent or removable.

THE SIZE, NUMBER, AND ARRANGEMENT OF FASTENERS DEPENDS ON THE WEIGHT AND FORM OF THE ARTWORK

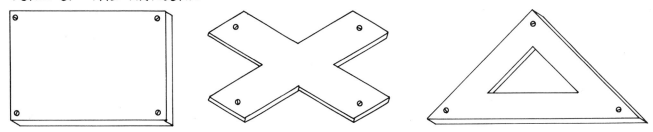

AND THE AMOUNT OF STRESS PLACED ON IT. THE WEIGHT OF THE ARTWORK WILL ORDINARILY CAUSE A STEADY, PREDICTABLE, DOWNWARD STRESS.

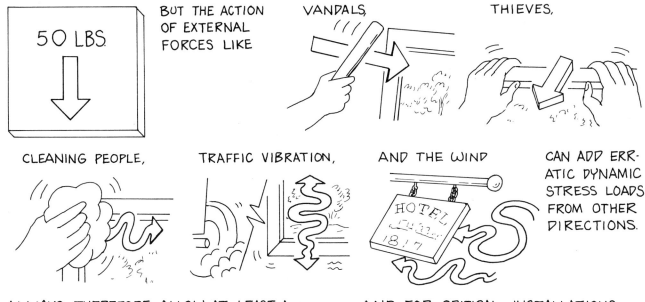

50 LBS.

BUT THE ACTION OF EXTERNAL FORCES LIKE

VANDALS,

THIEVES,

CLEANING PEOPLE,

TRAFFIC VIBRATION,

AND THE WIND

CAN ADD ERRATIC DYNAMIC STRESS LOADS FROM OTHER DIRECTIONS.

ALWAYS, THEREFORE, ALLOW AT LEAST A **FOURFOLD** SAFETY MARGIN BEYOND THE ACTUAL WEIGHT OF YOUR ARTWORK...

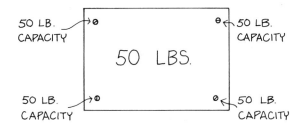

50 LB. CAPACITY 50 LB. CAPACITY

50 LBS.

50 LB. CAPACITY 50 LB. CAPACITY

AND FOR <u>CRITICAL INSTALLATIONS</u> ALLOW AT LEAST A **TENFOLD** SAFETY MARGIN.

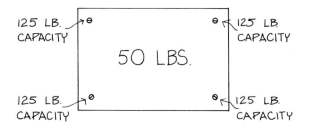

125 LB. CAPACITY 125 LB. CAPACITY

50 LBS.

125 LB. CAPACITY 125 LB. CAPACITY

Fasteners—their size, number, and arrangement depends on weight, form and stress.

NAILS

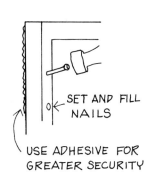

← SET AND FILL NAILS

USE ADHESIVE FOR GREATER SECURITY

SCREWS

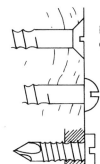

FLATHEAD - SET FLUSH OR SINK AND FILL

ROUNDHEAD - USE WITH THIN MATERIALS, FLAT WASHERS

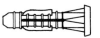

SELF-TAPPING METAL SCREWS

SPECIAL HEADS DETER THEFT

 ALLEN HEAD

 ONE WAY

 PHILLIPS HEAD

PLUGS

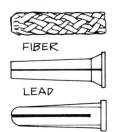

FIBER

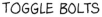

LEAD

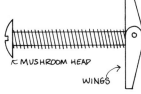

DRILL A HOLE AND INSERT THE PLUG. PLACE THE SCREW THROUGH THE OBJECT INTO THE PLUG TURN THE SCREW COMPRESSING THE PLUG.

POLYETHYLENE EXPANSION ANCHORS (POLY-SET)

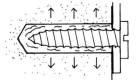

DRILL HOLE AND INSERT PLUG. PLACE SCREW THROUGH HOLE IN OBJECT INTO ANCHOR AND TIGHTEN IT.

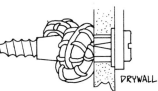 DRYWALL

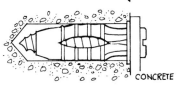 CONCRETE

TOGGLE BOLTS

MUSHROOM HEAD

WINGS

DRILL HOLES IN THE WALL AND IN THE OBJECT. INSERT BOLT THROUGH OBJECT AND ATTACH WINGS. FOLD THE WINGS BACK, INSERT IN HOLE IN THE WALL. PULL BACK TO SPREAD WINGS AND HOLD AGAINST WALL. TURN BOLT UNTIL TIGHT.

FOLD WINGS BACK AND INSERT

PULL BACK ON WINGS AND TIGHTEN

SLEEVE ANCHORS (ANCHOR BOLTS)

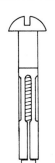

DRILL THE SAME SIZE HOLE FOR ANCHOR AND OBJECT. INSERT ANCHOR, TAP UNTIL FLUSH AND TIGHTEN TO FLARE.

LAG SHIELDS

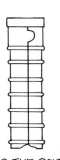

LAG BOLT →

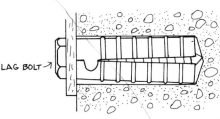

DRILL A HOLE IN THE WALL FOR THE SHIELD AND THROUGH THE OBJECT FOR THE LAG BOLT INSERT THE SHIELD IN THE WALL, SLIP THE BOLT THROUGH THE OBJECT AND TIGHTEN.

Nails, screws, plugs, polyethylene expansion anchors, toggle bolts, sleeve anchors, lag shields.

DIRECT

THROUGH FASTENING

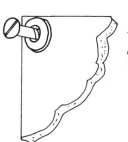

USE WITH SCREWS, NAILS, LAG BOLTS, TOGGLE BOLTS, SLEEVE ANCHORS AND OTHER FASTENERS

ADHESIVE, BY ITSELF OR WITH TAPE AND/OR FASTENERS

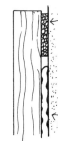

STRIPS OF TAPE, E.G. 3M DOUBLE COATED FOAM # 4016 ($\frac{1}{16}$" THICK) OR #4004 ($\frac{1}{4}$" THICK). USE THICKER TAPES FOR MORE IRREGULAR WALLS. THE TAPE HOLDS THE ART UNTIL THE ADHESIVE SETS

ADHESIVE, E.G. SILICONE ADHESIVE, MASTIC, OR CONTACT CEMENT

INDIRECT

BRACKETS

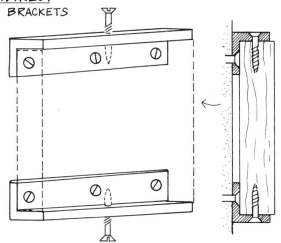

WITH HOLLOW ART, YOU CAN LOWER THE BRACKETS TO HIDE THEM

FIRST SECURE THE BRACKETS TO THE WALL. NEXT, PLACE THE ART AND FASTEN IT. FOR GREATER SECURITY, USE SELF-TAPPING SCREWS, AND OR ADHESIVE. YOU CAN LOCATE THE SCREW HOLES BY DRILLING UP THROUGH THE BRACKET HOLES BEFORE PLACE-MENT.

PAIRS OF BRACKETS

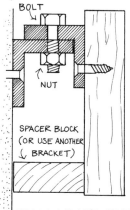

ATTACH ONE BRACKET TO THE ART WITH FASTENERS, AD-HESIVE, OR BY WELDING. IF YOU CAN'T REACH THE NUT, CEMENT OR WELD IT TO THE BRACKET OR TAP THE HOLE.

ANGLED BLOCKS

ATTACH ONE OF THE ANGLED WOOD BLOCKS TO THE ART AND THE OTHER TO THE WALL. FIT TOGETHER. GRAVITY WILL HOLD THE ART IN PLACE, OR ADD A LINE OF ADHESIVE.

NAILS AND BLOCKS

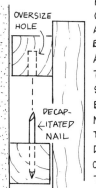

HAMMER A LINE OF NAILS 4"-8" APART IN ONE BLOCK OF WOOD. AND DECAPITATE THEM. PRESS AGAIN-ST THE SECOND BLOCK. THE CUT NAILS WILL MARK THE PLACES TO DRILL SLIGHTLY OVERSIZE HOLES TO RECEIVE THEM. ATTACH THE NAIL BLOCK TO THE WALL AND THE HOLE BLOCK TO THE ART. FIT THE ART ONTO THE WALL BLOCK.

Installation methods.

Base the selection of fastener *size*, *number*, and *arrangement* on the weight and form of the artwork, and the nature and amount of stress placed on it. The weight of the artwork will ordinarily cause a steady, predictable, downward stress, but the action of external forces, like vandals, thieves, cleaning people, traffic vibration, and the wind, can add erratic dynamic stress loads from other directions. Always, therefore, allow at least a fourfold safety margin beyond the actual weight of your artwork, e.g., for a 50-pound painting, allow 200 pounds of support. For critical installations, such as overhead signs, allow at least a tenfold safety margin, e.g., for a 50-pound painting, allow 500 pounds of support.

You can obtain pullout load-test data from most fastener manufacturers that will advise you on the capacity of various fastener types and sizes. A particularly useful booklet is *How to Anchor Anything to Masonry*, available from the Rawlplug Company; Inc., 200 Petersville Road, New Rochelle, New York, 10802. Another informative booklet on anchoring systems can be obtained from ITT Phillips Drill Division, P.O. Box 364, Michigan City, Indiana, 46360.

Pullout load-test data must be scientifically replicable. Therefore, the testing services use standard bearing surfaces, concrete being particularly favored. When transferring the test data to your own circumstances, realize that the bearing surface under consideration, e.g., drywall, may not have the performance characteristics of the test material, and that the material of your artwork or its construction may prematurely fail. In other words, while a particular togglebolt may, in concrete block, support 1,000 pounds, it could break out of half-inch drywall long before that maximum is reached. Or the frame through which you've inserted the toggle may disintegrate. Because of such imponderables, it's always wise to consult experienced people before specifying fasteners for critical installations.

IF YOU MUST MARK ON THE WALL USE VERY LIGHT PENCIL OR APPLY DRAFTING TAPE AND MARK ON IT.

USE PIECES OF WOOD TO MAINTAIN THE UNIFORM HEIGHT FROM THE FLOOR OF LONG OBJECTS OR GROUPS OF OBJECTS

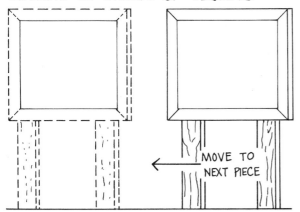

MOVE TO NEXT PIECE

Installing pictures and panels.

HOLD HEAVY OBJECTS WITH BAR CLAMPS WHILE SECURING THEM

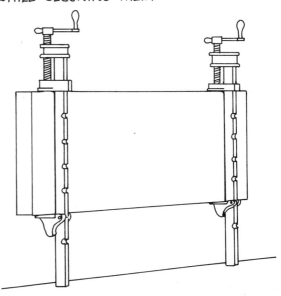

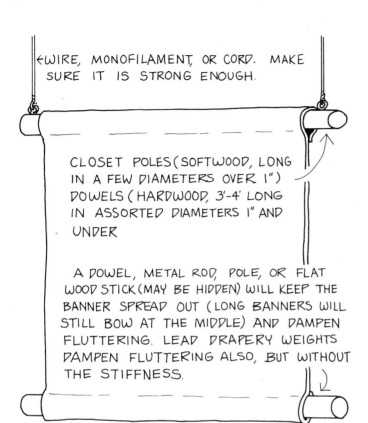

←WIRE, MONOFILAMENT, OR CORD. MAKE SURE IT IS STRONG ENOUGH.

CLOSET POLES (SOFTWOOD, LONG IN A FEW DIAMETERS OVER 1") DOWELS (HARDWOOD, 3'-4' LONG IN ASSORTED DIAMETERS 1" AND UNDER

A DOWEL, METAL ROD, POLE, OR FLAT WOOD STICK (MAY BE HIDDEN) WILL KEEP THE BANNER SPREAD OUT (LONG BANNERS WILL STILL BOW AT THE MIDDLE) AND DAMPEN FLUTTERING. LEAD DRAPERY WEIGHTS DAMPEN FLUTTERING ALSO, BUT WITHOUT THE STIFFNESS.

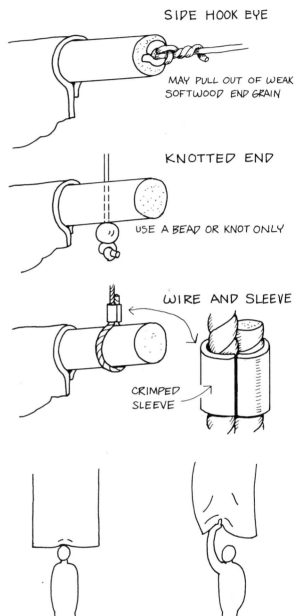

SIDE HOOK EYE

MAY PULL OUT OF WEAK SOFTWOOD END GRAIN

KNOTTED END

USE A BEAD OR KNOT ONLY

WIRE AND SLEEVE

CRIMPED SLEEVE

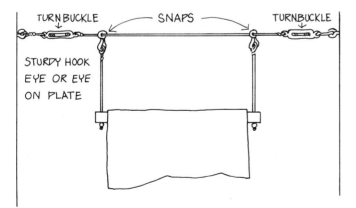

TURNBUCKLE — SNAPS — TURNBUCKLE

STURDY HOOK EYE OR EYE ON PLATE

A HORIZONTAL SUSPENSION ARRANGEMENT

ALWAYS ALLOW ADEQUATE HEAD ROOM AND DON'T FORGET THE GRABBERS.

Installing wall hangings.

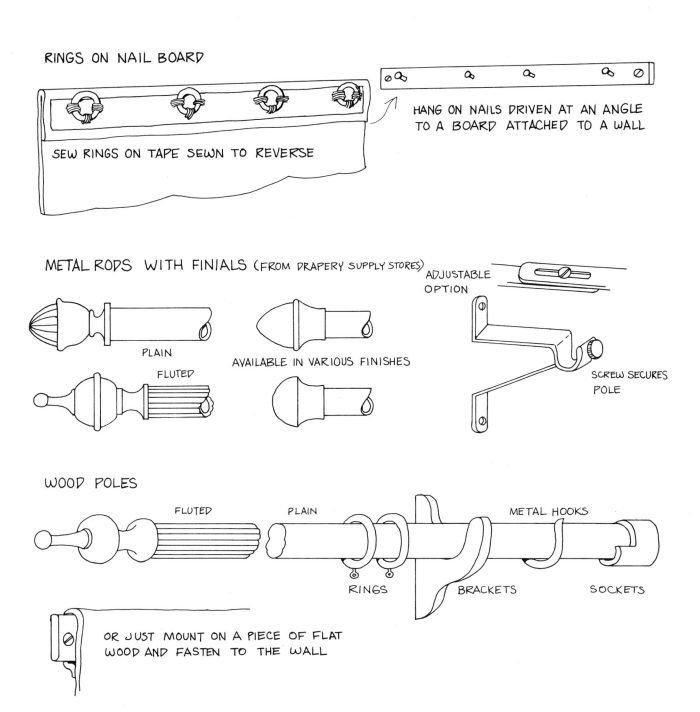

RINGS ON NAIL BOARD

SEW RINGS ON TAPE SEWN TO REVERSE

HANG ON NAILS DRIVEN AT AN ANGLE
TO A BOARD ATTACHED TO A WALL

METAL RODS WITH FINIALS (FROM DRAPERY SUPPLY STORES)

PLAIN

FLUTED

AVAILABLE IN VARIOUS FINISHES

ADJUSTABLE
OPTION

SCREW SECURES
POLE

WOOD POLES

FLUTED

PLAIN

METAL HOOKS

RINGS

BRACKETS

SOCKETS

OR JUST MOUNT ON A PIECE OF FLAT
WOOD AND FASTEN TO THE WALL

SCREW EYES ARE MOST COMMONLY USED. KEEP SEVERAL SIZES ON HAND

217
215
213
211

ACTUAL SIZE
ALSO MADE WITH LONG SHANK

USE WITH BRAIDED PICTURE WIRE AVAILABLE IN 15' COILS AND 5 LB SPOOLS

SIZE	STRANDS	BREAKING PT.	FT./SPOOL
1	8	34 LBS.	C. 2200
3	16	68 LBS.	C. 1025
5	24	102 LBS.	C. 740
8	36	145 LBS.	C. 500

① MEASURE DOWN FROM BOTH SIDES. START THE HOLE WITH A BRADAWL. DRILL A PILOT HOLE IN HARDWOOD

② WAX THE SCREW EYE. START IT BY HAND, THEN SLIP THE TIP IN THE EYE AND TURN THE SCREW EYE HOME.

③ KNOT THE WIRE

FOR GREATER SECURITY USE MIRROR HANGERS

HEAVY DUTY WALL HOOK

YOU CAN ALSO USE NAILS

HANG WIRE OR MIRROR HANGERS ON NAILS, SCREWS, HOOKS, MOLYS, ETC.

SOLID RING HEAVY DUTY MIRROR HANGER (ASSTD. SIZES)

WIRE TYPE MIRROR HANGER (ASSTD. SIZES)

USE TWO SUPPORTS FOR MIRROR HANGERS OR WITH WIRES TO REDUCE SLIPPAGE. ALIGN THEM WITH A LEVEL.

YOU MAY ALSO USE A MUSEUM INSTALLATION TECHNIQUE

BRASS OR STEEL FLAT MENDING PLATE

OR VARIOUS MIRROR CLIPS

BENDABLE

PUSH DOWN

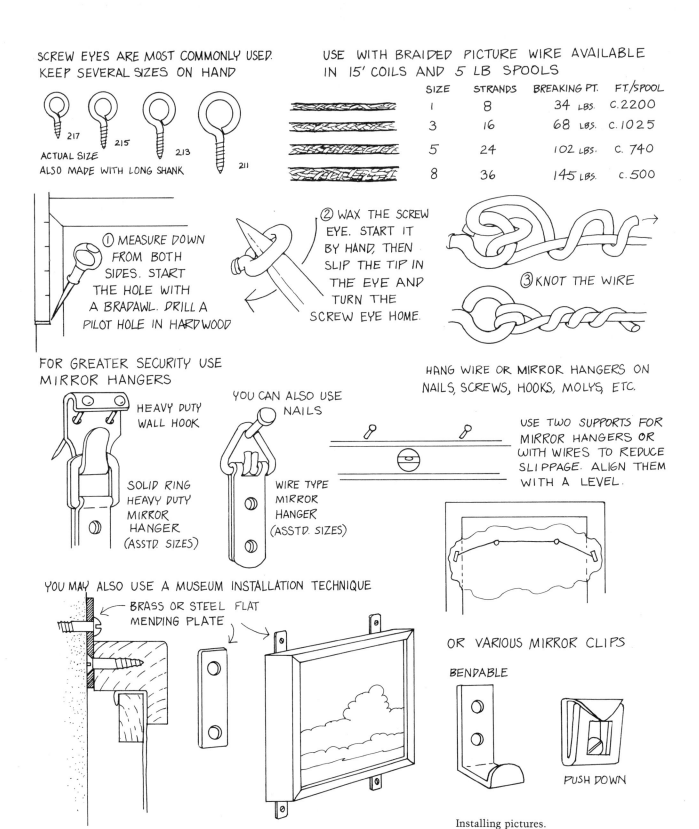

Installing pictures.

FASTENERS

Fastener	Use With	Comments
Nails	Wood, wood products, wood studs.	Crude, quick, and cheap. Danger of injury to art. Great range of styles and sizes. Casing and finishing nails can be sunk and filled for a neater job.
Screws	Wood, wood products wood studs. Metal and metal studs.	Quick and cheap. Great range of styles, sizes, and finishes. Countersunk heads can be sunk and filled. Round heads are used for thin materials. Self-tapping metal screws need no pilot hole and can be driven directly into metal studs.
Silicone Adhesive	Non-porous surfaces	One-part, tough, flexible, weather resistant. To hold art while adhesive cures, use nails, masking tape on the face, or double coated flat or foam tape. Foam tape bridges irregularities of rough surfaces like masonry.
Plugs	Drywall, concrete, brick, block, stone.	Used in conjunction with wood, or sheet metal screws, or lag bolts. Plastic plugs are cheapest and used for light loads. Lead plugs should not be used for loads subject to shock or vibration. Fiber plugs, e.g., Rawlplug, are good for general use. The holding power of Rawlplugs in concrete is: with a #10 x 1″ screw, 1,300 lbs.; and with a 3/8″ x 2¼″ lag bolt, 3,225 lbs.
Polyethylene Expansion Anchors (Poly-Set)	Drywall, plywood, block, concrete, brick, stone.	A multi-purpose anchor for general light use. The pullout of a #8 screw is in: ½″ drywall — 135 lbs. ½″ plywood — 240 lbs. light weight block — 290 lbs. solid concrete — 210 lbs. The pullout of a #14 screw is in: ½″ drywall — 180 lbs. ½″ plywood — 400 lbs. light weight block — 625 lbs. solid concrete — 865 lbs.
Toggle Bolts	Hollow surfaces, e.g., drywall, block.	Requires two different size holes. Drill the bolt hold through the object one size larger to allow maneuverability. A ¼″ Rawl toggle bolt has 650 lbs. holding power. A 3/8″ Rawl toggle bolt has 1,000 lbs. holding power.
Sleeve Anchors (Anchor Bolts)	Concrete, brick, block, stone.	A one-piece masonry fastener. Needs only one size of drill. A ¼″ x 2″ Red Head round head sleeve anchor holding a 1″ thick object in solid concrete tests at: 1,125 lbs. shear and 2,080 pullout. A 3/8″ x 2½″ Red Head round head sleeve anchor holding a 1¼″ thick object in solid concrete tests at: 3,000 lbs. shear and 3,600 pullout.
Lag Shields	Concrete, block, mortar joints.	Requires 2 different size holes. The pullout of a ¼″ Rawl long lag shield in concrete is 600 lbs., and a 3/8″ Rawl long lag shield is 2,000 lbs.

Installing Murals

You can spare yourself the added time, trouble, and expense of working on location if you can execute murals in your shop and have them installed on location by a paperhanger. The technique is not suitable, however, for large or complex sites that cannot be duplicated in your studio.

Locating a qualified paperhanger may not be easy. All paperhangers should know how to hang wallpaper, but few will have ever had the occasion to hang a mural, which requires skill, experience, self-confidence, and careful workmanship. You can ask mural artists or people who've specified murals for their recommendations. Or, have the business agent of your local painters' and/or paperhangers' union suggest his best qualified member.

Evaluate a paperhanger by first discussing your job with him to see if he seems credible. Does he answer your questions decisively or is he tentative and evasive? If he sounds okay ask for the names and locations of his recent work. You may then, as with any sub, contact his clients to learn their opinions of him and his workmanship, and visit the job sites for a personal inspection.

To evaluate a paperhanger's work, first check the mural's alignment. It should hang straight and the seams should match. Next check the surface; it should be free of bubbles, lumps, and other imperfections, and be clean of installation dirt. View the wall from a raking angle to see if subsurface irregularities like sloppy spackle, nail pops, and wavers have been removed. Finally, check his trim work. The edges should be cut smooth, not ragged, and lay flat and not curl up. Accessories like switch and outlet plates should be covered neatly and match the background.

Hanging a Mural

Before hanging the mural, the paperhanger must prepare the wall as necessary. This may involve as little as some spot sanding and spackling or as much as a complete priming or relining. If the surface is really bad, it may have to be plastered or drywalled.

Once the wall is ready, the paperhanger determines the placement of the mural. He then rolls out the mural, examines its condition, and finds its center. If the mural is in sections, he pastes up one roll at a time starting in the middle and working out. If it is in one piece, he first pastes up one half the mural, starting in the middle and working out, and then goes back and does the other half. He can, incidentally, for nonpermanent installations, use a paste that will permit the mural to be easily peeled off the wall.

After he hangs the mural, the paperhanger smooths out any imperfections with a soft, dry, smoothing brush, and trims all the edges with a sharp knife. That done, he washes the mural down with a soft sponge and clean water. Finally, when it's dry, he spackles the seams if need be. If the artist is not available, the paperhanger can touch up any minor holidays.

Under normal circumstances, a paperhanger will prefer one piece (railroaded) murals because he won't have to fool with seams. He should be able to handle a mural within the span of his arms, i.e., approximately six feet wide. Discuss larger murals with him to determine if he would prefer them in one piece, or would want to seam them.

Laying Up a Pieced Mural in the Studio

1. When you receive an order, calculate the total yardage, allowing for overage. With railroaded goods, the calculation is simple; with pieced goods you must figure the cuts by allowing for overage top and bottom and at either end. Check your inventory and order additional goods if necessary.

2. Measure piece goods on a cutting table. One or more sheets of homosote laid over 2 × 4's resting on sawhorses makes a good table. You can use the end of the table as a reference point. Measure the length required along both sides of the table and mark the points with a push pin. Then roll out your goods, connect both push pins with a straightedge, and make your cuts. Allow for slight errors in measurement by over-cutting an inch or so.

CALCULATE THE YARDAGE

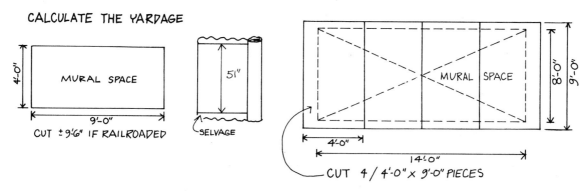

MURAL SPACE

4'-0"

9'-0"

CUT ± 9'-6" IF RAILROADED

51"

SELVAGE

MURAL SPACE

8'-0"

9'-0"

4'-0"

14'-0"

CUT 4 / 4'-0" x 9'-0" PIECES

CUT THE GOODS

MEASURE FROM THE END ALONG BOTH SIDES, MARK THE POINTS WITH PUSH PINS, CONNECT THE PINS WITH A STRAIGHTEDGE AND CUT ALONG IT.

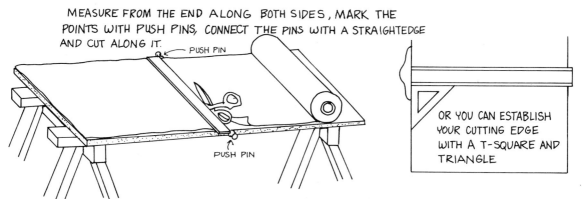

PUSH PIN

PUSH PIN

OR YOU CAN ESTABLISH YOUR CUTTING EDGE WITH A T-SQUARE AND TRIANGLE

HANG THE MURAL ON YOUR PAINTING WALL

STRING LEVEL

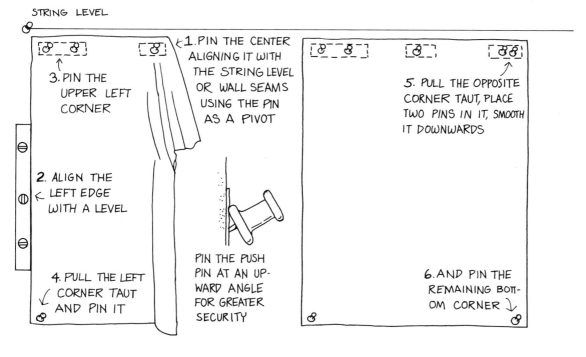

3. PIN THE UPPER LEFT CORNER

1. PIN THE CENTER ALIGNING IT WITH THE STRING LEVEL OR WALL SEAMS USING THE PIN AS A PIVOT

5. PULL THE OPPOSITE CORNER TAUT, PLACE TWO PINS IN IT, SMOOTH IT DOWNWARDS

2. ALIGN THE LEFT EDGE WITH A LEVEL

4. PULL THE LEFT CORNER TAUT AND PIN IT

PIN THE PUSH PIN AT AN UP-WARD ANGLE FOR GREATER SECURITY

6. AND PIN THE REMAINING BOTT-OM CORNER

Laying up a pieced mural in the studio.

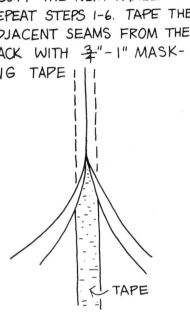

7. BUTT THE NEXT PANEL AND REPEAT STEPS 1-6. TAPE THE ADJACENT SEAMS FROM THE BACK WITH ¾"-1" MASKING TAPE

TAPE

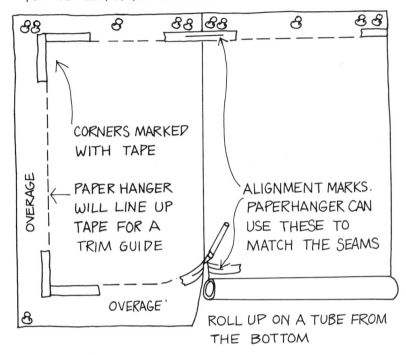

YOU CAN MARK THE MURAL FOR THE PAPERHANGER

CORNERS MARKED WITH TAPE

PAPER HANGER WILL LINE UP TAPE FOR A TRIM GUIDE

OVERAGE

ALIGNMENT MARKS. PAPERHANGER CAN USE THESE TO MATCH THE SEAMS

OVERAGE

ROLL UP ON A TUBE FROM THE BOTTOM

An alternative measuring method is to align your goods with the edge of the table and use a T-square and triangle.

3. If the material is thin, reinforce it along its top rear edge at both corners and the center with 3/4-inch-wide masking tape to prevent ripping when it's pinned up.

4. Roll the goods up on a tube.

5. Clear your painting wall of push pins. Establish a top edge for the mural, using either (a) the horizontal (8-foot) seams of the wall, or (b) a string made level either by measuring up to the end points from the floor, by attaching a line level, or by using a water level.

6. Hang the mural on the wall, proceeding from one side to the other. Use for a vertical either a mason's level or the wall seams (if they're level). Align the top of the mural with your string or the

wall seams. Place a 5/8-inch pin at an upward angle into the middle of the top edge of the fabric. Let the fabric unroll.

7. Using the pin as a pivot, align one vertical edge with your level and place two pins in the upper left corner above it. Place a pin in the lower corner beneath. Pull the opposite top corner taut, place two pins in it, smooth it downward, and pin the remaining bottom corner.

8. Butt the next panel against the first and repeat steps 7 and 8.

9. Tape the backs of the vertical edges together with a continuous strip of 1-inch masking tape. You may have to unloosen some of the adjacent pins if you don't have enough leeway for manipulation. Too much strain to join the fabric will make it stretch or even rip; not enough stretch and the seams will bulge.

Mural Fabrics

You should use a tough canvas for rough walls, long railroads, and high-abuse situations. Use a tight weave that won't stretch for linear designs and those with considerable detail.

Artists' canvas comes with the selvage untrimmed. If you must seam it, lay the adjacent pieces out together, place one edge over the other, and with a sharp knife simultaneously *double cut* a common joint.

Double-cut edges will not be as exact, however, as factory trimmed ones. One pretrimmed material is *vinyl-coated lining paper*. One manufacturer is Standard Coated Products, Humboldt Industrial Park, Box D, Hazleton, Pennsylvania, 18201. It is not really a paper, but a coated, lightweight cloth. While the surface accepts both water- and oil-based paint, one or more coats of primer will greatly improve its handling qualities. Besides murals, it's used for lining rough walls to provide a smoother surface for repainting or repapering. It's thinness is its principal disadvantage; you must handle it with care to avoid tears and punctures, and it won't hold up under abuse.

Working with a Paperhanger

Always review your intentions with your paperhanger to make sure you understand one another and to receive any suggestions that he might have.

The paperhanger will find the mural's center by folding it over on itself, but if the mural is off center, or its location on the wall is uncertain, provide centering marks. Mark these with drafting tape placed at the corners, edges, and wherever else he might benefit from guidance. Always clearly label abstracts; their direction and joints may be obscure to your paperhanger. If he may be confused matching the seams, as with a nebulous passage, run a few pieces of drafting tape across them, draw a line on the tape, and then cut through the tape at the seam line when you roll up the mural. The paperhanger will be able to align the marks on the tape rather than worry about matching the mural pattern itself.

Always overpaint your murals to compensate for inadvertent errors. Allow a more generous margin where measurements are uncertain, for larger murals, and for sites with doors, windows, switchplates, and similar obstructions.

There are no special mural paints or varnishes. Whichever you choose should be water resistant, dry hard enough to allow the mural to be rolled, and be sufficiently flexible to roll without cracking or flaking.

As soon as the paint is dry, you can roll the mural up on a cardboard tube—the greater the tube's diameter, the less the stress. A tube longer than the mural will help protect its ends, a particular consideration with pieced murals. If you must roll a tacky mural, you can interleaf its surface with polyethylene film as you roll it.

Mural Installation Costs

In his installation estimate, the paperhanger will consider:

1. *The mural site:* If the wall is simple, or if there are bends, columns, windows, doors, and switchplates; if the site is readily accessible, or if he will need scaffolds.

2. *The condition of the wall:* If it is smooth, primed, and ready to go, or if, and how much, he must prepare it.

3. *The mural, its nature, size, and value:* If it is one piece or seamed, small or large, fragile or rugged, inexpensive or valuable. He must take into account the mural's value, since he is responsible for its damage or loss while it's in his care.

The paperhanger may charge either a fixed fee or by the hour. Travel is usually charged as straight time, door to door. As with all subcontractors, have a written agreement and a copy of his insurance.

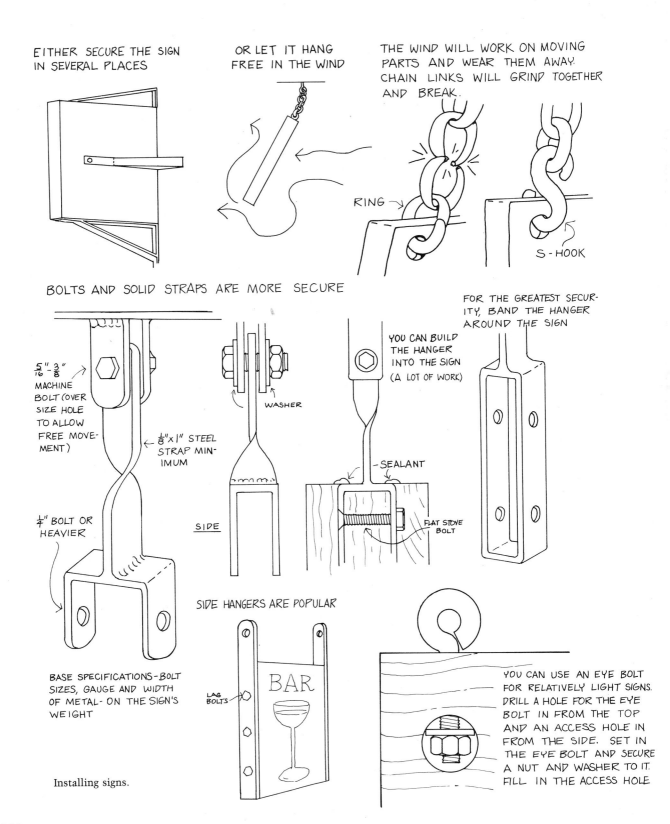

EITHER SECURE THE SIGN IN SEVERAL PLACES

OR LET IT HANG FREE IN THE WIND

THE WIND WILL WORK ON MOVING PARTS AND WEAR THEM AWAY. CHAIN LINKS WILL GRIND TOGETHER AND BREAK.

RING

S - HOOK

BOLTS AND SOLID STRAPS ARE MORE SECURE

FOR THE GREATEST SECURITY, BAND THE HANGER AROUND THE SIGN

$\frac{5}{16}" - \frac{3}{8}"$ MACHINE BOLT (OVER SIZE HOLE TO ALLOW FREE MOVEMENT)

$\frac{1}{8}" \times 1"$ STEEL STRAP MINIMUM

WASHER

SIDE

YOU CAN BUILD THE HANGER INTO THE SIGN (A LOT OF WORK)

SEALANT

FLAT STOVE BOLT

$\frac{1}{4}"$ BOLT OR HEAVIER

BASE SPECIFICATIONS—BOLT SIZES, GAUGE AND WIDTH OF METAL—ON THE SIGN'S WEIGHT

SIDE HANGERS ARE POPULAR

BAR

LAG BOLTS

YOU CAN USE AN EYE BOLT FOR RELATIVELY LIGHT SIGNS. DRILL A HOLE FOR THE EYE BOLT IN FROM THE TOP AND AN ACCESS HOLE IN FROM THE SIDE. SET IN THE EYE BOLT AND SECURE A NUT AND WASHER TO IT. FILL IN THE ACCESS HOLE

Installing signs.

Outdoor Signs

Don't attempt to design or install large or heavy outdoor signs if you haven't the experience—consult a skilled sign man. Be aware of local regulations and license requirements.

There are many factors to consider when installing signs—theft, clearance, visibility—but weather is key. You can either secure the sign in several places to resist the wind, or allow it to hang freely. The wind will work on moving parts and erode them away, much as the action of waves on a beach. Solid bolts will be more permanent than chain, the links of which will grind together and eventually break.

You can connect signs with rings, hooks, or brackets. The choice of a method depends on your budget and the size, thickness, design, and weight of the sign. Never use screw eyes in the end grain of wood, especially in plywood. The wood will quickly rot away, releasing the sign.

Signs should be inspected for wear regularly. No outdoor installation is permanent.

Estimating Installations

Installations can be even harder to estimate than artwork because of your uncertain control over events. If you must bid in advance, don't get burned. Better to overestimate and tell the client you'll charge less if possible, than the reverse.

You may require the following information for your estimate:

1. *Installation location(s):* You need precise instructions, preferably blueprints or dimensioned drawings, so you can estimate how long it will take to get your work to the location site(s) and how long it will take to install the work once you get there. Study the plans for difficult accesses, tight passages en route, heights that may require ladders, scaffolds, or even cranes—anything that will cause delays and increase your expenses.

If the job is complicated, you can proceed as though planning a military campaign. Run through the operation and estimate how much time it will take for each phase: parking your vehicle, unloading, carrying the work to the site(s), moving obstructions, and so forth. Add the estimates together and stir in a generous margin for error.

2. *Installation surfaces:* Determine the installation surfaces and subsurfaces. If you must drill or break into a wall, be certain that you won't interfere with any hidden pipes, wires, ducts, or the like. Confirm that the wall will, in fact, support the added weight of your artwork. Unusually heavy loads like sculpture will need special consideration and perhaps extra bracing.

3. *Installation method(s):* The installation method will depend on the installation surface and on the artwork—its size, weight, and permanence. Nailing, applying adhesives, and taping are quick. Screwing and lag-bolting are somewhat slower. Toggle-bolting and lag-bolting with expansion shields are slower still. Complicated blind-mountings are slowest of all.

4. *Expenses:* Expenses can include hardware, rentals of vehicles and special equipment, and parking. For overnight stays, add meals and lodging.

5. *Travel time:* Travel time is the distance between the job site and your and/or your crew's shop, or home. The crew may ask for travel time at the same rate as work time, at a reduced or negotiated rate, or not at all.

6. *Other:* Inquire about any unusual circumstances that might complicate the job. Common ones are: no power, water, or light at the job site; no place to unload or park your vehicle; odd hours of access; no storage space; conflicts of access with other work crews or the public; and a lack of working elevators in a multifloor building. If you must depend on an agent of the client to provide access, material, equipment, or directions at the job site, you may wish to have an understanding that delays caused by the nonappearance of the agent or the absence of the promised provisions will be billed extra.

Allow for imponderables:

1. *Downtime:* Delays are inevitable—traffic, getting lost, parking, finding the job site, finding the client's agents, assembling and disassembling

equipment, locating outlets, moving furniture, waiting for other crews or the public to move out of the way, unforeseen problems, e.g., a water pipe in a wall that was supposed to be empty or metal studs when they were to have been wood (and you only brought wood screws—off to the hardware store), cleaning up after the previous crew, etc.

2. *"Nobody works like the boss works"*: Don't assume your crew will be as well motivated as you. You're eager to see your work displayed and to return to your studio. For the crew, yours may be just another job.

Come Prepared

After you've participated in a number of installations, you'll learn to come prepared with everything remotely useful and then some. Thorough preparation is especially important when working at job sites that are either distant from supply stores or under construction. Consider: a ladder or stepping stool (or both); auxiliary lights; extension cords; marking implements; masking tape; drop cloths; newspapers; a means of cordoning off your work area; a full selection of hand and power tools, including levels, hammers, rulers, power drills, screwdrivers, nail sets, saws, chisels, wrenches, pliers, and clamps; extra drills and fasteners to replace those lost or broken; a mat knife and staple remover for unwrapping; scrap lumber for shims and braces; sawhorses; and clean-up materials like soap, erasers, water, paint thinner, towels, dust brush, broom, and vacuum cleaner. Also take repair and touch-up materials for your artwork: extra paint, thinner, medium, touch-up wax, spackle, varnish, and applicators like paint brushes and cotton swabs—whatever might be needed to mend transportation and installation damage.

26. Packing and Shipping

Packing

In this chapter, I often distinguish between *commercial* and *museum* shipments. Commercial shipments comprise relatively inexpensive, non-unique artworks like catalog and production items. The emphasis is on *price* rather than protection, and certain risks and shortcuts are acceptable that would be unthinkable in museum work. Museum shipments comprise high-value, unique items. The emphasis is on *protection* rather than on price, and all reasonable precautions are taken to ensure a safe passage. You as a shipper can choose between the two and make any suitable compromises in between.

The principles are the same for packing an inexpensive print or an invaluable painting. Economics and common sense, however, dictate that the amount of protection be proportionate to the value and uniqueness of the shipment. You can't expect a client to pay you $100 to build a plywood box for a $50 print, nor would you expect a museum to ship a Rembrandt in a fibreboard carton. Consider the artwork: its fragility, size, weight, replaceability, and value; and consider the carrier: its service, and restrictions of size, weight, and insurance. Think also of the packing budget and who's paying for it—you, or the purchaser.

Packing and arranging for shipment take considerable time—time that is difficult to charge off entirely to a client. If you're doing production (repeat) work, it is good sense to size and construct your pieces with a preferred carrier and packing method in mind.

Don't expect indulgent treatment from a carrier. Your shipment may be dropped, dragged, bounced, knocked about in the back of a truck, and ripped open by careless receiving clerks. Pack accordingly.

Don't make your filled boxes heavier than two people can comfortably handle; overloading makes damage more likely. Unless you can make special arrangements, pickups are ordinarily made by a driver and a truck without an automatic tailgate. If you don't have employees and a loading dock, you and the driver will have to haul the crate onto the truck bed yourselves. And all the way to its destination, probably only one or two people will be handling your shipment.

Commercial shipments, unless they are extraordinarily heavy or valuable, are normally made in corrugated fibreboard boxes. Museum shipments and others of high value are made in boxes of wood or of wood in combination with plywood, tempered masonite, fibreboard, or homosote. You can use wadded newpaper, egg cartons, and paper bags for packing, but commercial materials look better and are cleaner, more resilient, and won't compress in transit.

First, wrap each item in a protective, nonadhering layer of polyethylene, glassine, or tissue, taping the material to itself or stapling it (use staples only for commercial shipments, never for museum work) to the rear of or underneath the object. Then, wrap it in additional layers of cellulose wadding, tissue paper, flexible foam, or bubble pack. Always wrap unsupported extensions—like handles—separately.

Pad the corners of pictures with cushions made of cellulose wadding or flexible foam, then tape or staple the pads to the frame. You can often combine the corner padding with the first wrapping in one operation. Tape picture glass to hold it in place if it breaks. Run the tape in a checkerboard pattern, avoiding the frame. Never tape plexiglas—which is almost unbreakable anyway—the tape will be extremely difficult to remove. Screw eyes, wires, and other hardware may work loose in transit and damage the artwork. Pack them separately in a marked envelope. Circle the screw eye holes in the back of the frame so they may be found easily. Pack pictures face to face, with their backs to the outside of the box. If the corner pads separate the pictures' faces, the pictures may require no additional protection for commercial shipments. If you want to be cautious, and for museum shipments, separate the pictures with sheets of fibreboard, foamboard, or Styrofoam. You may also suspend pictures in racks as described under museum packing.

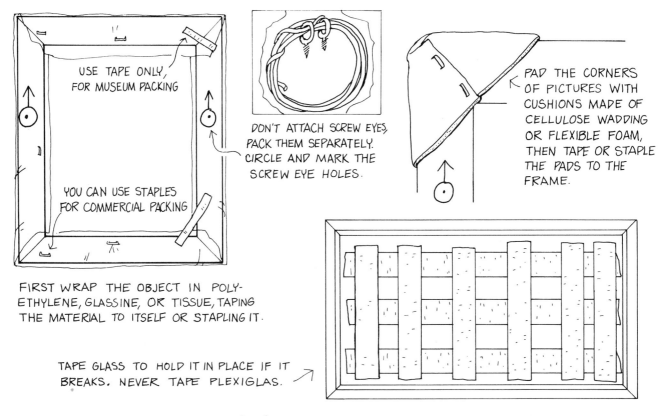

USE TAPE ONLY, FOR MUSEUM PACKING

YOU CAN USE STAPLES FOR COMMERCIAL PACKING

DON'T ATTACH SCREW EYES, PACK THEM SEPARATELY. CIRCLE AND MARK THE SCREW EYE HOLES.

PAD THE CORNERS OF PICTURES WITH CUSHIONS MADE OF CELLULOSE WADDING OR FLEXIBLE FOAM, THEN TAPE OR STAPLE THE PADS TO THE FRAME.

FIRST WRAP THE OBJECT IN POLYETHYLENE, GLASSINE, OR TISSUE, TAPING THE MATERIAL TO ITSELF OR STAPLING IT.

TAPE GLASS TO HOLD IT IN PLACE IF IT BREAKS. NEVER TAPE PLEXIGLAS.

First-wrapping, screw eyes, padding corners, taping glass.

Once you've wrapped your work, you may proceed to design a box. The idea is to "float" the contents within the crate to prevent shifting, a major cause of breakage. The type of crate will depend on a combination of factors already mentioned: size and value of the object, shipping method, packing budget, etc.

Measure the object, allowing for adequate additional padding. If you have several objects, measure them by stacking them together. Strong objects in strong boxes may need no more than the original one-half inch or so of wrapping or corner padding, while breakables may need as much as four to six inches. Place heavier things on the bottom, the lighter on top.

Box manufacturers want to know the inside box dimensions stated as: *length*, the larger of the two dimensions of the open side; *width*, the smaller open side dimension; and *depth*, the distance perpendicular to the length and width. The distinction is important, because you want to load the box from the easiest side.

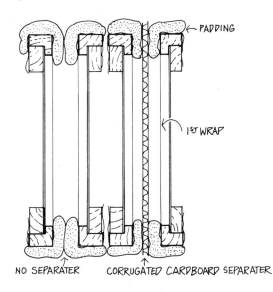

Separating pictures.

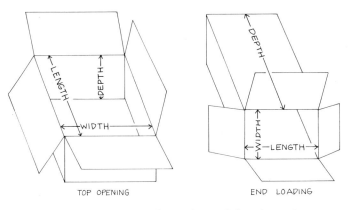

Box manufacturers need to know the inside box dimensions stated as: *length*, the larger of the two dimensions of the open side; *width*, the smaller open-side dimension; and *depth*, the distance perpendicular to the length and width. The distinction is important, because you want to load the box from the easiest side.

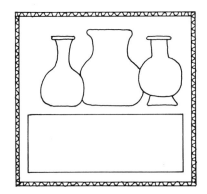

PLACE HEAVIER THINGS ON THE BOTTOM, THE LIGHTER ON TOP

Packing.

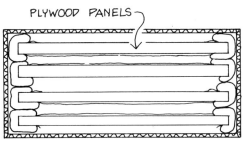

STRONG OBJECTS IN STRONG BOXES MAY NEED NO MORE THAN THE ORIGINAL ½" OR SO OF WRAPPING OR CORNER PADDING...

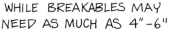

213

Pack all boxes so they are tight and free of rattles. You may hold light objects securely with dunnage, but heavier ones will need firm bracing and wedging. A box packed within a box is useful for valuable pieces.

Seal fibreboard boxes with reinforced sealing tape, box-sealing tape, or filament tape. You can use short tape lengths, but for maximum strength, run the tape around the box and overlap it on itself by at least four inches. Cover the flap seams with continuous lengths of tape.

Abundant rules regulate common carriers. You should become aware of them if you intend to do much volume shipping, especially of fragile articles. Railroad Classification Rule 41 (more commonly known simply as Rule 41) sets the standard for fibreboard boxes, not only for railroads but for general commerce as well. Section 5, for example, specifies that glassware and other fragile articles must not exceed a total of 65 pounds per container and be packed with "liners, partitions, wrappers, excelsior and other packing material that will afford adequate protection against breakage and damage,

and so the contents will completely fill the box." It then outlines tests of ten controlled drops on various sides of the packed carton onto a concrete floor from a height of 16 inches (if the carton is under 20 pounds) to 12 inches (if the carton is over 30 pounds). You will not be arrested if you disobey these rules, of course, but you may have trouble collecting insurance claims.

Museum Packing

In museum packing, the emphasis is on protection rather than economy. Since my experience is with commercial packing, I visited Kenneth Bush, manager of the Smithsonian's History and Technology Museum Objects Processing Facility to observe his highly regarded packing operation. Ken does his wrapping on tables covered with homosote and a tightly woven, rubber-backed commercial carpet—a soft and resilient combination. For especially delicate objects, he lays felt over the carpet for added protection. Each object is a unique challenge—the day I was there Ken and his staff were applying themselves to a covey of down-at-the-heels

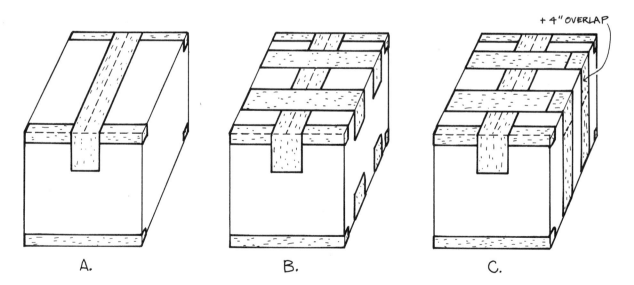

A. B. C.

Cover the flap seams with a continuous length of tape. You can use short tape lengths, but, for maximum strength, run the tape around the box and overlap it on itself at least 4 inches.

stuffed penguins—and he handles each job democratically regardless of value, the penguins as carefully as the Presidential china.

His general approach is to double-wrap everything—first an inner contact layer to protect the object's surface, then an outer bulk layer for overall protection. Finally, he secures the object in a carefully constructed wooden box.

These are his procedures by types:

Unframed paintings are first covered with glassine tissue and then with a layer of cellulose wadding, e.g., Kimpac, bubble pack, or similar material.

Framed paintings have, if the frame is simple, their corners padded with flexible foam. For elaborate frames, additional protection is given by tissue and felt layers along with the foam.

Paper is covered with acid-free tissue and sandwiched between sheets of foamboard or corrugated fibreboard that are lightly taped together.

Dimensional objects are first wrapped in cellulose wadding, tissue paper, or, rarely, polyethylene or glassine (polyethylene forms a vapor barrier, glassine is brittle). The wrapping is then taped to itself with plastic box-sealing tape.

Hollow objects are covered inside and out with tissue and second-wrapped with more tissue or packing cotton to lightly fill the interior. Ken avoids Styrofoam free flow. He finds that its lightness makes voids hard to fill and permits objects to shift in transit, and its dust sticks to things.

Unsupported areas like handles or extensions are wrapped separately with cotton pads that are rolled in tissue and held together with tape and then swathed in paper wadding or bubble pack.

Boxes

Most of Ken's boxes are wood. He only uses corrugated containers for lightweight or nonfragile items on short hauls in private vehicles or local carriers, or as a packing box within a wooden crate. For single-use corrugated boxes, he uses reinforced sealing tape. For multiple-use corrugated boxes, he cements Velcro to the flaps, the adhesive side to the top of the inner flap and the loop side to the bottom

of the outer flap. This allows the box to be readily opened and closed, and avoids tape residue build-ups.

He makes his boxes out of 1/4- to 3/4-inch exterior plywood, depending on the size, weight, and nature of the contents. The boxes are braced along all sides with # 2 white-pine battens, which reinforce and protect the box and enlarge its nailing and screwing surface. He nails thick skids to the bottom to raise the box off the ground and to provide a space for hand carts and lift trucks. The boxes are fully lined with waterproof asphaltic paper before they're assembled, and the joints are coated with PVA adhesive, wetting the paper. Then the bottom and sides are nailed together with coated box nails. Ken *always* screws the top on, never nails it, (nailed tops invite damage on placement and removal) with flathead screws and countersunk washers. The tops may also be attached with bolts and wing nuts for multiple use.

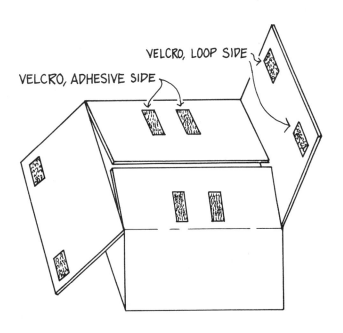

VELCRO, LOOP SIDE

VELCRO, ADHESIVE SIDE

For multiple-use corrugated boxes, cement Velcro to the flaps, the adhesive side to the top of the inner flap, and the loop side to the bottom of the outer flap. This allows the box to be readily opened and closed, and avoids tape-residue build-up.

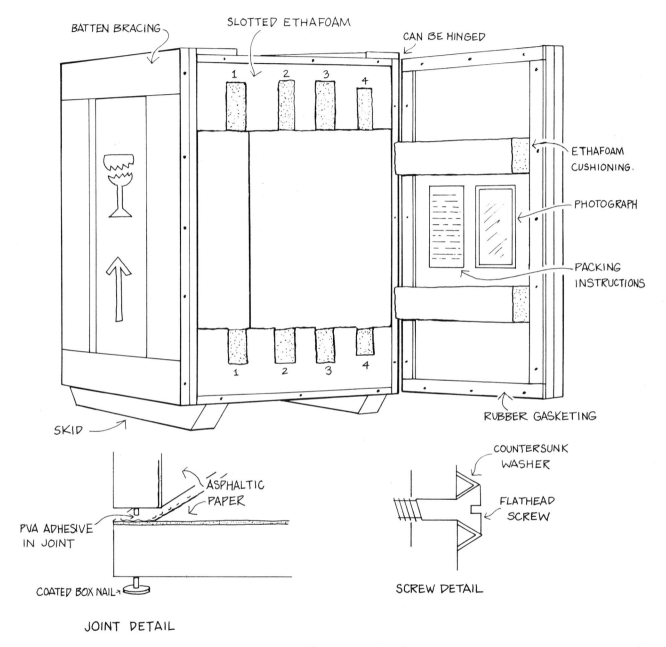

BATTEN BRACING

SLOTTED ETHAFOAM

CAN BE HINGED

1 2 3 4

ETHAFOAM CUSHIONING

PHOTOGRAPH

PACKING INSTRUCTIONS

1 2 3 4

RUBBER GASKETING

SKID

ASPHALTIC PAPER

PVA ADHESIVE IN JOINT

COATED BOX NAIL

JOINT DETAIL

COUNTERSUNK WASHER

FLATHEAD SCREW

SCREW DETAIL

A museum-grade picture-packing box.

Securing the Object in the Box

Ken secures the object in the box with tissue paper or a variety of packaging materials and dunnage in combination with braces made of either flexible Ethafoam or padded wood. Strips of 1/8-inch-thick self-adhesive rubber covered with tissue, or with high-density flexible foam, may also be attached to the braces for cushioning between the brace and the object. Wood braces are glued and screwed in place, and foam is adhered with either double-coated tape or with solvent-based contact cement. Ken frequently lines the boxes with flexible or rigid packing materials. He finds that the dense flexible foams like Ethafoam make excellent racks for paintings. Slots are cut with either a band saw, a sharp, thin knife, or a hand saw.

Ken emphasizes that his methods work for him but are certainly not the only solutions to packing problems. The important thing, he feels, is to be versatile, and do what works for "the objects first and for you second."

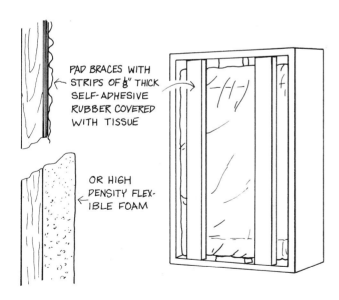

PAD BRACES WITH STRIPS OF ⅛" THICK SELF-ADHESIVE RUBBER COVERED WITH TISSUE

OR HIGH DENSITY FLEXIBLE FOAM

Bracing.

Materials
Fibreboard Boxes

Fibreboard boxes are the standard commercial shipping container. Look for manufacturers' names in the Yellow Pages under "Boxes, corrugated" or "Packing and shipping supplies"; ask business people who ship goods, your local chamber of commerce, or state department of commerce; or consult *Thomas's Register of American Manufacturers* or the "Sources" at the end of this book. A sympathetic packing salesperson can be an invaluable source of advice and information, and will keep you up-to-date on new techniques and materials.

Manufacturers will make boxes to your specifications, and often they have overruns or stock sizes on hand for sale. For ease in storage and delivery, boxes are delivered either partially assembled or completely knocked down. You put them together as needed.

Corrugated fibreboard comes in four thicknesses: (1) *single face*, (2) *single wall* (double faced), (3) *double wall*, and (4) *triple wall*.

(1) *Single face*, a sheet of corrugated glued to a sheet of linerboard, is the cheapest form of corrugated and the only flexible one, especially when it is bent along the grooves. It is sold in rolls or flat sheets, and is principally used for wrapping objects to be packed in boxes.

(2) *Single wall*, which accounts for 90 percent of all shipping containers, is a sheet of linerboard glued to either side of a sheet of corrugated. It can be scored and folded in either direction.

(3) *Double wall* consists of three flat and two corrugated sheets, and is used for heavier boxes.

(4) *Triple wall* consists of four flat and three corrugated sheets, and is used for the heaviest boxes. Single- and double-wall corrugated have a gross weight limit of 65 pounds. Triple wall has over five times the puncture resistance of single and double wall, and a gross weight limit of 275 pounds.

Fibreboard boxes come in dozens of styles, several joint designs, and in many inner-partition configurations. Discuss your needs with your supplier and choose a style that will simplify your packing and provide maximum strength at the seams, always the weakest points.

An important consideration is which side of the box is best for the opening. For example, if you are shipping rolled murals, will you want to load through the end of the box (which will mean less taping but more trouble loading and cushioning) or through the long side (which is easier loading and cushioning but more trouble taping)? We load through the long side. We once had trouble with heavy, painted panels and framed paintings. At first we used boxes that opened from the narrow side. One of us held the box open while the other dropped in the panels. We always had to laboriously shoehorn the last piece. In desperation, we consulted the box manufacturer. He hadn't realized what we were packing. He made the next set of boxes open from the wide side so we could lay the panels in flat, and our problem was solved.

Regular slotted containers (RSC), the standard box style, are cheapest and more adaptable. The center flaps may be designed to overlap for extra reinforcement. *Telescope boxes* come in two parts; the top slips (or telescopes) over the bottom. The extra side wall provides reinforcement for stacking, and the box is easy to open for inspection. Other styles are the *double-cover box*, which can be readily cut down for smaller shipments; *the bulk bin*, an oversized fibreboard box with a pallet base that takes shipments of up to 3,000 pounds; and *slide* and *folder boxes* for light weight shipments.

Shells, tubes, partitions, and inner packing forms provide additional protection inside boxes. Inner packing forms may be die-cut for repeat shipments of odd shaped objects.

Padded shipping bags, cushioned with cellulose wadding or Styrofoam pellets are used for small, lightweight shipments or for additional protection within boxes. They are available in many different sizes.

Wood crates are used for heavy or valuable artwork. They are expensive, take time to build, and require skilled carpentry.

Corrugated fibreboard comes in four thicknesses.

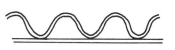

SINGLE FACE

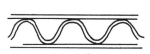

SINGLE WALL

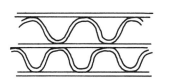

DOUBLE WALL

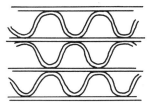

TRIPLE WALL

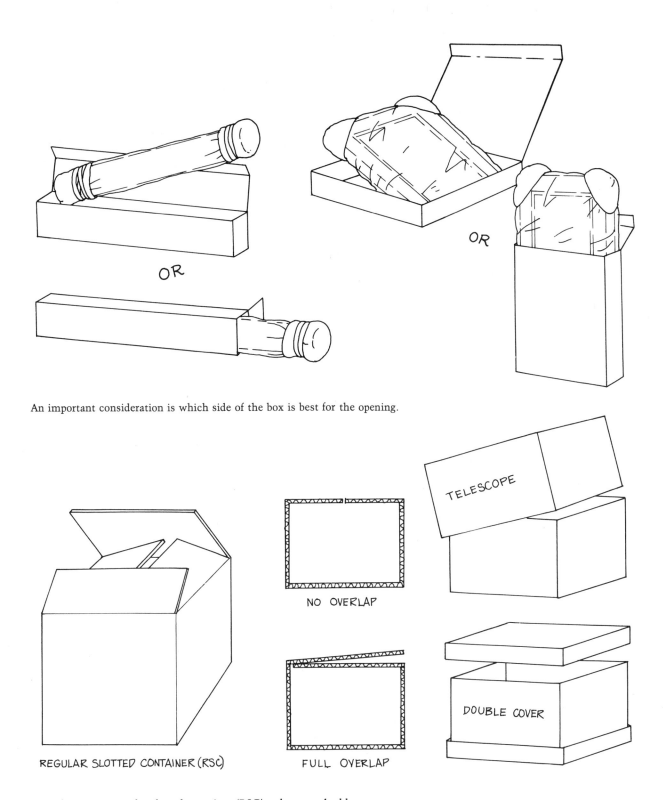

An important consideration is which side of the box is best for the opening.

NO OVERLAP

FULL OVERLAP

TELESCOPE

DOUBLE COVER

REGULAR SLOTTED CONTAINER (RSC)

Some box types: regular slotted container (RSC), telescope, double cover.

Flexible Foams

Polyethylene foams: Resilient, white, clean, nonabrasive, long-lived, closed-cell foams. Can be stapled, glued, heat sealed, and cut. Come in various densities and thicknesses from fractions of an inch to several inches. The thinner sheets are used for wrapping and wadding; the thicker for racks, lining, and braces. Examples: Ethafoam, Jiffyfoam.

Polyurethane foams: Similar to polyethylene foams, except they are yellowish, open cell, cheaper, more compressible, and disintegrate with age. Example: Polyfoam.

Foam rubber: Similar to polyethylene foam except it is more expensive and more resilient. Used where more compression resistance is required.

Polypropylene foams: Similar to polyethylene foam, but tears more easily. Example: Microfoam.

Rigid Sheets

Single-Wall Corrugated Fibreboard: A sheet of linerboard glued to either side of a sheet of corrugated. It can be scored and folded in either direction. Used for liners, shells, inner partitions, and boxes.

Polystyrene Foam: Rigid, lightweight, nonresilient, white or blue, closed-cell foam. Comes in various densities and thicknesses. Can be glued, nailed, and cut with a saw, knife, or hot wire. Used for interior packaging, liners, inner partitions, wedges. Example: Styrofoam.

Foamboard: Lightweight sheets of paper-covered polystyrene foam. Much more expensive than corrugated.

Free Flow

Polystyrene foam pellets in various shapes according to the manufacturer—noodles, peanuts, silver dollars. The shape is not important. Lightweight, used for filling packages with irregularly shaped, often hollow, contents. While it is widely used for commercial packaging, museum packers complain that its lightness allows shifting in transit and that the pellets cling electrostatically.

Cellulose Packaging Materials

Cellulose Wadding: Rugated (waffle pattern) cellulose, like multilayer crepe paper. Comes in various thicknesses, softnesses, and degrees of shock absorbency. Clean, resilient, inexpensive. A good choice for general-purpose wrapping and dunnage. Examples: Kimpac (used as a generic), Jiffy Custom Wrap.

Kraft Wadding: Cellulose wadding bonded to kraft paper in various weights and styles. Stiffer and stronger than cellulose wadding, it's used primarily for dunnage. Example: Jiffy Kushion Kraft.

Excelsior: Fine wood shavings, loose or in paper packages. Messy, dusty, and hygroscopic. Largely replaced by other materials. *Not recommended.*

Films

Bubble Pack: A cushioning film composed of air cells sandwiched between layers of clear polyethylene film. Clean, lightweight, more expensive but less resilient than cellulose wadding. Examples: Air Cap, Kim-Cel, Vistaflex.

Polyethylene: Tough, clean, transparent, waxy, nonsticking surface. Comes in many widths and thicknesses; four mil is standard. Used for first-wrapping paintings, sculpture, and other artwork. Be careful not to hermetically seal the object or condensation may form within the package—always allow for air circulation.

Mylar: Excellent, very tough, stable, clear polyester film in various widths and thicknesses. More expensive than polyethylene but more reusable.

Glassine: A glazed, nonsticking, nonstatic, somewhat brittle, translucent paper. Used for first-wrapping flat surfaces, especially if they are tacky. It is too brittle to use for dimensional objects, and may adhere to very sticky surfaces like fresh paint (try polyethylene or wax paper).

Tissue: Thin, soft sheets of paper excellent for first-wrapping delicate objects. Available in sheets and rolls. Special types are *acid free* tissue for wrapping valuable papers and textiles, and *anti-tarnish* tissue for wrapping tarnishable metals like silver and brass.

Fasteners

Coated box, annular ring, screw, and spiral nails: The coated box nail is a slimmer version of the common nail. The cement coating increases the holding power. Annular ring, screw, and spiral nails are common nails with ridged or threaded shanks to increase their holding power. Used for nailing the sides of boxes together. (*Never use nails for lids.*)

Square-headed plate nails: A short, common nail with a one-inch-square plate fastened to the head. Used to nail cardboard to wood. The plate increases the bearing surface.

Flathead, oval, and roundhead wood screws: Flathead and oval screws are countersunk screws. Either countersink, or better yet, use with a countersunk washer. Roundhead screws have a flat base; use them with flat washers. All three are used for fastening the lids of boxes.

Bolts and Wing Nuts: Wing nuts are flanged nuts that can be tightened or loosened by hand. Used for fastening multiple-use box lids.

Self-Adhesive Tapes

Box-sealing tape: A strong, pressure-sensitive film tape used for general sealing purposes. Example: 3M #355 High Performance Box Sealing Tape.

Filament tape: A very strong, transparent, pressure-sensitive film tape reinforced with glass fiber. Used for general sealing of heavy boxes. Example: 3M Scotchpar #898.

Water-Adhesive Tapes

Keep in a cool, dry place. Always use with hot water to activate the adhesive properly.

Gummed tape: Gummed kraft paper, available in various widths, colors, and weights; 60-pound is the most common. Used for sealing lightweight packages only.

Reinforced sealing tape: Heavy duty, quite strong, inexpensive, reinforced with glass fiber. Available in various widths. Has a quick tack for a fast grip. Most widely used tape for general sealing.

Labelling and Record Keeping

Each box should have at the minimum:

Return address (consigner, shipper, sender): Your name and address.

Address (consignee, receiver, recipient): The name and address of the person or company to whom you're sending the box. If to a person within a company, mark "Att:" and his or her name and title.

Additional useful information includes:

Boxes in shipment: Whenever there is more than one box in a shipment, use either: box number/number of boxes in the shipment enclosed in a circle, example: 2/4 means Box #2 in a shipment of four boxes; or "Box #_____ of _____ in Shipment."

Net weight: The total weight of the box and its contents.

Net size: The length, width, and height of the outside of the box.

Contents: An itemized list or general description of the contents.

Purchase Order Number or other identifying information

Packing slip: A statement that can include: the consigner, consignee, purchase order or contract number, contents, weight, size, packer, value, and carrier. It may be a copy of your bill with the prices excised, or a printed form. If you wish, you may substitute an invoice for the packing slip to eliminate later billing. Attach the packing slip to the box in a clear polyethylene shipping envelope printed "Packing List Enclosed."

OPEN THIS SIDE: Mark the preferred side to be opened, especially with screwed-on tops. May be accompanied by "OPEN OTHER SIDE" on the opposite side to alert recipients.

THIS SIDE UP: When tipping is undesirable, mark on top and with accompanying arrows on sides. Tip-N-Tell labels will show if a package has been tipped (see Sources).

FRAGILE: Either the words, a printed label, or the symbol—a broken wine glass. Used for delicate contents.

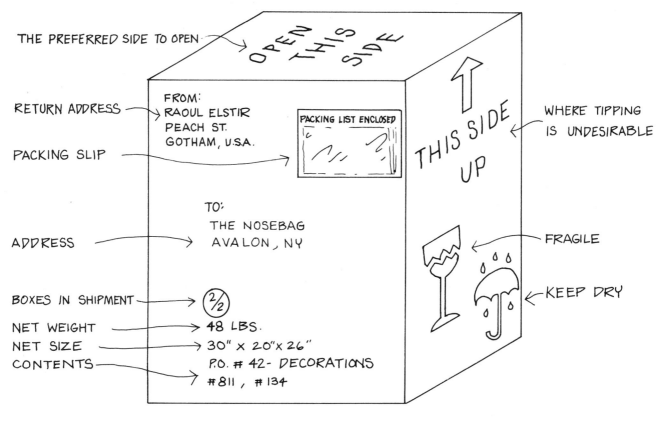

THE PREFERRED SIDE TO OPEN → OPEN THIS SIDE

RETURN ADDRESS → FROM:
RAOUL ELSTIR
PEACH ST.
GOTHAM, U.S.A.

PACKING SLIP → PACKING LIST ENCLOSED

THIS SIDE UP

WHERE TIPPING IS UNDESIRABLE

TO:
THE NOSEBAG
ADDRESS → AVALON, NY

BOXES IN SHIPMENT → 2/2

NET WEIGHT → 48 LBS.
NET SIZE → 30" X 20" X 26"
CONTENTS → P.O. # 42- DECORATIONS
#811, #134

FRAGILE

KEEP DRY

A fully labelled box.

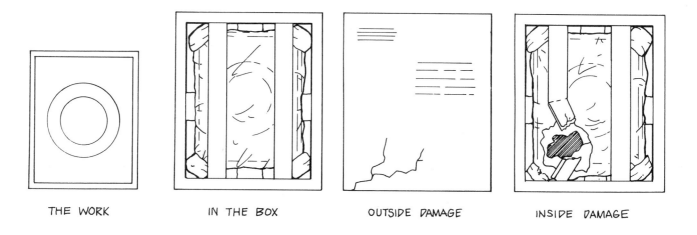

THE WORK   IN THE BOX   OUTSIDE DAMAGE   INSIDE DAMAGE

Photographs of your work provide a record in case of theft or damage in transit or thereafter.

KEEP DRY: Either the words, a printed label, or the symbol—an umbrella with rain drops. Used where dryness is critical.

Photographs of your work provide a record in case of theft or damage in transit or thereafter. If your work is out on loan or consignment and returns damaged, photograph it as soon as the damage is apparent, still in the box if possible. If damage is apparent before opening, photograph the outside of the box as well. This "before and after" evidence pinpoints when the damage occurred and who caused it, and provides firm substantiation for insurance claims.

If you are shipping several pieces together, identify each with a title, purchase-order number, or other designation. To avoid confusion, you can mark abstractions on their backs with an "UP" in a circle and an arrow pointing in the correct direction, or you can mark the screw eyes with a circle and directional arrow.

Enter each box with its itemized contents into a manifest:

The Nosebag, P.O. #42

Box	Item	Description
1/2	2002	Ped Xing
	412	Gloucester Fishermen
2/2	811	Mrs. Rumpelmeyer's Flesh
	134	The Butter Churn

You may also include other information like addresses, sizes, weights, values, etc. Thus, if any problems arise with the shipment, you will know from your manifest that #2002 *Ped Xing*, is in box #1.

Carriers

Your carrier options as a shipper of artwork are: private vehicles; parcel services like UPS; freight forwarders; and common carriers like bus and air lines, and moving lines. Truck lines are effectively eliminated because they cannot handle "extraordinary value" goods worth more than $5.00 per pound.

Select a carrier on the basis of: (1) the carrier's service, availability, cost, speed, and insurance coverage; (2) the shipment—its number of items, value, and packaging; (3) the purchaser's preference; (4) the distance to be covered—long or short haul.

Your experience and those of other shippers of artwork, e.g., museums, galleries, shops, and other artists, will help guide you in your choice.

Considering the time involved in selecting a carrier and arranging shipments, you'll be better off settling on a few methods and becoming familiar with them, rather than shopping around for the lowest possible rate each time you make a shipment. Rates depend on so many variables that it's difficult to make an accurate cost comparison. The regular UPS and bus-line service is at the lower end of the rate scale and air freight at the higher end, but the special options of one ordinarily less expensive carrier may make it in fact cost more than another.

Your studio insurance doesn't cover your work once it leaves your studio. To be protected, you'll need shipping insurance. (See Chapter 13.) You can, of course, overinsure your artwork, or, in an effort to circumvent a carrier's restrictions, claim that a package contains toothpaste rather than a painting. You'll be okay until you try to collect on a lost or damaged shipment. The Interstate Commerce Commission (ICC) requires that carriers have minimum insurance, investigate claims promptly, and be liable for the full value of a shipment, but *you* are responsible for establishing the shipment's value. Requirements may differ slightly from carrier to carrier but, in general, to document a claim, you must have a recent bill of sale, invoice, contract, or insurance policy that states what your work is worth. Also, in cases of damage rather than loss, if the carrier can demonstrate that the injury is due to your negligent packing rather than his careless handling, your claim may be disallowed.

FOB (Free on Board) indicates the point where the goods and the responsibility for them transfers from the seller to the carrier or purchaser. For example, *FOB Studio* means that the responsibility for your artwork transfers from you at your studio to the carrier who picks it up, and then to the purchaser when he accepts delivery. *FOB Delivery* (or

Destination) means that the responsibility remains with the seller, through the carrier, until the purchaser accepts delivery. The distinction is important when goods are lost or damaged in transit. *FOB Studio* means the purchaser must try to collect from the carrier; *FOB Destination* means it's your headache.

Private Carriers

Private carriers include you and your vehicle, your client and his vehicle, and local truckers not regulated by the Interstate Commerce Commission.

Transporting work yourself is often the simplest procedure, although it may not be the best use of your time. You can reduce packaging, because you know the care you'll give and you'll eliminate making arrangements with a carrier, but you'll have the compensating (and often greater) hassle of coordinating with the client. If you don't have an adequate vehicle, investigate truck rentals.

Bill the client for the delivery either as a contract or sales inclusion, or as an add-on. If you can combine your delivery with other business in the same area you will have, in effect, a free trip.

Of all methods, the client's making the pickup is usually the easiest one for you. If you think he has the facilities, present it as an option. Be sure you have the driver sign a receipt on pickup.

Unregulated local movers and shippers are more flexible and less expensive than the interstate giants, but they may be less dependable. Get recommendations from people who've used them, ascertain the mover's delivery range (some are intrastate only), and obtain a copy of their insurance.

Local movers are especially useful for shipments within a one or two day's drive, shipments that are too awkward or expensive to crate, or those that are too big for you to handle by yourself.

United Parcel Service

Service: Fast, inexpensive, reliable, convenient. Door-to-door pickup and delivery over most of the United States. UPS keeps good records, makes three delivery attempts, and offers COD service. They accept any type of artwork, except unique art for air delivery.

Weight limits: 50 pounds per package. 100 pounds from one shipper to one recipient per day.

Size limits: 108 inches length and girth (distance around the package) combined. A measuring chain is available on request.

Insurance: Automatic insurance of $100 per shipment and additional coverage at 25¢ per $100. To document a claim you must provide: "(1) a bill of sale or invoice that establishes value if it's [the art] been sold within the past year, or (2) a statement of value from a certified appraiser within one year." Proper packing is another requisite.

Comments: Although many people think UPS will not accept original artwork or glass in frames, headquarters has assured me that this is a misapprehension. They say, "UPS has no upper limits on the value placed on works of art. However, paintings of high value demand special handling which UPS does not provide. Such art works should be crated and sent via carriers that provide special handling." UPS is a general commodities carrier, which means they have no special-handling provisions. Your package will be treated the same as any other, no matter how many fragile stickers you paste on it.

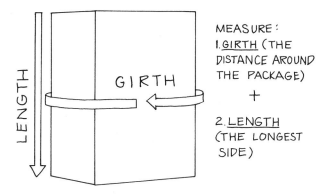

MEASURE:
1. GIRTH (THE DISTANCE AROUND THE PACKAGE)
+
2. LENGTH (THE LONGEST SIDE)

Measure length and girth.

UPS has an excellent information packet, which includes a packing guide and current details about their service. Obtain a copy and further information from your local office listed in the phone book.

Air Freight

Service: Commercial airlines are fast, dependable, and price competitive. The larger lines in fact have separate cargo planes and jumbo jets that can accommodate items as big as automobiles. The smaller lines have stricter size and weight limitations but may serve more out-of-the-way areas. If the company you call first cannot help you, they will usually refer you to one that can. Airlines pick up and deliver under arrangements with trucking companies.

Weight limits: Differs from line to line and from destination to destination. Depends on the capacity of the planes in operation.

Size limits: Same as weight limits.

Insurance: Differs among the carriers, but coverage can be in six or seven figures. United Airlines, for example, requires that in case of loss you submit a copy of the airbill along with documentation, such as an invoice, an appraisal, or an insurance policy; and a repair invoice in case of damage. "Articles of extraordinary value," such as valuable paintings, must be handled individually. United's maximum claim is $1.5 million per airbill or shipment.

Comments: An excellent all-around means of shipping artwork. Individual lines may offer special services. United, which is the nation's biggest carrier, has "Small Package Dispatch" and "First Freight" service, which guarantees a specified flight. You can get more information by writing: United Airlines, Public Relations Department, P.O. Box 66100, Chicago, IL 60666. Contact your local agents for addresses of other carriers. Look in the Yellow Pages under "Air Cargo Service" or "Airlines."

Have a supply of airbills in advance of your pickups. You will save the driver's time, avoid hasty mistakes, and can include the shipping number on your invoice. If the driver doesn't have your carrier's airbills, you may have to alter that of another line, which can create confusion if you have to trace your shipment.

Bus Lines

Service: Round-the-clock service seven days a week between any bus station within a line's system, and there may also be interline connections that broaden the network. Rates, which are regulated by tariff, are quite economical. Greyhound and Trailways offer door-to-door pickup and delivery service in many cities at an additional cost. Shipments may be sent prepaid, collect and/or COD.

Weight limits: 100 pounds per package.

Size limits: 141 inches length, width, and height combined, and a length of 60 inches or less.

Lot limits: A maximum of three packages per lot.

Insurance: Free valuation for the first $50, and additional coverage at 25¢ per $100. No shipment worth more than $250 will be accepted.

Comments: Greyhound, the largest busline, serves 14,000 cities and towns nationwide, and has pickup and delivery service in over 200 major cities at an additional cost. They also offer rush service, door-to-door rush service (800-528-6077), and airbus interconnections from small communities without air service (800-426-2827). For more information call your local bus station or write: Greyhound Lines Inc., Package Express Department, Greyhound Tower, Phoenix, AZ 85077.

Freight Forwarders

Freight forwarders are shipping agents. They pick up and deliver with their own or leased trucks and planes. Two of the largest are:

Federal Express

Service: Picks up and delivers in their own trucks and airplanes, serves over 15,000 cities, operates their own airplanes, and offers overnight priority service and collect service.

Weight limits: 70 pounds per package.

Size limits: 108 inches length and girth combined.

Insurance: Varies with service. Automatic insurance of $100 per shipment for "Priority One" and "Standard Service" with additional coverage at 25¢ per $100 up to $2,000, except for "Signature Security Service," which has a $5,000 maximum.

Comments: For more information and a service guide, call: 800-238-5355; in Tennessee call: 800-542-5171, or write: Federal Express Corp., AMF Box 30167, Memphis, TN 38130.

Emery Air Freight

Service: The largest air freight forwarder, Emery has 144 offices around the world, 103 domestic, 41 international. Operates door to door in their own or leased vehicles, and so offers single-party responsibility in case of claims or the need to trace a shipment. Overnight service.

Weight limits: Basically unlimited, depends on the planes used on each route segment.

Size limits: Same as weight limits.

Insurance: Automatic insurance of $9.06 per pound, and additional coverage of 40¢ per $100 to a maximum coverage of $500.

Comments: For more information call the local office or write: Emery Air Freight, Old Danbury Rd., Wilton, CN 06897.

Interstate Moving and Storage Companies (Van Lines)

Service: Van lines are licensed to handle valuable objects like expensive artwork and furniture. They will pick up, deliver, and place articles inside buildings as directed, distinguishing them from other types of carriers, which are confined to door-to-door operation. They have crating and storage facilities, and will also handle uncrated items. They are required to charge a 500-pound minimum rate per shipment. Movers will interconnect with other lines to provide coast-to-coast coverage.

Weight limits: Varies with the mover.

Size limits: Varies with the mover.

Insurance: Adequate. Check with the mover.

Comments: Select a company by its reputation. *Consumer Reports* periodically evaluates the industry and makes recommendations.

U.S. Parcel Post

Service: Offices in large cities and hamlets all over these United States. They have been overtaken by UPS and other carriers who offer cheaper, faster, more reliable service.

Weight limits: 40 pounds from first class post offices, 70 pounds from smaller post offices.

Size limits: 84 inches combined length and girth from first class post offices, 100 inches combined length and girth from smaller post offices.

Insurance: No automatic insurance. Sliding coverage available from $100 to $400. Claims forms are available at the post office.

Comments: Consider parcel post if you're outside the UPS or other parcel networks, or if your package weighs over 50 and under 70 pounds, or if you're in no hurry and nostalgic.

CARRIERS

Carriers	Service	Weight Limits	Size Limits	Insurance
Private Carriers: You	Often simplest procedure	Dependent on your vehicle and your strength	Dependent on your vehicle and your strength	Self insurance
Client	Usually easiest method for you	Dependent on the client's vehicle and on the strength of his employees	Dependent on the client's vehicle and the strength of his employees	Client's insurance (have client accept responsibility on pick up)
Unregulated local movers and shippers	Use for local shipments and those too awkward or expensive to crate, and those too big to handle by yourself	Dependent on the carrier's vehicles and on the strength of his employees		
United Parcel Service (UPS)	Fast, inexpensive, reliable, convenient, good records, three delivery attempts, C.O.D.	50lbs./package 100 lbs./one shipper to one recipient per day	108″ length and girth combined	Automatic insurance of $100/shipment. Additional coverage at 25¢/$100
Air Freight	Fast, dependable, price competitive, door to door, or terminal to terminal	Differs from line to line and from destination to destination	Same as weight limits	Differs among carriers, can be six or seven figures
Bus Lines (Greyhound)	Economical, round-the-clock, seven days a week. Shipments may be prepaid, collect, or C.O.D. Door-to-door pick up and delivery may be available, otherwise terminal to terminal	100 lbs./package A maximum of 3 packages/lot	141″ length, width, and height combined, a length of 60″ or less	Free valuation for the first $50. Additional coverage at 25¢/$100. No shipment over $250 accepted

Carriers	Service	Weight Limits	Size Limits	Insurance
Freight Forwarders: Federal Express	Door-to-door. Overnight, priority, and collect available	70 lbs./package	108″ length and girth combined	Varies. Automatic insurance of $100 per shipment for "priority one" and "standard service" with additional coverage at 25¢/$100 up to $2,000, except for "signature security service" which has a $5,000 maximum
Emery Air Freight	Largest air freight. Door-to-door. Overnight available	Depends on the planes used on the route segment	Same as weight limits	Automatic insurance of $9.06/lb. Additional coverage of 40¢/$100 to a maximum of $500
Interstate Moving and Storage	Licensed to handle valuable objects. Pick up, delivery, and placement of objects. Crating and storage available. Must charge 500 lb. minimum rate/shipment	Varies with the mover	Varies with the mover	Varies. Adequate
U.S. Parcel Post	Erratic	40 lbs. from first class post offices, 70 lbs. from smaller post offices	84″ combined length and girth from first class post offices; 100″ combined length and girth from smaller post offices	No automatic insurance. Sliding coverage available from $100 to $400

Sources of Supply

Find sources of supplies through recommendations obtained from other artists, art schools, art centers, and art suppliers; through directories (I list a few under references); through the Yellow Pages of your telephone book; and through magazines.

Two useful trade magazines which may be unfamiliar to artists are *Decor*, for framing, packaging, and installation equipment and supplies; and *Signs of the Times*, for signmaking and installation materials and supplies. (See Periodicals)

Sources for some of the supplies that may be less familiar follow. Some firms listed under one entry may carry other items as well.

Drafting Equipment and Materials

Adcom, 502 West Broad Street, Falls Church, VA 22046.

Alvin and Company, Inc., Box 188, Windsor, CT 06095.

Arthur Brown and Brothers, Inc., 2 West 46th Street, New York, NY

Charette Corporation, 31 Olympia Avenue, Woburn, MA 01801.

Keuffel and Esser Company, 20 Whippany Road, Morristown, NJ 07960.

MacMillan Arts & Crafts Inc., 9645 Gerwig Lane; Columbia, MD 21046.

Fabric Finishing

Kiesling-Hess Company, 1011 Wood Street, Philadelphia, PA 19107.

Framing: Die Cut Mats, Mat, Backing, Museum and Other Boards

Cardcrafts, Inc., 115 Wooster Street, New York, NY 10012.

Miller Cardboard Corporation, 75 Wooster Street, New York, NY 10012.

National Card, Mat and Board Co., Box 2306, City of Industry, CA 91746.

Framing Supplies

Bull Dog Lock Company, 4636 North Ravenswood Avenue, Chicago, IL 60640.
Picture accessories, hangers.

Juhl-Pacific Corporation, 7518 Washington Avenue South, Eden Prairie, MN 55344.
Complete framing source.

Kenneth Lynch and Sons, 78 Danbury Road, Wilton, CN 06897.
Hanging devices, lights, cases.

Sommer and Maca Industries, Inc., 5501 West Ogden Avenue, Chicago, IL, 60650; 800/323-9200.
Cut polystyrene and a few molding lengths.

United Manufacturers Supplies, Inc., Box 731, Hicksville, NY 11802.
Very large, full catalog; wholesale only.

Matboard

Charles T. Bainbridge's Sons, Inc., 50 Northfield Avenue, Edison, NJ 08817.

Crescent Cardboard Company, 100 West Willow Road, Wheeling, NY 60090.

Molding Lengths, Chops, Ready-Made Frames

ASF Sales, Box 6026, Toledo, OH 43614; 800/537-7083.
Aluminum section frames.

Milton W. Bosley Company, Box 576, Glen Burnie, MD 21061.
Lengths, extrusion chops, custom-made moldings, custom frames.

Classic, Box 73, New Brunswick, NJ 08902.
Extruded moldings.

Furst Brothers Company, Inc., 1215 Leadenhall Street, Baltimore, MD 21230.
Lengths, chops, ready-made frames, custom frames.

Gaines-American Moulding Corporation, 45 West 21st Street, New York, NY 10010.

Chops and lengths.

Woltman Margol, Inc., 4000 Cedar Springs, Dallas, TX 75219; 800/527-7570.

Chops, lengths, supplies.

Stringer Factory and Gallery, Box 4437, Davenport, IA 52808; 800/553-1861.

Lengths, chops, custom frames, supplies.

Structural Industries Inc., 96 New South Road, Hicksville, NY 11801; 800/645-3993.

Aluminum and wood sectional frames, ready-made frames, complete frame units including glass, mat, backing, and hangers.

Packing and Shipping

Arnold's Factory Supplies, Inc., 1800 South Hanover Street, Baltimore, MD 21230.

Complete line of packaging materials, including full 3M line, custom fibreboard, and wood boxes.

Bee Paper Company, 1800-8th Street, Passaic, NJ 07055.

Kimpac, kraft paper, glassine.

Dow Chemical Company, Olefin Plastics Department, Midland, MI 48610.

Ethafoam; wholesale only, write them for their local distributor.

E. I. DuPont De Nemours and Company, Inc., PR & R Department—Microfoam, Chestnut Run, Wilmington, DE 19898.

Microfoam; wholesale only, write them for their local distributor.

Index Packaging, Inc., 331 West Mountain Road, Sparta, NJ 07871.

Tip-N-Tell labels.

Jiffy Manufacturing Company, 360 Florence Avenue, Hillside, NJ 07205.

Packaging materials, including shipping bags, wadding, and rugated papers; wholesale only, write them for their local distributor.

Ollendorff Fine Arts, 21-44 Forty-Fourth Road, Long Island City, New York, NY 11101.

Art packing, transporting, and warehousing.

Robbins Container Corporation, 222 Conover Street, Brooklyn, NY 11231.

Packing supplies, stock boxes.

Sealed Air Corporation, 19-01 State Highway 208, Fairlawn, NJ 07410.

Aircap (mfg.); wholesale only, write them for their local distributor.

TALAS, Technical Library Service, 104 Fifth Avenue, New York, NY 10011.

Acid-free tissues, archival supplies.

3M Company, Tape and Allied Products Groups, St. Paul, MN 55101.

All manner of tapes (mfg.); wholesale only, write them for their local distributor.

Bibliography

The following annotated bibliography is intended as a guide to supplementary reading. Following a list of general books, the readings are arranged by chapters or groups of chapters. Some areas, photography, for instance, are especially rich, while for others there is no material that I can suggest.

General

Boyd, Margaret A. *The Mail Order Crafts Catalogue*. Radnor: Chilton, 1975.
Lists mail-order suppliers of crafts materials.

Clark, Leta W. *How to Make Money With Your Crafts*. New York: William Morrow, 1973.
Discusses going into business, bookkeeping, purchasing and manufacturing, craft fairs, etc. The author's background in the textile trade makes her particularly authoritative in that area.

Cochrane, Diane. *This Business of Art*. New York: Watson-Guptill, 1978.
The business side of art written in a question and answer format by the editor of the *American Artist Business Letter*. Contents include contracts, copyright, selling and exhibiting, commissions, dealers, coops, original prints, print publishers, museums, legal questions, insurance, bookkeeping, and taxes.

Colin, Paul, and Lippman, Deborah. *Craft Sources*. New York: Evans, 1975.
Lists and evaluates books and magazines on crafts. Lists suppliers of crafts without evaluations, and schools offering crafts programs. Also includes interviews with craftspeople.

Conran, Terence. *The House Book*. New York: Crown, 1974.
A one volume course in applied interior design. Profusely illustrated and chock full of practical and creative advice. Very useful for artists working with designers and for anyone integrating art in environments.

Cummings, Paul, ed. *Fine Arts Market Place*. Ann Arbor: R. R. Bowker, 1977.
Lists services: photographers, packers and movers, restorers, insurers; suppliers of wholesale and retail art materials and gallery equipment; art organizations; and exhibitors.

Glassman, Judith. *National Guide to Craft Supplies*. New York: Van Nostrand Reinhold, 1975.
Lists hundreds of wholesale and retail craft supply houses.

Gray, Bill. *Studio Tips for Artists and Graphic Designers*. New York: Van Nostrand Reinhold, 1976. *More Studio Tips*, 1978.
Two attractive, hand-lettered, profusely illustrated compilations of very useful information. Partial contents include: handling artwork; mechanicals, paste-ups and layouts; type; lettering; making your own tools, circle formulas; and metric equivalents.

Holden, Donald. *Art Career Guide*. New York: Watson-Guptill, 1973.
A guide to schools, jobs, and job hunting in the visual arts. Contains much solid advice on career opportunities and how to go about marketing yourself.

Holland, John. *Photo Decor*. Rochester: Kodak, 1978.
This 88 page guide is loaded with practical advice and illustrations on using photography, and by extension other art forms as well, in decor. Contents include sources; techniques; designing a photo wall; working with a lab; mounting, matting, and framing; installations; and lighting.

Holz, Loretta. *How to Sell Your Art and Crafts.* New York: Scribner's, 1977.

Contents include markets, pricing, publicity, legal aspects, finances, selling, mail-order, and coops.

Lapin, Lynne, and Wones, Betsy. *Art and Crafts Market.*Cincinnati: Writer's Digest, revised annually.

Brief synopses of subjects like selling and packing and lists of potential markets, exhibitions, and galleries.

Mehrabian, Albert. *Public Places and Private Spaces.* New York: Basic Books, 1976.

A highly informative, popular work on environmental psychology. Invaluable for understanding actions of people in public environments.

Meyer, Karl E. *The Art Museum: Power, Money, and Ethics.* New York: William Morrow, 1979.

A fascinating, informative study of art museums and the art market. Educational for artists curious about where their occupation fits in the art game.

Nelson, Norbert. *Selling Your Crafts.* New York: Van Nostrand Reinhold, 1967.

One of the first works on the subject. Includes information on pricing for profit, your own retail store, mail-order selling, special markets, publicity and advertising, and legal pointers.

Scott, Michael. *The Crafts Business Encyclopedia.* New York: Harcourt Brace Jovanovich, 1977.

The best reference on business practices for the production craftsperson. Most of the basic information is usable by artists as well. Scott is the editor of the valuable monthly newsletter, *The Crafts Report.*

Wettlaufer, George and Nancy. *The Craftsman's Survival Manual.* Englewood Cliffs: Prentice-Hall, Inc., 1974.

A down to earth guide to running a crafts business written by husband and wife potters. Includes getting started, bookkeeping and financial matters, pricing, selling at shows, and selling through shops.

Chapter 2. Marketing

American Federation of Arts. *American Art Directory.* New York: Bowker, 1952-date.

Triannual directory of art organizations, art schools, museums, art educators, art magazines, newspapers carrying art notes, and scholarships and fellowships.

Bachner, John Phillip, and Khosla, Naresh Kumar. *Marketing and Promotion for Design Professionals.* New York: Van Nostrand Reinhold, 1977.

While written primarily for large architectural, design, and engineering firms, it contains a wealth of practical information on standard professional practices, such as letter writing, telephone technique, slide shows, presentations, and interviews. I am indebted to it for ''Marketing'' and for ''Identifying Yourself.''

Berlye, Milton K. *How To Sell Your Artwork.* Englewood Cliffs: Prentice-Hall, Inc., 1978. (A revision of the 1973 edition.)

Includes advice on selling artwork in the commercial and fine art fields; on protecting artwork, e.g., insurance coverage, financial and legal considerations; and on art education. Many of the illustrations are curiously unrelated to the text.

Chamberlain, Betty. *The Artist's Guide to His Market.* New York: Watson-Guptill, 1975.

A very useful guide to selling through galleries. The author, an expert in the field, has run the Art Information Center in New York for many years. Subjects include how the art market (New York's in particular) works, how to look for a gallery and work with dealers, and how to exhibit.

Cultural Directory: Guide to Federal Funds and Services for Cultural Activities. New York: Associated Councils of the Arts, 1975.

A guide to the art and cultural resources of the federal government. Lists over 350 programs that assist individuals and cultural organizations.

Genfan, Herb, and Taetzsch, Lyn. *How to Start Your Own Craft Business.* New York: Watson-Guptill, 1974.

The business side of crafts.

Goodman, Calvin J. *Marketing Art: Art Marketing Handbook.* Los Angeles: Gee Tee Bee, 1975.

While many artists will be alienated by the hard-sell techniques advocated by the author, a management consultant to the arts, some may find his viewpoint and advice useful, especially for his insights into the aggressive marketing of art and the complexities of running a gallery. Topics include promotion, marketing planning, making sales presentations, what to do after the sale, sales aids, elements of an art-sales training program, pricing, artist/dealer relations, and accounting, budgeting, and planning.

Hillman, Bruce. *Writers Market.* Cincinnati: Writer's Digest.

Describes how and where to place and sell articles. Lists publishers by type with instructions for submission of manuscripts. Revised annually.

Millsaps, Daniel. *The National Directory of Arts Support by Private Foundations.* Vol. 3. Washington: Washington International Arts Letter, 1977.

Lists over 1,200 foundations according to areas of interest with the grants they give.

——. *The National Directory of Grants and Aid to Individuals in the Arts.* Washington: Washington International Arts Letter, 1976.

Lists 1,800 government and private grants, prizes, and awards.

Chapter 3. Specifying and Purchasing Materials

Flame Retardant Application Concerns Fabrics, Materials and Chemicals.

California requires that drapes and similar articles like wall hangings and banners used in places of public assembly be fire retardant. Their annual approved list, in pamphlet form, is a good source for fire retardant fabrics. Write: State of California, Documents Section, Box 20191, Sacramento, CA 95820. Revised annually.

Larsen, Jack Lenor, and Weeks, Jeanne. *Fabrics for Interiors.* New York: Van Nostrand Reinhold Company, 1975.

A solidly written professional book highly valuable for artists working with fabrics. Topics include aesthetics; using fabrics; fabric facts: cloths, fibers, yarns, constructions, finishing, compound cloths; coloring; and professional practice. Also useful for its insight into the thinking of a top designer.

National Fire Protection Association. *The NFPA Life Safety Code No. 101.* Boston: National Fire Protection Association, 1976.

A standard manual for fire officials.

Chapters 5, 10, 11, 14. Contracts, Bookkeeping, Law, Copyright

Crawford, Tad. *Legal Guide for the Visual Artist.* New York: Hawthorn, 1977.

A widely used guidebook to artists' legal problems but not, in my opinion, particularly written for the layman. Discusses in detail copyright law (predates the 1976 Act), artists' rights, contracts, sales, income tax, and many other issues. An appendix lists 28 artists' organizations, and all the state art agencies.

———. *Visual Artists Guide to the New Copyright Law.* Philadelphia: Hastings, 1978.

A comprehensive guide to the Act of 1976.

Duffy, Robert E. *Art Law: Representing Artists, Dealers, and Collectors.* New York: P.L.I., 1977.

A comprehensive source for attorneys and others who represent or advise artists.

Lidstone, Herrick K., and Olsen, Leonard R. *The Individual Artist: Recordkeeping, Methods of Accounting, Income and Itemized Deductions for Federal Income Tax Purposes.* New York: Volunteer Lawyers for the Arts, 1976.

A 52-page excerpt from the authors' longer *Tax Guide for Artists and Arts Organizations.* Discusses essential theories and practices, with an explanatory list of 30 potential tax deductions.

Peters, Marybeth. *General Guide to the Copyright Act of 1976.* Washington: U.S. Copyright Office, Library of Congress, 1977.

An extensive training manual prepared to explain the new act to employees of the Copyright Office.

Van Caspel, Venita. *Money Dynamics.* Reston, VA: Reston Publishing Company, 1975.

Advice on building financial independence from a leading financial planner. Topics discussed include: inflation, stocks, bonds, mutual funds, real estate, life insurance, and retirement programs for the self employed.

Your Federal Income Tax (For Individuals).

Washington: Department of the Treasury: Internal Revenue Service.

The IRS's free manual explaining the operation of the income tax law and providing full information on preparing returns. Revised annually.

Chapters 17, 18. Architectural Blueprint Reading, Architectural Drafting

Curden, Ernest. *Architectural Delineation: A Photographic Approach to Presentation.* New York: McGraw-Hill, 1971.

An explanation of the camera and perspective, techniques of drawing, and presentations. Profusely illustrated with top-quality architectural renderings.

Ching, Frank. *Architectural Graphics.* New York: Van Nostrand Reinhold, 1975.

A handsome paperback illustrated and lettered by the author. Chapters are: equipment and materials, architectural drafting, architectural drawing conventions, rendition of value and context, graphic symbols and lettering, freehand drawing, and architectural presentations. Useful for all artists involved with drafting and blueprint work.

Dagostino, Frank R. *Contemporary Architectural Drawing.* Reston: Prentice-Hall, 1977.

An excellent introduction to architectural drafting, sketching, and blueprint reading. Includes equipment, basic techniques, lettering, dimensioning, projection, views, schedules, and perspective. Profusely illustrated.

Hepler, Donald E., and Wallach, Paul. *Architecture, Drafting and Design.* New York: McGraw-Hill, 1971.

A standard text.

Jacoby, Helmut. *New Techniques of Architectural Rendering.* New York: Praeger, 1971.

A collection of exemplary architectural renderings with a brief explanatory text by a master renderer.

Ramsey, Charles G., and Sleeper, Harold. *Architectural Graphic Standards.* New York: John Wiley, 1970.

A standard reference manual for architects.

Snyder, John. *Commercial Artist's Handbook.* New York: Watson-Guptill, 1973.

A useful reference book that describes graphic art equipment and materials in detail, tells how to use them, and what to do if things go wrong.

Chapter 19. Presenting Designs to a Client

Hohauser, Sanford. *Architectural and Interior Models.* New York: Van Nostrand Reinhold, 1970.

Although already a decade old this superb guide to model making promises to remain the last word on the subject for many years to come.

Leach, Sid Del Mar. *Techniques of Interior Design Rendering and Presentation.* New York: Architectural Record Books, 1978.

A thorough, profusely illustrated course on interior design rendering including preparing story boards, making presentations, and selling designs.

Chapter 21. The Studio

Bureau of Naval Personnel. *Tools and Their Uses.* Washington, D.C.: Government Printing Office, 1971; Dover, 1973.

Intended as a training manual for naval personnel, it provides for the general public an inexpensive introduction to hand and power tools, measuring devices, fasteners, grinding, metal cutting, and other operations. Many illustrations.

Callender, John, ed. *Time-Saver Standards.* New York: McGraw-Hill, 1974.

A standard architectural reference work. A storehouse of valuable information not only on lighting design, but also on such subjects as: graphic symbols; building materials, components, and techniques, like waterproofing, skylighting, windows, flashing and hardware; and environmental-control, like acoustics, insulation, and heating.

Manner, David X. *Home Workshops.* New York: Harper and Row, 1969.

The best guide I know to designing and outfitting the home workshop. Includes descriptions of different types of shops, e.g., metal and crafts, as well as storage, tools, and shop aids. His *How to Plan and Build Your Workshop*, New York: Arco, 1977, is the reprinted 1955 version.

Readers's Digest Complete Do-It-Yourself Manual.

Pleasantville: Reader's Digest Association, 1973.

An invaluable illustrated guide to tools, equipment, fasteners, hardware, and adhesives, plus clear chapters on home repair and working with building materials.

"Skylights: better technical performance for an architectural favorite." *Architectural Record*, June 1979, pp. 141–148.

Lighting Manufacturers

General Electric has a number of useful free publications that are available from: General Electric Company, Lamp Business Division, Nela Park, Cleveland, OH, 44112, or from their many regional offices.

These include:

TP–101 *General Lighting Design*

TP–110 *Incandescent Lamps*

TP–114 *Office Lighting*

TP–119 *Light and Color* (highly recommended)

TP–128 *Footcandles in Modern Lighting*

Lightolier also has free publications of interest. Obtain them from their executive offices at: Lightolier, 346 Claremont Avenue, Jersey City, NJ, 07305, or from one of their regional showrooms.

Two in particular are:

Notes on the Lighting of Walls, Pictures, Draperies, and Other Vertical Surfaces (ideas for lighting painting walls)

Recessed Fluorescent Lighting

GTE Sylvania, 100 Endicott Street, Danvers, MA 01923, has two valuable booklets:

Jerome, C.W. *Basic Colorimetry.* An illustrated technical booklet prepared for the lighting industry. Describes light sources, the physiology of color, color rendering, and color systems.

Color is How You Light It. A popular discussion of color and lighting.

Chapter 22. Photography

Blaker, Alfred, *Field Photography.* San Francisco: W. H. Freeman, 1976.

While written for nature photographers, this large book with over 150 illustrations is a thorough guide to all the complexities of taking photographs of publication quality. Subjects range from equipment and materials, exposure and filters, to darkroom procedures.

Kodak, 343 State Street, Rochester, NY 14650, has many excellent publications. Consider:

AR–21 *Kodak Master Photoguide*

AW–1 *How To Make Good Pictures*

E–77 *Kodak Color Films*

M–1 *Copying* (shows copying set ups and gives specific advice for different subjects)

O–22 Holland, *Photo Decor.* (See page 231.)

S–30 *Planning and Producing Slide Programs* (lots of good advice on taking slides and putting on a slide show).

Molitor, Joseph W. *Architectural Photography.* New York: John Wiley and Sons, 1976.

A brief discussion intended for photographers. The main interest is in the excellent photographs and the insight into how a pro goes about his business.

Schmid, Claus-Peter. *Photography for Artists and Craftsmen.* New York: Van Nostrand Reinhold, 1975.

An excellent introduction to photographing art and crafts. Following a discussion of film, equipment, and lighting, Schmid provides much practical advice on photographing different subjects and on making camera set-ups. He includes many drawings and photographs, but no index.

Time-Life Books. *Life Library of Photography.* 15 Vols. New York: Time-Life, 1970-72.

A multivolume series of very handsome, beautifully illustrated, entertaining, and informative books.

Veltri, John. *Architectural Photography*. Garden City: Amphoto, 1974.

A thorough discussion of architectural photography by a professional. Contents include: photographing architecture, equipment, films and negatives, printing, and photographic communication. It is profusely illustrated in color and black and white, but has no index.

Chapter 23. Paint

Mayer, Ralph. *The Artist's Handbook of Materials and Techniques*. New York: Viking, 1970.

Still the standard reference work for the subject.

Chapter 24. Framing

Duren, Lista. *Frame It*. Boston: Houghton Mifflin Company, 1976.

A do-it-yourself guide to picture framing. Included: how-to information on choosing a frame, archival framing, types of frames and non-frames, mats, tools and materials, measuring frames and mats, etc. Thorough, with illustrations, but no index.

Rogers, Hal, and Reinhardt, Ed. *How To Make Your Own Picture Frames*. New York: Watson-Guptill, 1966.

An old standard, straightforward and reliable.

Toscano, Eamon. *Step-by-Step Framing*. New York: Golden Press, 1971.

An attractive, popular treatment with good decorative ideas.

Chapter 26: Packing and Shipping

Dudley, Dorothy H., and Wilkinson, Irma Bezold. *Museum Registration Methods*. 3rd ed. Washington, D.C.: American Association of Museums, 1978.

A manual on museum registration practices for registrars, administrators, students, and other museum professionals, in two parts. Includes information on condition reports, shipping and packing, insurance, cataloging, importing and exporting, and loan procedures.

Fibre Box Handbook. Chicago: Fibre Box Association, 1976.

All you ever wanted to know about the fibre box: definitions, construction, styles, testing procedures, rail, truck, and air regulations.

Hanlon, Joseph F., ed. *Packaging Marketplace*. Detroit: Gale Research Company, 1978.

A guide to suppliers of materials and services in the packaging field. Over 4,000 manufacturers, distributors, and wholesalers.

Keck, Caroline. *Safeguarding Your Collection in Travel*. Nashville: American Association for State and Local History, 1970.

An excellent, inexpensive, well-illustrated small book that is a must for anyone packing and shipping valuable art.

Packing/Shipping Crafts. New York: American Crafts Council, 1977.

General and specific media recommendations for packing crafts; listings of packing supplies and suppliers and shipping agents. 12 pages.

Periodicals
Architectural

Architectural Record, Box 430, Hightstown, NJ 08520.

1 year, $19.00.

Progressive Architecture, Reinhold Publishing Corporation, 600 Sumner Street, Stamford, CN 06904.

1 year, $20.00 (non-architects), $10.00 (architects).

Interior Design

Contract, P.O. Box 2775, Clinton, IA 52732.

1 year, $18.00, contract (nonresidential) interior design.

Interior Design, Box 2780, Clinton, IA 52732.

1 year, $22.50, contract (nonresidential) interior design.

Interiors, 1515 Broadway, New York, NY, 10036.

1 year, $18.00, contract (nonresidential) interior design.

Artists' Magazines, Artists' Newsletters, and Newspapers

Art Letter, Art in America, Inc., 850 Third Avenue, New York, NY 10022.

Published monthly, $28.00 per year. A newsletter for art professionals. Grant programs and opportunities to show and sell, detailed reports on news developments, issues affecting visual artists.

American Artist, 1 Color Court, Marion, OH, 43302.

$17.00 per year. A magazine for artists. Art tips, new products, shows, technical information, current events, interviews, features, marketing.

American Artist Business Letter, Subscription Department, 2160 Patterson Street, Cincinnati, OH 45214.

10 issues per year, $15.00. A newsletter for art professionals. Business issues such as marketing, evaluating dealers, contracts, taxes, grants. Some news.

Art Management, 408 West 57th Street, New York, NY 10019.

Five issues per year, $10.00. A newsletter for administrators of cultural activities. It also may contain information of use to individual visual artists. The editor, Alvin H. Reiss, is the author of the well-received *The Arts Management Handbook*.

Arts Reporting Service, 1110 Fidler Lane, Suite 1615, Silver Spring, MD 20910.

24 bi-weekly issues, $35.00 per year. A newsletter for artists, art administrators, and those interested in art events.

Artweek, 1305 Franklin Street, Oakland, CA, 94612.

44 issues per year, $12.50, $0.75 per issue. An illustrated newspaper for artists. The art scene; reviews of shows,

books, and events; interviews; opinions; ads; gallery and competition news.

Crafts Business Management, P.O. Box 10, New Paltz, NY, 12561.

Monthly, $18.00 per year, $12.00 to ACC members. A newsletter for professional craftspeople. Business subjects.

The Crafts Report, 700 Orange Street, Wilmington, DE, 19801.

11 monthly issues, $13.50 per year. A newspaper for professional craftspeople. Government activities, shows, fairs, exhibitions, current events, articles, book reviews, ads, crafts outlets. The editor, Michael Scott, is the author of the highly useful *Crafts Business Encyclopedia*.

North Light, Fletcher Art Services, Inc., 37 Franklin Street, Westport, CN, 06880.

9 issues per year, free to members of the North Light Book Club, annual subscription, $7.50. A magazine for artists. Artists and their work, interviews, and technical advice.

Ocular, 1539 Platte Street, Denver, CO, 80202.

Quarterly, 1 year, $14.00. A magazine for art professionals. Information and opportunities in the visual arts: competitions, grants, workshops, exhibits, employment opportunities, artists, health hazards, current arts legislation.

Woman Artists News, Box 3304, Grand Central Station, New York, NY, 10017.

10 issues per year, $6.00. Newspaper with emphasis on women artists. Conferences, government, interviews, book reviews, current events, shows, jobs, exhibitions, grants.

Washington International Arts Letter, Box 9005, Washington, DC, 20003.

10 issues per year, $16.00. A newsletter. Grants and assistance by government and private patrons of all the arts. They also publish *The National Directory of Arts Support by Private Foundations* and *The National Directory of Grants and Aid to Individuals in the Arts*.

Organization Newsletters

American Crafts Council, 25 West 55th Street, New York, NY, 10019.

Annual membership, $18.00. Annual membership entitles you to bimonthly editions of *American Craft*, which, in addition to informative illustrated articles on all aspects of the crafts scene, now contains "Craft World," which includes an up-to-date survey of news, an ACC events calendar, and grants, marketing, and exhibition information.

American Council for the Arts (ACA), 570 Seventh Avenue, New York, NY 10018.

Student membership, $20.00, individual membership, $30.00. ACA is an umbrella organization for the promotion of all the arts. Its members include state and community arts councils, arts institutions and facilities, as well as individual artists. It publishes *Word from Washington*, a monthly newsletter about government activities; *ACA*

Reports, a regular newspacket of topical information; and publishes or distributes a wide range of valuable books. Free book list on request.

The American Federation of Arts (AFA), 41 East 65th Street, New York, NY, 10021.

Active membership, $25.00, includes a subscription to *Arts* magazine. A national nonprofit cultural service organization that originates and circulates art exhibitions and film programs to arts organizations.

The American Institute of Graphic Arts, 1059 3rd Avenue, New York, NY 10021.

Membership, $40.00 to $100.00. A professional organization of graphic designers. Benefits include six competitive exhibitions of members' works per year, plant tours, and seminars.

Artists Equity Association, Inc., 3736 Albermarle Street, N.W., Washington, DC, 20016.

Annual dues $8.50 to $30.00. An organization of professional artists that works with government at all levels for the improvement of artists' welfare. Benefits include group insurance, information kits, and a newsletter, which contains articles, information on pending legislation, and news.

Artists Equity of New York, 1780 Broadway, New York, NY, 10019.

Annual dues, $20.00. An organization of art professionals. Benefits include information on legal rights, group medical insurance, interest-free loans or gifts to needy artists, cultural programs, employment assistance, exhibitions, promotion of arts-related legislation, public relations, and a newsletter, which contains articles, news, book reviews, and show information.

ASMP—The Society of Photographers in Communications, 60 East 42nd Street, New York, NY, 10017.

Annual dues $75.00 to $500.00. An organization of professional photographers. Applicants must prove professional status and be sponsored. Benefits include group insurance, free accident insurance, the *ASMP Guide to Business Practices in Photography*, a press card, education programs, a membership directory, and a monthly bulletin, which includes current ASMP activities, market and business information, job prospects, and member news.

Business Committee for the Arts, Inc., 1700 Broadway, New York, NY 10019.

A private, tax-exempt national organization of businesses active in promoting the arts. They publish two free newsletters, *BCA News* and *Arts Business*, that may be of value to some artists.

Foundation for the Community of Artists, 220 Fifth Avenue, New York, NY 10001.

Annual membership, $10.00, subscription only, $7.00. An artist-run service agency. Benefits include occupational assistance for New York artists, group insurance, art-hazards resource center, and *Art Worker News*, a newspaper published ten times a year, which includes articles on grants, galleries, housing, censorship, cultural policy, and service organizations.

Graphic Artists Guild, 30 East 20th Street (Room 405), New York, NY, 10036.

Membership, regular $75.00, provisional $45.00, student $20.00. An organization of graphic artists and illustrators. Benefits include a pricing and ethical guideline booklet, group health insurance, referral listing, art material and travel discounts, a standard contract, and a bimonthly newsletter, which contains news, articles, and letters on the graphic arts.

The Society of Illustrators, 128 East 63rd Street, New York, NY, 10021.

Initiation fee, $100.00, annual nonresident dues, $75.00, annual resident dues, $160.00. An organization of professional illustrators. Applicants must prove professional status and be sponsored. Benefits include projects, group shows, group insurance, *Annual of Illustration*, use of society building, a quarterly publication, and a monthly newsletter.

There are also nonprofit artists' information centers around the country. One of the more active is the Center for the Study of Public Policy and the Arts, P.O. Box 5395, Berkeley, CA, 94705. They are developing materials on the economic enhancement of artists, new applications for the arts, government relationships with the arts, and the arts in society. They also have an Artists and Craftspersons Housing and Studio Space Exchange Program.

Trade Publications

Two of the biggest problems artists face when entering unfamiliar fields are learning the state of the art and finding sources of supplies. Trade publications fill these needs, and each profession or trade has its special literature. The following three are representative.

Decor, Commerce Publishing Company, 408 Olive Street, St. Louis, MO, 63102. Monthly, 1 year $10.00. *Decor* is a storehouse of decorative accessories and artwork, frames and frame supplies. You may be amazed by the profusion and inexpensiveness of the artwork.

Restaurant Design, 633 Third Avenue, New York, NY 10017.

Quarterly, free to professional restaurant designers. A new magazine. Current events, outstanding restaurant designs, sources of supplies.

Signs of the Times, 407 Gilbert Avenue, Cincinnati, OH 45202.

Monthly, 1 year $15.00. *The* signmaker's magazine. Informative articles (especially the cost study series), sources of supplies.

References for additional periodicals

Ayer Directory of Publications. Philadelphia: Ayer.

An annual directory of newspapers and magazines by state, listing addresses, editors, circulation, etc.

The Standard Periodical Directory. New York: Oxbridge.

Includes house organs, yearbooks, etc.

Ulrich's International Periodicals Directory. New York: Bowker.

The Encyclopedia of Associations. Detroit: Gale.

A multivolume listing of organizations by type, including trade associations.

Business Newsletters

Dodge Reports, F. W. Dodge Division, McGraw-Hill Information Systems Company, 1221 Avenue of the Americas, New York, NY (or look in the phone book for the local office).

Dodge Reports are daily computer printouts of construction projects, including such information as the stage of the job: pre-plan, plan, pre-bid, bid, etc.; project name; location; stage of development; owner; architect; engineer; and project description. The service is sold in minimum three-month units and is based on geographical areas, the larger the area covered the more expensive the service. Current minimums are $34 per month per city. Purchasers can select the type of construction they are interested in, e.g., theaters, religious buildings, public buildings. Large architectural, engineering, contracting firms and others connected with the building industry usually get Dodge Reports. You may be able to have their old copies. Dodge Reports are useful not just for the projects listed, which may be too early or late, but for leads to active prospects.

Herb Ireland's Sales Prospector, Prospector Research Services, Inc., 751 Main Street-Waltham, Boston, MA 02154.

A monthly ''prospect research'' report for salesmen and other businessmen interested in industrial, commercial and institutional expansions and relocations in new and existing buildings. Reports are available for regional or national coverage. An edition covering one region costs $68 per year.

Marketing Directories

Most public libraries own a variety of business directories that contain useful information. Two are *The Dun and Bradstreet (D & B) Million Dollar Directory* and *The Dun and Bradstreet Middle Market Directory*. Between them they include 76,000 of the nation's largest businesses. They list companies alphabetically and identify principal officers, owners or partners, annual sales volume, lines of business, mailing addresses, and telephone numbers. There are also sections in both directories that list companies by lines of business and by geographical location. In addition, the *Million Dollar Directory* has two new sections that list, in alphabetical order, 250,000 officers and directors of 42,000 U.S. companies.

Index